# CRAFTING EXPOSITORY ARGUMENT

## PRACTICAL APPROACHES TO THE WRITING PROCESS FOR STUDENTS AND TEACHERS

Michael Degen, Ph.D.

TELEMACHOS
PUBLISHING

Dallas, Texas

Fourth Edition
Third Printing 2004

Telemachos Publishing
PO Box 460387
Garland, TX 75046-0387
www.telemachospublishing.com

Library of Congress Catalog Card Number: 2002110521
ISBN: 0966512588

Printed in Canada

For my teacher and friend

## Sarah Greer Bush

who not only taught me how to write, to examine language,
and to admire well-crafted prose, but also taught me how to
teach students—working with young writers individually, showing
them how to improve sentences, paragraphs, and papers.
Each time I meet with a student I remember Sarah's gift—
hours at her kitchen table and office desk explaining, guiding,
and shaping my knowledge of prose.

# TABLE OF CONTENTS

## CHAPTER THREE: CONSTRUCTING A PAPER

## CHAPTER FOUR: GRAMMAR FOR STRUCTURE AND SYNTAX

# FOREWORD TO TEACHERS

## ARGUMENTS AND LESSON PLANS

### Definition of Expository Argument

Nonfiction prose contains an introduction with a thesis statement—a sentence asserting a claim that must be demonstrated or proven—body paragraphs that illustrate and prove the elements of the thesis statement, and a conclusion.

### Quick Overview: What This Book Is About

These are the beliefs that inform this book.
- Writing well is a difficult and complex task, one that demands more than one year of concentrated study.
- Students do not become better writers merely by reading.
- Students do not become better writers by completing a series of writing assignments with little teacher feedback and no option for revision.
- Students learn to write better if the teacher models the assignment, states directions clearly, offers opportunities for students to practice the skills necessary to achieve high expectations, provides specific feedback toward improvement, and requires students to revise written work after thoroughly instructing them in the revision process.
- The teaching of writing has been made more complex because of academic and social distractions. One academic distraction includes English curricula that emphasizes the quantity of material studied rather than the quality. One social distraction includes our media-driven culture that supports instant gratification and little self-discipline.
- Almost all English teachers battle time restraints because they must teach both literature and composition in one course.
- Serious writers revise; serious teachers expect revision.
- Research demonstrates that teaching grammar without applying it to writing assignments does not improve student writing, but the teaching of writing with simultaneous instruction in the specifics of grammar usage and sentence structure will produce writers skillful in using language.

### Four Key Teaching Concepts

This manual/resource book is in response to the aforementioned assertions. Moreover, it focuses on four key concepts with regard to teaching secondary students expository argument.

#### • Clear directions

Write down for students all expectations for written work: whatever length requirements you wish students to achieve, position of topic sentences, location of thesis statement, type of introduction, minimum number of quotations, etc..

#### • Repetition

Use consistent directions for each paper all year. For the majority of major writing assignments, require (for a paper) a thesis statement located near the end of the introduction or (for an essay test question) a topic sentence positioned as the first sentence in the paragraph.

#### • Revision

Each major writing assignment should provide a revision option.

#### • Modeling

Use class time to model the steps of the writing process: brainstorming, drafting, revision, editing. Use class time to model examples of introductions, thesis statements, topic sentences, body paragraphs, and conclusions. The effectiveness of modeling has been discussed by Janet Emig and Robert Zoellner, who advocate "that instructors demonstrate writing to their students by composing aloud while writing on the blackboard...composing a draft of an assignment at least once and discussing your writing process with the class for fifteen to twenty minutes" (qtd. in Connors and Glenn 106). Other researchers have also emphasized the importance and efficacy of using models to improve student writing, among them Charney, Carlson, and Stolarek. Charney states that "models do influence the content and organization of students' texts. Reading models seems to have reminded writers of concepts that they otherwise would not have included in their texts" (111).

### Teaching Expository Argument

At the secondary level there exists an urgency for ensuring that students can write cogent, concise, and coherent exposition. After all, when students leave the classroom, they will be asked in almost any profession to write exposition, to move from data to conclusion with clarity and sophistication. Throughout students' lives they will be frequently asked to draw conclusions from facts, to reorder information, to argue from information, to explain and to describe, whether they be preparing a legal brief, an argument to an insurance company to pay for medical treatment, a proposal to corporate executives, or a computer instruction manual. Moreover, students must learn to write on topics that are not particularly appealing, for they will discover that we do not always have a choice of topics. As Robert Connors and Cheryl Glenn write in *The St. Martin's Guide to Teaching Writing*, "Composition teachers today must turn out students who can write on assigned subjects and demonstrate their engagement with a topic"(154).

Fortunately, research clearly demonstrates that students can learn these skills and that teacher instruction plays a significant role in improving student writing. Studies completed by Sandra Perl demonstrate that student writing improves in classrooms where writing is taken more seriously (19). Not only does writing improve, but also students' general level of self-confidence increases when they see they can perform these critical thinking skills with competence.

### • It is not enough to assign the five-paragraph essay

The urgency exists for educators to become more aggressive in the teaching of expository argument for two reasons. First, many teachers underestimate the complexity of writing expository argument and hence merely assign a "five-paragraph essay" without providing students instruction in the composing process. For some reason, many believe that, by high school, students should have developed these skills, a belief affirmed by research completed by A.N. Applebee. Amazingly, Applebee writes, "only three minutes elapsed from the time the teacher began explaining a writing topic until the time students were expected to begin to write"(102). Perhaps this myth may be due in part to the inaccurate belief that writing is merely talk recorded. Jane Emig points out, in her essay "Writing as a Mode of Learning," that writing is not recorded talk and that writing is a skill emanating "from different organic sources and represents quite different, possibly distinct, language functions"(123). Second, perhaps the reason why some teachers assign essays without teaching students how to write the essay and how to improve it is a more personal one—many teachers are not sure how to teach writing or are intimidated by the detail such teaching may require. Because writing expository argument is a complex process, developing skills takes time; it is something learned through practice and feedback and more practice, not during one year, but year after year through direct teaching by the educators responsible for such instruction. It is learned as well through interaction among the student writers themselves under the guidance of teachers who not only provide feedback but also offer numerous opportunities for such practice after they have shown students how to write exposition and how to continue to increase the sophistication of their writing. By the ninth grade, students are running out of time. It is naïve to think that a high school student can quickly learn how to write effective expository argument after a few assignments.

Moreover, though the narrative, reflective, and descriptive types of writing are important elements of good expository composing (journaling, personal experience writing, the short story, poetry) and are effective exercises in creativity and thinking, an emphasis or reliance on these types of writing will not teach a student the complex task of expository argument. To think otherwise is unfortunate, for it fails to recognize the complexity and arduousness of helping a young person respond intelligently to an essay test or essay topic.

### Teacher's Role

English teachers greet students who have a vast range of writing skills. Few students are truly competent, even by the twelfth grade. This challenge is presented in August or September. With a 50-minute class that meets on average four to five days a week until May or June, a teacher must sandwich a curriculum filled with literature and a host of sundry objectives plus attempt to help students write a coherent, cogent argument. It is a daunting task. Little help comes from 400-page writing textbooks that categorize a myriad of forms and sequences. Too much material. Where does a teacher start? And if one started from the beginning, working from writing assignment to writing assignment, would students have time to master any one form? Or should we work on the short story? The poem? Journal writing?

## • Focus on the expository form

With little time and an extensive curriculum guide, it seems wise to keep it simple. Focus primarily on one form, the form most useful and practical—the expository argument. If the teacher keeps assigning and explaining the same form all year, mere repetition will affect even the most intellectually withdrawn students. My experience teaching writing suggests that I can be most effective if I primarily teach students throughout the year how to argue a simple but clear thesis, if I teach repeatedly the creation process of the expository paragraph and essay, and if I require the same directions for the composing process. If the expectations stay high and consistent, even the most reluctant students will develop specific writing skills. For those on task and ready to plunge into each assignment, their skills will quickly move beyond competence; some of their essays will sparkle and amaze readers.

Another benefit to this procedure is that it becomes easier to hold students accountable for performance. Grading becomes more fair, more objective, and more valid. It becomes more difficult for a student to cry, "I don't know what you want. I don't know what you mean by blending."

For these reasons this manual focuses on the expository argument. It assumes that most expository, nonfiction writing contains a thesis and body paragraphs that illustrate the thesis. Instead of introducing the classification essay, the compare/contrast essay, or the definition essay as separate units, we discuss these as methods for organization once students have narrowed topics and have begun to formulate thesis statements.

## • Demonstrate the writing process repeatedly

Perhaps the most salient element of this manual is that teachers must show their students how to create each part of the paragraph and each part of the essay. Students need to see how to write a topic sentence, how to write a thesis statement, how to make paragraphs more coherent. Teachers must take time in class to show examples, to work with student papers in a positive, constructive, caring fashion in front of the class, so students can see how one improves writing. Research completed by Steven Graham, Karen Harris, and the University of Maryland faculty demonstrates that teaching students writing strategies in a deliberate manner "increases the number of revisions and results in a much longer, better-quality final product" (Pressley and Woloshyn 169). In their study of helping learning disabled students improve writing skills, they emphasize a series of steps all writing teachers should implement: 1) discuss and model the writing strategy repeatedly; 2) practice repeatedly the steps with the students; 3) provide repeated opportunities for independent practice of the strategy. This research is further supported by Hillocks, Brown, Lave, Williams, Smagorinsky, Raphael, Flower, and Cheng, all of whom advocate the explicit teaching of writing strategies. Unfortunately—and I did this, too—too many teachers merely assign a paper, provide little instruction over the methods for achieving expectations, and scream while grading "these terrible essays." Simply because students are in the ninth, tenth, eleventh, or even twelfth grade, we can no longer assume that they know how to select and think about a paper topic, craft a thesis, organize a paper, and construct paragraphs. I don't even assume, when assigning the tenth paper of the year, that I can simply pass out the instructions and move onto the literature. We often forget that "the ability to communicate through writing develops at a much slower rate than does the ability to communicate through speech and requires much more formal instruction" (Connor and Glenn 111–112). Even after a year's instruction, there may remain a handful of students who need me to go through one part of the process or another once again. To keep assigning papers without teaching how to write them is professional negligence.

### Lesson Plans That Lead Toward Exposition

The lesson plans that follow begin with exercises intended to develop the writing skills students will use in expository composition. These "Writing to Show" exercises use the modes of description and narration to teach *universal writing skills* of elaboration, concrete diction, active verb usage, and sentence variety. These exercises develop a positive, enjoyable foundation and environment for writing instruction that continues throughout the year, a foundation for writing that significantly improves student outcomes, as illustrated by research done by Frank Pajares and Margaret Johnson. Later, when you begin writing about literature, students will, with your guidance, apply these "Writing to Show" skills to their expository compositions.

Bear in mind, too, that the "Suggested Lesson Planning Sequence" is a type of blueprint that explains the basic approach toward the teaching of writing as well as how to integrate successfully practical grammar instruction that students will employ in their writing. It is a *flexible blueprint*. The grammar instruction (see chapter four) may be woven into the fabric of the writing process by you at a different pace than I have approached it here.

### WEEKS ONE-TWO

#### Objectives
- To introduce the skills for extending the elaboration of an idea with concrete and singular detail;
- To introduce these editing symbols: **SH, E3, V, C, L, G, WC,** and ⬭;
- To introduce the year-long practical integration of grammar in the writing process—with an emphasis on the clause and the phrase as tools for using sentence structures that improve meaning, clarity, and sophistication.

#### Day One
1. Explain "Writing to Show." During the next few weeks, students will be writing "showing" exercises that will provide the foundation for universal writing skills. Discuss the sample Telling v. Showing paragraphs in chapter one, pp. 34–35.
2. Homework. Writing to Show assignment one, p. 42. Explain to students Gabriele Lusser Rico's clustering activity. For example, place the word "fear" or the sentence "He is scared" in a circle on the blackboard or overhead. Ask students then to list concrete words or images that they think of when they see the word "fear." The composition requires students to show fear—to elaborate the details of it fully and to do so with vivid present tense verbs.

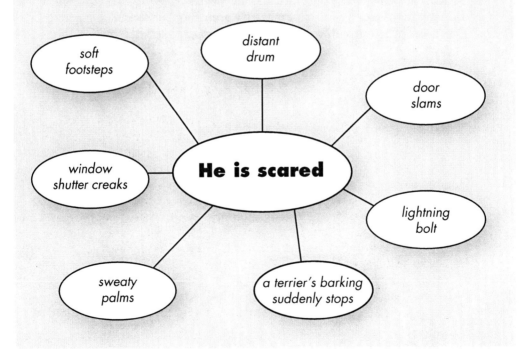

### Day Two

1. Students turn in their first assignment. To encourage class discussion of writing and revising, I read some assignments turned in that day to the homework box. I randomly select a few compositions from the box and read them aloud. Then I ask my students, "Where in this composition is the writer beginning to show well?" After a few examples are stated, I ask, "Where is the writer telling rather than showing, where could something be shown, or elaborated, more, and what could the writer do to show it more?" The point is not to make judgements about the writing, I assure them; after all, everyone is in the learning stages here. The point is to begin thinking about our writing and what makes writing effective, what makes it communicate vividly to the reader. We briefly discuss how specific details could be elaborated more extensively and how plurals can be more effectively shown when they are turned into singulars. For example, a student might write, "All my shoes were under the bed" and another student might suggest this to replace it: "My grass-stained Adidas running shoes rest beside the bedpost."

2. For these "Writing to Show" exercises, I employ a checkmark system: If the student has followed the directions and has clearly attempted to show and extend elaboration, I give a check plus, which I later translate into a homework grade of 95; a check—an 85—means that the student is starting to show but that much more showing can be done and/or that directions were not followed completely (for example, the composition may be in past tense rather than present); a check minus—a 75—indicates that the composition is basically all telling. When reading student compositions, I usually highlight parts of a few sentences where the students are showing, describing specific action or items in precise, singular sensory details. I will often circle a few nouns or verbs, in this manner indicating that what is going on here is mere telling rather than showing. You'll especially want to encourage students at this point to focus on singular rather than plural details. Plurals are almost always too vague in any type of writing.

3. Grammar instruction. Explain the different between clauses and phrases, p. 132, and explain that our study of grammar will involve learning the function of these structures and how to use them in the writing process.

4. **Present participial phrase.** See pp. 137–138 in chapter four. I begin with this phrase because it is a dynamic structure that is fairly easy for most students to master (although mastery is nothing anyone expects to occur within a mere day or two, or—for some students— even one or two weeks). After teaching the concept, we practice sentence combinations.

5. Teaching a structural concept in grammar requires the teaching of the punctuation rule for that structure. Rather than throwing all of the punctuation rules at students at one time and expecting that a

unit on punctuation will make an appreciable difference in their use of correct punctuation in their writing, experience demonstrates that teaching the specific punctuation rule with a specific structure—and repeatedly asking students to explain what that rule is with that structure throughout the year—will be much more likely to ensure compliance.

6. Homework. Their first grammar assignment, p. 167, is to combine related sentences by turning one into a present participial phrase. The idea is to help students move away from a reliance on simplistic sentence structures, and adding a present participial phrase actually becomes a fun way to do it. This is the first of many practices with various sentence structures, primarily phrases or clauses. I let students know we'll be combining quite a bit and that all structures, once taught, are expected to be clearly evident in their writing. The regularity of this requirement is important. As Connor and Glenn have stated, "You will see little improvement unless you work on the exercises regularly and expose your students to as many kinds of sentences as you can" (225). Moreover, the research of Faigley, Kerek, and Daiker emphasize the positive relationship between growth in "syntactic maturity" and the "overall quality of the writing" (227).

### Day Three

1. Check homework in class, then turn it in to the teacher. I give each student a red pen, and they make corrections in red on their own work whenever a combination is incorrectly done. No other writing instruments are allowed on the desk, and a failure to correct the sentence earns a double deduction. This procedure is standard on all combining assignments—no paper exchange; students correct their *own* work in red.

2. Introduce the second "Writing to Show" assignment, p. 42. You might consider doing something a bit crazy as a preparation—for example, throw a number of books into a pile somewhere on the floor. Ask students what they see. The most common responses will be "a mess" or "a pile of books." Tell them you can't see "a pile," you can't see "a mess." Tell them that they will have to show you what is there: "Who can show me what is *really* there?" Once someone goes to the singular and mentions a specific book, have the student pick up that book and talk about it in great detail. This can be very imaginative and great fun—and very elaborated. Have another student show one of the other books in detail. What you are demonstrating is this: That for the reader to see the whole, the writer must show the parts, each part extensively elaborated.

3. Homework. Here students will be seeking to elaborate extensively a single part of their room (a desk, a bed, a closet) or a single object (a teddy bear, a t-shirt, a shoe). See p. 39. Added to the requirements for the first "Writing to Show" assignment—*vivid present tense verbs, full elaboration*—is the highlighting of *two present participial phrases correctly punctuated.*

### Day Four

1. Read a few of the second "Writing to Show" compositions turned into the homework box. Use the same system as described in #1 for Day Two.
2. Grammar instruction. **Adverb subordinate clauses,** p. 133. This is the clause that most of these students use already. I want them to know they are using it and that, as with the present participial phrase, they can begin taking two sentences and turning one of them into an adverb clause and attaching it to the independent clause to make a longer, more elegant sentence, a complex one they can intersperse among their simple ones. Again, punctuation is taught and repeated; some combining is practiced.
3. Homework. Sentence Combining Using Adverb Clauses, p. 162.

### Day Five

1. Check homework in class, then turn it in to the teacher. The red pen procedure is used.
2. Preparing for "Writing to Show" assignment three: Athletic Action, p. 43. Discuss writing about one single athletic action. To allow students to visualize an action, I pantomime match point of a tennis match. (Another teacher acts out a football play that focuses on a running back from the moment he receives the ball from the quarterback to the end of that play.) Or the class and teacher can examine the models in chapter one. What I want the students to do is visualize an action moment by moment or, as I tell them, milli-second by milli-second. Look at it as though it were being replayed in super slow motion. And write about it with that kind of detail in mind. Often at this point in the week, a few students will begin asking questions like, "Can't you show too much, Dr. Degen? No one writes with *this* much detail. It would get boring." These comments indicate that students do not understand that these writing assignments are exercises that allow students to *practice* the skill of making details concrete and extensively elaborated. They are similar to athletic or musical drills where the athlete or musician is developing particular skills he or she will implement at will during a game or performance. Later in the semester when students begin essay writing, they will decide where to elaborate and where they need more concrete detail. Before they get to this point, however, they need to make sure they have the skills of elaboration and concrete detail.
3. Homework. Students will show an athlete in action at one moment in time or during one particular play. The list of requirements is longer now: *Extensively elaborate each concrete detail, use vivid present tense verbs, highlight two present participial phrases and two adverb clauses.*

**Day Six**

1. Review present participial phrases and adverb subordinate clauses, as well as the punctuation rules that govern them. I have students do a few combinations in class, and we go over them.

2. Introduce peer review in the revision process. See appendix for various peer review methods. Research supports that students can be taught revision strategies that can eventually lead to the self-editing of their own work. Garrod Beal has explained that students fail to revise because they cannot detect the problems with the text. Once taught strategies, "students...detected more errors and constructed more revisions" (Pressley and Woloshyn 177). Additional research by David Wallace and John Hayes suggests that significant improvements in students' abilities to revise occur after teachers provide instruction (54). Moreover, studies suggest that teachers should first focus on one or two editing strategies (Pressley and Woloshyn 176). Focus only on editing for one or two symbols. (Editing symbols, pp. 196–197.) First, review the samples for **E3** in chapter one, p. 36. Next, assign for homework (or do in class) a few of the exercises for the **E3** and **SH** editing symbols at the end of chapter one, p. 45. Explain to students that, when working with peers, they need to offer precise suggestions. Simply saying "You need to show more" is not helpful. Ask students to think of their peer's paper as their own. How would they revise certain sections? In addition, throughout the year, remind students that peer review has two purposes: 1) to read how other students write, which might provide them with new ideas about their paper topic; 2) to share their particular writing gifts with another student. Remember that writers don't have to use all or any of the suggestions. I tell my students that I hope a few ideas trigger additional reflection.

3. Peer review workshop: Everybody reads and suggests (for symbols **SH**, **E3**). Before they begin, we talk about peer review (see #2 above) and workshopping papers and what my expectations are in terms of their behavior and attitude toward one another's writing. Instead of reading compositions aloud, I have students work in triads and read their compositions to one another. After the composition on the athletic action is read, the other members of the triad are to point out at least three different places where the writer is starting to elaborate well and three areas where the writer is telling and could show more. The writer is to add those suggestions at the bottom of the paper. When every group is done—and before the compositions are turned back in to the teacher—more than one student will volunteer to read his or her composition aloud to the class. You might ask the reader to share the comments made by his or her peers.

### Day Seven

1. Grammar instruction. The compound sentence and the three ways that two independent clauses can be joined together with emphasis on the solo **semicolon,** p. 136.
2. Introducing assignment four, an ordinary action, p. 44. I usually role play a man sitting in the park reading a newspaper. While I pantomime/role play, I ask students to jot down every singular action I perform in the form of a present participial phrase (e.g. *folding* the newspaper, *conversing* with the dog, *swatting* a mosquito).
3. After the role is done, students share the specific details they have noted, and they state them in the form of present participial phrases.
4. Explain ordinary action assignment. The requirements for the composition include these: *Extensively elaborate each concrete detail; use vivid present tense verbs; highlight two present participial phrases, two adverb clauses, and one compound sentence, its independent clauses joined by a solo semicolon.*

### Day Eight

1. Grammar instruction. The compound sentence and the three ways that two independent clauses can be joined together with emphasis on the **conjunctive adverb,** correctly punctuated. See pp. 136, 152.
2. Homework. Students will consult p. 152: Using five different conjunctive adverbs, they will create five very well-elaborated compound or compound-complex sentences. I expect that each sentence will also contain either a present participial phrase or an adverb subordinate clause (no more than three total of one structure for the overall assignment). I give students ten generalized or abstract words; they choose five from the list, each one inspiring the content of the sentence without the word actually being used. Sample words used have been, among others, *music, football, hobby, basketball, math class, book, Mexican food, car, television show, friend.* We practice creating a few in class. For example, someone writing a sentence having to do with *football* might write the following: *The quarterback, grasping the ball tightly in his right hand, quickly leaps sideways to avoid a collision; however, his left foot does not miss the gopher hole in his friend's backyard.*
3. Peer review workshop. Students work in triads on their ordinary action compositions (similar to #2, Day Six, but with different people in each triad). Writers will again seek feedback for **SH** and **E3**; add **V** as well.

### Day Nine

1. Brief quiz over present participial phrases and adverb subordinate clauses.
2. Students share some sentences from previous night's homework before turning them in.
3. I explain to students that their next major composition assignment will be a thorough revision of one of the "Writing to Show" compositions. We discuss the revision requirements that will produce a truly rough draft, an edited draft, and a final draft, p. 48. Their job right now is to decide on which composition to revise.

### Day Ten

1. We begin the revision process for the *one* "Writing to Show" composition. Teaching students that revision does not mean "rewrite" is very important; revision means "re-see," and following an organized revision process allows that re-seeing to occur.   One teacher makes this a publishing project, with the students' final drafts anthologized, pp. 46–48; while that is certainly not necessary, you do want to make sure that students understand that this is a major writing grade and their first major effort at using constructively the revision process.
2. Select a peer review format that works for you and your students. I often experiment with a variety of workshopping/editing formats. See "peer review/editing activities," pp. 198–204. For today I have students work in triads with partners they have not previously worked with. The writer reads his composition twice to the listeners. After the first reading, the listeners ask questions of clarification about the composition to make sure they have understood each detail; they also mention particular places so far where the writer is starting to show well. The writer needs to know what is working. After the second reading, the listeners make specific suggestions as to **E**, **SH**, **V**, and **WC**. The writer carefully jots down the suggestions without considering at this time whether or not to use them. Tonight, upon reflection, he or she can best make such decisions.
3. Homework. Students will type a new draft. On this draft will be highlighted the following structures: *three present participial phrases, three adverb clauses, and two compound sentences—in one case its independent clauses joined by a solo semicolon, in the other, by a correctly punctuated conjunctive adverb.* The composition will be between 25 and 50 typed lines, all verbs vivid and in present tense, every detail extensively elaborated.

### Day Eleven

1. Peer editing of the second draft. Use the alternative one or alternative two of the individual/class editing techniques, explained on pp. 203–204. Students create, or are given, an editing sheet, p. 204. If, for instance, you use alternative two, the students will exchange their papers (their composition and their editing sheet) and read their partner's composition looking only for one type of detail (places for **E3**, for example), and they edit or suggest for that, making all their suggestions on the editing sheet. I give *x* number of minutes for this detail, and then students on one side of the rows—and always just this same side—move down one. Students exchange papers again, this time checking for either the same thing or something different (**WC**, for instance). In a peer editing situation, I always have students check for required structures, so at some point I ask people to look at their peer's paper for highlighted adverb clauses, for example, and make sure they are actually adverb clauses and that they are punctuated correctly. I walk about the room, prepared to answer questions as they come up, and I watch the time to let students in the designated "moving" rows know when to move again. Using this process, many pairs of eyes see the paper, and so by the end, students will have a great deal of feedback from various sources to work with as they prepare final drafts.
2. Give due date for final draft.

### Weeks Three–Six

For the next three or four weeks, I'm teaching a work of literature, which will become the subject of our first expository paragraph. Before that assignment, I will teach the **past participial phrase,** pp. 137–138. Students will observe the similarities of the past and present participial phrases, how to distinguish between a past participle as a verb and as an adjective, and practice combining sentences with past participial phrases, pp. 168–169. This now becomes part of the basic structural requirements for all future writing assignments.

### Week Seven: Teaching the Paragraph

#### Objectives

- To transfer the showing writing skills to expository literary analysis and to introduce symbols **A, B, O, TS, P**;
- To continue the practical application of grammar; and
- To continue emphasizing the writing process: drafting, revising, publishing.

#### Preparation

- Before the first class discussion on crafting paragraphs, I give the students a preparatory assignment, which is printed below. This assignment refers to *The Great Gatsby, but you will want to have yours apply to the work of literature your students are currently studying.* I explain to students that I want them to search for showing details (direct quotations from the text, for this example) that would prove one of the listed topic sentences. The assignment does not ask students to write a paragraph yet. The focus is to begin seeing what "showing" detail means when discussing literature.

***This is a model only; adapt it to the literary work you are studying.***

### Writing Assignment

*Directions:* Choose one of the following topic sentences. Do not write a paragraph! List only the textual passages that you would use as evidence to support your argument. Textual evidence = showing details. Include page and chapter numbers.

- **Topic sentence choices**
    1. Daisy copes with the cruelty of the world with an effervescent and fatuous personality.
    2. Tom's actions reveal his desire to control people.
    3. Myrtle's primary objective is to pursue material wealth.

- **Example of what your homework should look like**
    TS: Daisy copes with the cruelty of the world with an effervescent and fatuous personality.
    
    "Well, I've had a very bad time, Nick, and I'm pretty cynical about everything" (21; ch. 1).
    
    "I woke up out of there with an utterly abandoned feeling" (21; ch. 1).
    
    "Nick. You remind me of a—of a rose, an absolute rose" (19; ch. 1).

Students come to class the next period with this assignment based on the topic sentence choices you have given them from the work of literature you have been studying. At that point we begin discussing the steps for constructing the paragraph, explained below.

### Day One

1. It's important that you stress to students that they will be using the same universal showing writing skills we used before: **SH, E, V, C, WC,** etc. The showing writing skills will now be used to write about literature: extending elaboration of ideas; focusing on concrete, singular detail; using a variety of sentence structures; choosing vivid active-voice verbs; and controlling verb tense. Now the showing details will be scenes from the literature. The elaboration will be the analysis of those concrete details.

2. Read together the passage from *A Christmas Carol,* pp. 105–107. Use this material to demonstrate how to construct a paragraph.

3. Begin the suggested strategy for constructing the paragraph, pp. 51–64.

4. Review the definition of a topic sentence, p. 50. Brainstorm topic sentence possibilities in response to the following essay question: *What is Dickens showing us about Scrooge's character in this passage?* Or *What is significant about what Dickens shows us in this opening passage from* A Christmas Carol? Write these brainstorming responses on the board or the overhead so that students can see them. After all suggestions have been written, you may go through each, circling words that may be too vague, phrases that are wordy, etc., showing students how you might revise and arrive at the most precise topic sentence possible.

5. Have students read through the passage of *A Christmas Carol* to gather evidence. Mark passages together as a class. Have students, after they gather additional evidence, revise the brainstormed topic sentence based on further reflection of that evidence.

6. Discuss the organization methods/options, pp. 51–55.

7. Examine the completed paragraph for Scrooge on pp. 61–62. As you work through this paragraph ask the following questions:

   A. Does the topic sentence contain information that further focuses the main idea? (What's the function of the prepositional phrase *by the repetition of diction...?*) This phrase and the second sentence act as a transitional sentence before the writer begins his first example. I use symbol **A1** or **A2** to designate the need for this type of sentence. You'll want to focus particular energy on developing transitional sentences.

   B. How is the writer organizing the information? How does the reader know this?

   C. Where are the "showing" details?

   D. Cite examples of where the writer is extending the elaboration of ideas.

   E. What structures is the writer using? Phrases, clauses, sentence types?

8. Explain homework. Students have previously gathered evidence for a topic sentence on the work of literature they have been reading. Have them develop a paragraph similar to the Scrooge model discussed in class. Ask students to write at the top of their papers the type of organizational method they have chosen. They should also circle the words in the paragraph that indicate this method of organization.

Place a box around their transitional phrase or sentence, the **A1** or **A2** sentence.

### Day Two

1. Read student homework samples aloud and ask students if they can tell how the writer is organizing the evidence.
2. Review pp. 55–57 and work on exercise over **A1/A2.**
3. Peer edit the paragraph students have been revising for homework. Editors should concentrate on making suggestions for revising the topic sentence, the transitional sentence, and organization. Remember to encourage student editors to provide suggestions for an actual sentence revision on the editing sheet. Merely writing "need a better transition" doesn't help. Peer edit for **TS, A1/A2,** and **P1.**
4. Homework. Revise paragraph, with particular attention to **A1/A2** sentence. Students should bring to class tomorrow a new copy of their paragraph, and they should highlight words, phrases, or sentences that are new. Each night they are to make additional revisions and to highlight these changes. I give students a completion grade for each required revision they bring to class.

### Day Three

1. Discuss with students word glue and logic glue, pp. 58–60, and maintaining topic focus, pp. 57–58. Do the exercises together as a class. You'll want to begin explaining the most difficult concept of argument—namely, that the writer must show and explain to the reader how he or she has arrived at the conclusions of the argument. *Glue* and *topic focus* help the reader understand the complicated thought process the writer has recently been engaged in. Even though the audience has read the literary material, they have not viewed the evidence in the same manner as the writer.
2. Homework. Continue revising homework paragraph based on the new knowledge of word-logic glue and topic focus.

### Day Four

1. In-class activity. In small groups—triads—assign students an essay question for which they formulate a topic sentence (**TS**), the transitional sentence (**A1/A2**), and the initial showing examples from the literary text (**SH/B3/E3**). Use the literary text that you are currently studying. It is important for each group member to write the sentences the group creates. Research by William Sweigart demonstrates that "small-group discussion was significantly more effective in improving the students' knowledge as they prepared to write than teacher lecture" (469). Additional research by Crawford,

Haaland, and many others echoes the positive benefits of cooperative learning, namely, improving motivation and promoting interaction among different intellectual levels of students. Moreover, James D. Williams adds, in *Preparing to Teach Writing*, that "a key to improving students' writing skills does not lie in simply having them write. They must write and receive meaningful feedback on work in progress and then they must use that feedback to revise" (87). What occurs in these writing groups, say researchers Flavell, Botkin, Fry, and others, is that students begin to develop alternative ways of approaching the writing process; in fact, students internalize new skills that will assist them in becoming better writers. In order to foster these benefits, I assign each group a different level of student, an A student, a B student, a C student, and so on.

2. In large letters, students in each group print three-to-four sentences of their completed paragraph on newsprint to explain to their classmates why they think the topic sentence is effective, how the transitional sentence assists the reader in understanding the manner in which the writer will proceed to organize the evidence in the text, and which words represent word glue.

3. Homework. Continue revising paragraph assignment given on day one. At this point the student's paragraph should contain several showing examples. They should continue highlighting the changes.

### Day Five

1. Groups will begin or continue presentations over yesterday's in-class activity (#1 and #2 from day four.) During presentations, encourage students to see the application of the universal showing strategies. These discussions also emphasize how important the writer-reader relationship is: that the writer must consciously and vigilantly work to show the reader how he has arrived at the conclusion. Research demonstrates that engaging students in the discussion of writing can help them improve their skills. Moreover, the transitional sentence is one of the more difficult sentences for young writers. Finally, using newsprint during discussion allows the teacher to mark on it suggestions for improvement. This helps students visualize a process of revision.

2. Homework. Final revision of paragraph. Students should follow the paragraph requirements listed on p. 185 under "Requirements for Smaller Compositions." Explain that they will revise this until it reaches "B" or "A" level. After students receive their paragraphs back from the teacher, in addition

to providing another revision (I make the revision due one week later), they write the teacher a memo explaining why they made certain revision choices. See the sample "Memo."

---

**Sample "Memo"**

I first realized that I did not have an appropriate transitional sentence after the topic sentence. My original second sentence started with "His nephew keeps trying to persuade his uncle to come over for dinner." I added, instead, after the topic sentence, "Scrooge faces several occasions where he makes conscious decisions to think only about himself. His first altercation occurs with his nephew." I also worked on improving transitions between sentences and on extending elaboration. For example, I improved the transition between sentences in lines 18–20. The original looked like this: "Scrooge scrutinizes his visitors' every suggestion by replying with 'Nothing!' Scrooge then says, "I wish to be left alone." With these sentences, I'm just listing text without explaining why it supports my topic sentence. I changed it to the following: "Scrooge scrutinizes his visitors' every suggestion by replying with, 'Nothing.' He feels this way because he believes that his money should only go to himself. Scrooge further displays his selfish attitude by insisting, 'I wish to be left alone.'"

---

### Day Six

1. Students turn in completed paragraph. This assignment includes a typed copy, plus the drafts and memo.

### Week Eight

Again at this point, you must decide whether you need to continue with the literature, or you want to work more with paragraph development. If the latter, consider additional work with peer editing required for symbols **B** and **O**, as well as **T**, taking time to help students learn these symbols adequately. Moreover, editing symbols **P1, P2, P3, P4,** pp. 81–84, symbols that will appear on student papers throughout the year, should be carefully examined.

By this point, I'm ready to give my first essay test. For essay tests, I spend a day reviewing with students how to write a topic sentence in response to an essay question. The answer to the question creates the topic sentence. Review examples in chapter two, pp. 61–64. I stress that they must apply the paragraphing skills we've been practicing. After the essay test and moving on to other pieces of literature, I'm about ready for teaching the entire paper.

Before I do, I introduce another sentence structure—**adjective subordinate clauses,** p. 134. Students work with combining exercises involving adjective clauses, learn where adjective clauses are located in relation to the word modified, and practice correct punctuation for nonessential adjective clauses. Once they are comfortable with using adjective clauses, they practice distinguishing between the use of *who* and *whom* as well as *that* and *which.* Their first essay will, thus, require highlighted examples of *present and past participial phrases, adverb and adjective clauses,* as well as *compound or compound-complex sentences joined by the solo semicolon and the correctly punctuated conjunctive adverb.*

### Week Nine or Ten: Writing Essays

#### Objectives
- To introduce the process of generating paper topics, gathering evidence, and organizing material;
- To continue emphasizing the practical use of grammar; and
- To emphasize the writing process: drafting, revising, publishing.

#### Day One
1. One of the most difficult tasks for students is to find a topic and to construct a thesis statement that asserts an idea beyond plot or general observation. The thesis should present the reader with a lens through which to examine the literary text. This viewpoint may explore more closely a pattern in the text, for instance, or a character. Students, however, need strategies to arrive at a general topic, theme, or subject—to find, in other words, something to argue. First, suggest that students answer the questions about literature in chapter three. Have them also consider Aristotle's three topics, pp. 110–111. At this point, students should be able to decide on a general topic. For example, they may want to write about a character, a symbol, a setting, an archetype, etc., but they might not yet know what to say about their topic or not yet be able to write a thesis statement. Here I have my students freewrite, a process designed to move students further toward a possible thesis statement by exploring aspects about the topic. Students should write without stopping for five, ten, or fifteen minutes, without regard to organization, style, or sense. After freewriting, have students return to the literary text and reread, then write down possible pieces of evidence that may relate to their topic. Once students compile a list of possible evidence and carefully peruse it, they will be more successful in writing their argument. Often, beginning students attempt to write a thesis statement and decide on

the organization of the entire essay before gathering evidence or rereading sections of the literary text that pertain to their topic. This proves very frustrating. We want to teach students to *reflect* on the textual evidence and, therefore, allow the discovery of further ideas.

2. Discuss the elements of writing the thesis statement. Complete the thesis statement exercise at the end of chapter three, p. 129.
3. If time, students brainstorm possible thesis statements. Discuss and evaluate.
4. Homework. Students continue search for textual evidence, write thesis statement, plus possible topic sentences that will support the thesis. (Bring in two copies, one for turning in.) See models in chapter three.

### Day Two

1. Review section in chapter three regarding diction of topic sentences, p. 115.
2. Choose one of the editing activities in the appendix. Have students focus only on the thesis statement and topic sentences.
3. You may collect students' thesis statements and/or topic sentences for brief comments before the next day's class.
4. Homework. Revise thesis statements and topic sentences; write one of the body paragraphs that will support the thesis statement.

### Day Three

1. Choose a peer-editing model. (See appendix.) Have students examine topic sentences and thesis statements again. It is in the best interest of the teacher to help ensure thesis statements and topic sentences are viable before students turn in their final essays for evaluation.
2. Examine the function of body paragraphs in light of paragraph written the night before. Emphasize components of a topic sentence within a larger essay: *topic sentence = an aspect of the thesis + an organizing element.* See chapter two.
3. Homework. Revise thesis + topic sentences; complete writing other body paragraphs. As students revise, they place new copies on top of the old.

### Day Four

1. Edit body paragraphs. As students edit, encourage them to make two suggestions on one of the body paragraphs and move onto the next paper. This allows more students to read more papers. It also provides more feedback for each student.

2. After students return papers, read samples; discuss possible improvements.
3. Homework. Revise body paragraphs.

### Day Five
1. Discuss "Showing-Telling" introductions. Go over samples, pp. 118–121.
2. If time, have students brainstorm possibilities.
3. Homework. Write the showing-telling introduction. I prefer to concentrate on the introduction after body paragraphs because the body of the paper is often the most arduous. (You may wish to switch the order.)

### Day Six
1. Continue discussing sample introductions.
2. Work in partners making suggestions about the introductions.
3. Discuss conclusions. Review the samples, pp. 122–124.
4. Homework. Write a conclusion.

### Day Seven
1. Choose the larger "Day Four: Final Evaluation" editing activity. Use this with partners or in the large group setting.
2. Assign a due date for your paper.

### Weeks Eleven–Eighteen
For the remainder of the semester, we read other works of literature, write other compositions based on the literature, and prepare to take an essay exam. An additional sentence structure taught is the **appositive phrase,** p. 142, which is added to the list of required structures for remaining compositions for the semester. Students also spend time revising their major essays and meeting with me outside of class. For the final exam, students write an essay during the exam period. They are allowed to bring to the exam an outline containing textual evidence, topic sentences, and a thesis statement.

## SECOND SEMESTER

As the first semester began with the present participial phrase, the second semester grammar instruction begins with a close relation, the **absolute phrase,** p. 139. This allows for a review of present and past participial phrases and a smooth, logical connection to the absolute phrase, which involves the noun + participial phrase combination. All compositions will now include highlighted absolute phrases, along with all structures learned first semester.

Very soon thereafter, students focus on *composing another paragraph.* This time I provide students with a series of essay test questions based on the current literary material we are studying. They choose one to answer, their response constructed into a topic sentence from which they must construct a paragraph. They need to follow the paragraph directions in the appendix. I make them revise the paragraph *until they reach "A" level.* It takes some students the entire semester to achieve this goal, but they do make it. Along the way, I set occasional due dates and deduct points if they are late.

Throughout the semester I repeat an abridged version of the paragraph-constructing lesson plans prior to an essay test. Whenever I assign additional expository paper assignments, I move through a modified version of the aforementioned lesson plans.

At a certain point, I explain that we will add the **noun subordinate clause,** p. 135, and the **gerund phrase,** p. 139, to our repertoire of required sentence structures. Because they both act as nouns, we review the function that any noun may have in the sentence. They refresh (or learn for the first time) how to distinguish between nouns as subjects, direct objects, indirect objects, predicate nominatives, objects of prepositions, and appositives. Once they are comfortable with this, the teaching of the noun subordinate clause proves to be relatively easy. Students are used to clauses by now; they look for *subject-verb combinations—the sign of the clause—*and they apply what they know about the functions of a noun (the location of each function, for example: predicate nominatives follow linking verbs, indirect objects—if there are any—exist only between action verbs and direct objects, etc.) when they make their own sentence combinations. When students have learned noun subordinate clauses, they soon figure out that gerund phrases function in the same way. The major problem with the learning of gerunds is their similarity to present participles. However, this not only provides the excuse to review participles but also allows everyone to see how to determine if a phrase is a present participial phrase or a gerund phrase by what it is doing in the sentence. Teaching the punctuation rules for these two structures is a breeze: With the exception of a noun clause or a gerund phrase functioning as a nonessential appositive, no commas are needed. Everyone likes that.

All writing now requires the following: *present and past participial phrases, gerund phrases, appositive phrases, absolute phrases, and all three types of subordinate clauses, as well as the use of the solo semicolon and the conjunctive adverb.*

The final major structure is the **infinitive phrase,** pp. 140–142. Here the students are asked to take another step backward. These students recognize prepositional phrases from their previous years in grammar instruction; some, though not all, can distinguish between the adjective and the adverb prepositional phrase. My students look again at the prepositional phrase in order to focus on exactly how to tell the difference between an adverb and an adjective phrase and then apply what they have learned to what they have already been taught this year about adverb and adjective subordinate clauses, thus more review. Where are the adverb and adjective prepositional phrases usually located? What questions might adverbs and adjectives answer, whether they be single words, clauses, or phrases? Now, they apply this information to the adverb and adjective infinitive phrase. Finally, the noun infinitive phrase becomes easy to teach because students see how noun infinitive phrases act in the same way as gerunds and noun subordinate clauses.

Student papers during the remainder of the year contain highlighted examples of everything taught: *present and past participial phrases; gerund phrases; adverb, adjective, and noun infinitive phrases; appositive phrases; absolute phrases; all three types of subordinate clauses; as well as the correct usage of the solo semicolon and the conjunctive adverb.*

## BIBLIOGRAPHY

Applebee, A.N. *Writing in the Secondary School.* Urbana, Illinois: National Council of Teachers of English, 1981.

Beal, C.R., A.C. Garrod, and G.J. Bonitatibus. "Fostering Children's Revision Skills Through Training in Comprehension Monitoring." *Journal of Educational Psychology* 82 (1990):275–280.

Brown, J.S., A. Collins, and P. Duguid. "Situated Cognition and the Culture of Learning." *Educational Researcher* 18.1(1989):32–42.

Charney, Davida H, and Richard A. Carlson. "Learning to Write in a Genre: What Student Writers Take from Model Texts." *Research in the Teaching of English* 29.1(1995): 88–125.

Cheng, Xiaoguang, and Margaret S. Steffensen. "Metadiscourse: A Technique for Improving Student Writing." *Research in the Teaching of English* 30.2(1996): 149–181.

Connors, Robert, and Cheryl Glenn. *The St. Martin's Guide to Teaching Writing.* 3rd ed. New York: St. Martin's Press, 1995.

Corbett, Edward P.J, and Robert J. Connors. *Classical Rhetoric for the Modern Student.* 4th ed. New York: Oxford UP, 1999.

Crawford, J. and C. Haaland. "Predecisional Information Seeking and Subsequent Conformity in the Social Influence Process." *Journal of Personality and Social Psychology.* 23 (1972):112–119.

Faigley, Lester. "Problems in Analyzing Maturity in College and Adult Writing." *Sentence Combining and the Teaching of Writing.* Eds. Donald Daiker, Andrew Kerek, and Max Morenberg. Conway, AK: L&S, 1979.

Faigley, Lester, and S. Witte. "Analyzing Revision." *College Composition and Communication.* 32 (1981):400–414.

Flavell, J., Botkin, P., Fry, C., Wright, J., and P. Jarvis. *The Development of Role-Taking and Communication Skills in Children.* New York: Wiley, 1968.

Flower, Linda. "Taking Thought: The Role of Conscious Processing in the Making of Meaning." In *Thinking, Reasoning, and Writing.* E.P. Maimon, B.F. Nodine, and FW O'Connor (Eds). New York: Longman. 185–212.

Gunderson, B. and D. Johnson. "Promoting Positive Attitudes Toward Learning a Foreign Language by Using Cooperative Learning Groups." *Foreign Language Annuals.* 13 (1980):39–46.

Hawkins, T. "The Relationship Between Revision and the Social Dimension of Peer Tutoring." *College English.* 40 (1980): 64–68.

Hillocks, G. Jr. *Research on Written Composition: New Directions for Teaching.* Urbana, IL: National Council of the Teachers of English. 1986.

Huff, R. and C. Kline. *The Contemporary Writing Curriculum: Rehearsing, Composing, and Valuing.* New York: Teachers College Press, 1987.

Johnson, D. and A. Ahlgren. "Relationship Between Students' Attitudes About Cooperation and Competition and Attitudes Toward Schooling." *Journal of Educational Psychology.* 68 (1976):92–102.

Johnson-Laird, P. *Mental Models.* Cambridge, MA: Harvard University Press, 1983.

Kerek, Andrew, Donald A. Daiker, and Max Morenberg. "The Effects of Intensive Sentence-Combining on the Writing Ability of College Freshmen." *The Territory of Language.* Ed. Donald McQuade. Carbondale: Southern Illinois UP, 1986.

Lave, J. and E. Wegner. *Situated Learning: Legitimate Peripheral Participation.* Cambridge: Cambridge University Press, 1991.

McCann, Thomas M. "Student Argumentative Writing Knowledge and Ability at Three Grade Levels." *Research in the Teaching of English* 23.1(1989):62–76.

Pajares, Frank, and Margaret J. Johnson. "Confidence and Competence in Writing: The Role of Self-Efficacy, Outcome Expectancy, and Apprehension." *Research in the Teaching of English* 28.3(1994):313–331.

Perl, S. "How Teachers Teach the Writing Process." *The Elementary School Journal.* 84 (1983): 19–24.

Pressley, Michael, and Vera Woloshyn. *Cognitive Strategy Instruction That Really Improves Children's Academic Performance.* Cambridge, MA: Brookline Books, 1995.

Raphael, Taffy E, et al. "Students' Metacognitive Knowledge about Writing." *Research in the Teaching of English* 23.4(1989):343–379.

Rico, Gabriele Lusser. *Writing the Natural Way.* Los Angeles: Tacher, 1983.

Smagorinsky, Peter. "The Writer's Knowledge and the Writing Process: A Protocol Analysis." *Research in the Teaching of English* 25.3(1991):339–364.

Sperling, Melanie. "I Want to Talk to Each of You: Collaboration and the Teacher-Student Writing Conference." *Research in the Teaching of English* 24.3(1990):279–321.

Stolarek, Elizabeth A. "Prose Modeling and Metacognition: The Effect of Modeling on Developing a Metacognitive Stance toward Writing." *Research in the Teaching of English* 28.2(1994): 154–174.

Straub, Richard. "Students' Reactions to Teacher Comments: An Exploratory Study." *Research in the Teaching of English* 31.1(1997):91–119.

Sweigart, William. "Classroom Talk, Knowledge Development, and Writing." *Research in the Teaching of English* 25.4(1991): 469–496.

Wallace, David L, and John R. Hayes. "Redefining Revision for Freshmen." *Research in the Teaching of English* 25.1(1991): 54–66.

Williams, Joseph M., and Gregory G. Colomb. "The Case for Explicit Teaching: Why What You Don't Know Won't Help You." *Research in the Teaching of English* 27.3(1993): 252–264.

Williams, Joseph. "Coherence and Cognitive Style." *Written Communication.* 2 (1985): 473–491.

Yagelski, Robert P. "The Role of Classroom Context in the Revision Strategies of Student Writers." *Research in the Teaching of English* 29.2(1995): 216–238.

# 1

DEVELOPING WRITING SKILLS

**OBJECTIVES**

Writing "to show" develops universal writing skills:
• learning to elaborate ideas with concrete singular detail;
• strengthening the writer's usage of active verbs;
• controlling verb tense; and
• incorporating a variety of sentence structures to eliminate redundancy and wordiness.

To improve critical thinking/reading by
• analyzing and observing details closely;
• considering thoughtfully the power of diction; and
• transferring these skills to readings in other disciplines.

## WRITING TO SHOW[1]

When authors write, they don't just *tell* the reader something; they *show* the reader what is meant. What are the pictures and images writers see, hear, smell, touch, and taste? Writers might think of themselves as photographers. What images will be shot to convey meaning? Writing to show, however, does not mean creating sentences with multiple adjectives that are vague, abstract, or general.

**Editing Symbol**

For example, the following list of adjectives reflects the type sophisticated writers *avoid*: great, immense, huge, scary, dangerous, bad, strong, powerful. The showing sentence relies on active verbs, concrete singular nouns, and concrete adjectives. For example, "His right foot catches a pile of crumpled white shirts in the doorway."

The following two paragraphs attempt to describe the same scene. Read them, noticing all the places where the second paragraph shows the reader details that the first paragraph doesn't.

### A telling paragraph

He gets ready for the race by tying his shoes. Feeling pretty nervous, he examines his shoes. His ankle hurts. He hears the announcer tell the athletes to get ready. After he gets in a position, he hears the gun start the race. All his limbs are moving fast and his feet pound on the concrete.

### A showing paragraph
*by Mauricio Delgado*

*Items in bold refer to the accompanying commentary in shaded area.*

The muscles in his left leg tense up as he shifts the weight of his body to one side while kneeling down to **tie his right shoe. Cross the first with the second, pull. Loop across, bring around, pull, braiding together the frayed gray laces of his Adidas spikes as skillfully as a seamstress weaves with thread**.

Extends elaboration: tying the shoe

With the pride of even the fleet-footed Achilles, the athlete inspects his sacred wings of land attentively as he quickly brushes off a few blades of grass and dirt collected on the instep of his sneaker. His ankle soon begins to throb with a lack of blood circulation to his foot; in fact, the knot of his shoe is so tightly laced that he can hardly feel his toes suffocating inside his shoe **like sardines packed in a tin can**. "Participants in the

Uses a simile

100 meters, report to the starting blocks. Third and final call." The announcement, monotonous and resounding, trumpets over the loudspeaker, abruptly breaking his current thoughts. At once he reaches down and relieves the pressure of the knot and walks briskly towards the crowded starting line. Crouching down on the red asphalt track, he stretches his hamstrings as a final precaution and positions himself on the starting blocks. "Runners on your marks!" His left leg fully extends backwards with the base of his foot resting gently on the shiny metal block. His right leg is bent almost at 90 degrees directly underneath him,

Absolute phrase

**sweat beginning to drip from his chin to his thigh**. He finally drops his shoulders and lowers his arms to the blistering asphalt, setting

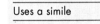

---

1 Adapted from Caplan, Rebekah, and Catharine Keech. *Showing Writing: A Training Program to Help Students Be Specific.* University of California, Berkeley, 1980.

his hands directly behind the painted white starting line. "Get set!" Immediately his rear ascends in the air, followed by his back and then his head. He rocks backwards then forwards, his heart racing anxiously, awaiting the crack of the gun. "Pop!" The whip-like crack of the metal hammer against the cartridge puts his muscles and joints in action. He shoots off the blocks with a sudden electrical vigor. His burning calves energize his quadriceps, which thrust the rest of his body forward. Right leg, left arm forward. Left leg, right arm forward. His limbs propel in rhythmic action while his heart pumps blood to the palpitating muscles. Inhale. His chest grows and his lungs expand with oxygen. Exhale. The body repels harmful gasses as the cycle continues. His breathing grows deeper and faster; the finish line grows more imminent and attainable. **Implanting themselves into the loose gravel and cracked asphalt**, the spikes on his cleats tear up the track as his heels pound the ground. Using his peripheral vision, he spots a blurry figure half a step in front of him in the next lane.

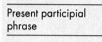

Present participial phrase

### Telling vs. showing

A **telling paragraph** is very general. It doesn't show the reader pictures and images; any effort that allows the reader to see, hear, taste, and touch concrete objects is weak or nonexistent. The reader does not see the *person* "tying his shoes" nor does the reader see the *actual tying* of a shoelace.

The **showing paragraph** is very specific. It is full of details and examples, which are elaborated—and can continue to be elaborated even more—so that we see what is being talked about as though we were viewing a picture. The writer shows the reader an athlete "who shifts the weight of his body to one side while kneeling down to tie his right shoe." The writer, therefore, is like a painter: The pen is his or her brush that is used to make everything come alive.

## WHEN "WRITING TO SHOW," SHOW FROM THE FIRST!

When writing the first sentence, the author begins with images that the reader can see, hear, smell, taste, touch. The goal is to grab the reader's attention and never let it go.

*Five threads poke out on the bottom left edge of the cap where the stitching has broken loose.*

*His brown, greasy hair swats his scarred face with each galloping stride. Gripping his Smith & Wesson in his left hand, he plummets through a pant pocket with his right, in futile search of an additional clip that he knows does not exist.* Instead, his bony index finger protrudes through a hole to reach a sticky thin layer of blood on his right quadriceps, where a single shotgun shell met its target.

*Tom begins to slide his fingers underneath the corners of the rectangular envelope.* He gently breaks the seal and can hear the loud ripping sound as the solid white envelope dismantles.

*His clenched fist shoots forward like a bullet out of a barrel as it digs its way into the boy's soft flesh just below his right eye, leaving a bright red trail of warm blood.* Trickling down the side of his face, the stream of blood slowly drags itself over the smooth curve of the boy's jaw, and then it drips on to the stiff pocket of the freshly starched shirt just above his rapidly beating heart.

## EXTENDING ELABORATION

**Editing Symbol**

**E3**

When the writer first introduces an image or idea, he or she should not immediately move to a new image after one sentence or phrase. Take time to make additional comments about the image, extending our understanding of it.

*by Michael Spurlin*

His right foot catches a pile of crumpled white shirts on the floor in the doorway, causing him to stumble as he enters the room, the side of his left ankle sliding across the purple burbered carpeting. As he puts down his left foot he hears the loud snap of the pencil breaking beneath his bare foot. The splintery wood begins to dig into the arch of his foot. As he slowly lifts his left foot, one-half of the yellow number two pencil sticks to his foot. He shakes his leg and the pencil piece bounces off the wall and falls to the floor.

*by Matt Connolly*

A jet black tomcat springs out from underneath the debris on the desk, soaring over a vast array of knives, needles, and thumb tacks scattered across the carpet. The cat lands safely on the yellow stained mattress wedged into the far right corner of the room. Oblivious to the rusty springs that have burst through the mattress cover, the cat stretches out on a pile of dusty pillow feathers at the head of the bed. It begins to swat at a fat green caterpillar crawling slowly toward a small hole in the wall. Being denied the opportunity to complete its destination, the caterpillar is hurled onto the floor a few feet in front of me.

*by Chris Hampton*

A bead of salt-watery sweat slowly drips down the marred and contorted features of his face. He feels the sting of salt as it travels down and through the three-inch gash just above his left eyebrow; down it creeps, over what would have been the bridge of his nose had it not been smashed into tiny fragments of cartilage, pus, blood, and mucus. The bead continues across the face, a tiny mirror of agony, as it follows each and every groove in the man's face: the jagged and irregular "v" in the nose, the size twelve hiker's boot with the three-inch sole and steel toe that cut his right cheek bone to white ribbons with a touch of red, the lipless mouth, long ago empty of tongue and but a few chipped teeth, once brilliant, now dull and grotesque with fragments of bone, enamel, and vomit caked over his three thousand dollar smile. The sweat finishes its trail of tears where it deems to rest on his chin, the only area of his face left just as it began. Promptly it falls to the floor, making what the man appears to believe is a huge thud. Where an angelically pure bead of saltwater began, a hellish collage of bone, blood, pus, and oozing vomit now end.

### How Writing to Show Connects to Expository Argument

To begin developing writing skills of students by working with "writing to show" exercises before working with "pure" exposition is to put the horse where it belongs. In my experience with the teaching of writing, one of the major problems is that most exposition by young writers lacks a spark of interest, a touch of creativity that distinguishes the writing and makes a reader—including the teacher—want to read it. Great writing is not a lackluster vanilla exercise, and that includes the expository essay form. The narrative and descriptive aspects of "writing to show" that allow students to, among other things, hone their elaboration techniques, their manipulation of sentence structures, and their abilities to work with concrete nouns and vivid verbs prepare students for the crafting of lively expository argument.

## SAMPLE WRITING TO SHOW COMPOSITIONS

*Assignment: "Show" an athlete in action at a specific moment in time*

*by Adam Klugiewicz*

Strong hands violently massage Johnny's aching back muscles. Ebony fingers, dancing nimbly, dig into the quivering brawn and knead the soft white dough. **Johnny's glassy stare falls upon the shiny blue mat, cool and azure as a gentle mountain lake; rocking his head back slowly upon its rusty hinges, his gaze opens up to the other side of the ring.** There sits his opponent, nearly a thousand miles away, waiting. For an instant their eyes meet: Blue piercing orbs stab Johnny, scorching white hot lances puncture him for a brief fiery instant, forcing him to

> A compound sentence, its two independent clauses joined by a semicolon

look away. A voluptuous walking carnival of sequins, make-up, and softly colored silk scarves parades around the ring bearing a large white board adorned with the number 12. Johnny **glances** down into a gray rusted steel bucket into which he **spews** a grisly mixture of spit and blood. It **splashes** and **ripples** into a miniature whirlpool for an instant, then **sinks** into the cool

> Note the vivid verbs throughout the piece.

depths of the tiny cesspool. Dozens of hands without faces attend to him. Fingers **strap** a bandage upon the gouge, splitting his left eyebrow, while others **cram** a water bottle into his cracked, parched lips and **squeeze** lukewarm water into his dry burning mouth; still others wipe the sweat from his brow with a velvety white Nike towel. **Floating directly in front of him,** the only face Johnny can see is Coach O'Reilly's. Finally, Johnny tunes into the coach's

> Two present participial phrases

gravel-filled voice. "Let's go now, kid! Bring this one home." He can barely distinguish the brass bells' high coppery chime from the low iron bells **already ringing in his head.** A final disembodied hand forces the grimy mouthpiece into Johnny's throbbing jaws, **criss-crossed by haphazard stitching** and **lined with shattered teeth.** With hip flexors painfully groaning and knees

> Two past participial phrases

cracking sharply, he draws himself up upon two shaky rubber planks. Johnny tediously swings the lead pendulums up from his sides and holds his aching hands in front of him in the fighting position. He valiantly marches to meet his opponent in the middle of the ring. The two opponents' eyes meet again.

Johnny's opponent glares at him from behind two red walls of padded glove, **his wiry torso swaying back and forth as the cobra prepares to strike.**

<aside>An absolute phrase extends the elaboration further.</aside>

**Assignment: "Show" someone who is afraid without telling the reader that the person is afraid**

<aside>*by Derek Rollins*</aside>

His brown greasy hair **swats** his scarred face with each galloping stride. Gripping his Smith & Wesson in his left hand, he **plummets** through a pants pocket with his right, in futile search for an additional clip that he knows does not exist. Instead, his bony index finger **protrudes** through a hole to reach a sticky thin layer of blood on his right quadriceps, **where a single shotgun shell has met its target.** His dark blue-stained velvet coat flies in the wind like the cape of Superman; his reputation proves he is far from heroic. Coming to a stop, he covers himself in the blanket of the far-reaching shadow of a garbage container, hitting against its side with a metallic cling. Sitting down to catch his breath, the seat of his hole-ridden pants crunch against a large brown, abhorrent cockroach, ending its menial existence with a repulsive squish. **A multicolored concoction oozes from the roach's intestines, the roach's blood staining the concrete, but the man remains oblivious to all but the crunching sound.** Off in the distance, past the garbage can that affords him minimal but necessary hiding, and beyond the decrepit old bum that on most occasions inhabits it, he hears the sound. The soft but ever-present rhythmic tapping of the hooves and metal horseshoes of the solitary steed, drawing with it the infamous brown wooden stagecoach, with a wheel that squeaks loud enough to warn any nearby criminals to flee, beats against the worn cobblestone pavement. Commanding the vehicle is, as always, Chief Quimbey, the stout, sloppy, yet respectable chief of police for the small English county of Westmorland. He stands semi-upright, knees bent, chubby hands clinched to the reins, holding on for dear life. The hot wind rushes by his fat face, leaving a tingling, burning sensation. He rhythmically casts out the black leather strips, crashing onto his engine's flesh. For the first time, after nearly an hour of swift pursuit, he reaches into the tight left jacket pocket, **retrieving his monogrammed off-white silk handkerchief. He swipes the thick lather of his own warm sweat from his hairy wrinkled brow. He returns the handkerchief to the pocket, hitting another pool of sweat under his arm on the way down. His thin, blue cotton shirt shows off many other such pools.** Immediately, his focus returns to the chase. **As the end of the dark alley approaches**, he slows the horse to a quick trot, a relief from the feverish pace that has been steadily maintained. The panting of the beast is quite audible. He turns his head and glares at the vagabond, who points an unsteady, dirty, drunken finger past his beloved dump

<aside>Vivid verb choices enhance the concrete detail.</aside>

<aside>An adjective subordinate clause</aside>

<aside>This compound sentence, its first independent clause containing an absolute phrase, extends the elaboration of the cockroach mentioned in the previous sentence.</aside>

<aside>The writer extends the elaboration of both the handkerchief and the sweat.</aside>

<aside>An adverb subordinate clause</aside>

site. Quimbey abruptly pulls the reins up toward his chest, his arms slightly shaking. Glancing down the slope of his belly and with a quick, deft hand, the chief returns a single, golden button that has come undone back to its proper place. **Reaching behind him, he grasps the uncomfortable but official standard English police hat, tall and red with a golden lion crest, and he mounts it on his round head. Out of habit, he pulls the thick plastic arc under his unshaven chin.** Dismounting from the great height of the worn-down coach, he sniffs the air, only to meet the stench of a week-old carcass of a mid-sized rat, which lies adjacent to his left steel-toed boot. The body looks to have been generously ravaged by fellow creatures of the night. Kicking the gut-wrenching body aside, he casually turns the corner to face his longtime evasive foe.

> The writer's attention to the singular detail of the hat and what its wearer does with it creates a solid concrete image.

### Assignment: "Show" that a specific object is old without telling the reader that it is old

*by Travis Baggett*

**A warped label desperately clings to the inside of the collar by mere threads, as though a previous owner had decided to rip it from the shirt and then changed his mind after the job was more than half-done.** The tag's faded orange letters read "X-Large," although the actual size of the article to which it clasps has shrunken to more of a "medium" over the years. The front of the shirt bears a monogrammed logo and name in the middle of the chest; the top of the logo, reaching to within an inch of the collar, extends down approximately seven inches below this peak height. At its widest point, the logo and lettering are eight inches in breadth. The white, monochrome design reeks of age. The once solid-white screen paint has acquired a mosaic quality, **a composition of thousands of tiny, yet discernible, broken tiles trying desperately to seek freedom but bound by their enduring chemical properties, which hold them fixed to the fabric.** The areas of white are like the baked floor of a vast drylands: cracked, weathered, beaten, hard, and flat—coarse to the eye and to the touch. The dull blue permeates the cracks between the broken tiles of paint and, for once, begins to assume a certain vitality against the cold contrast of faded white, as though nourishing the cracked, depleted surface. **The monogram's design features a soccer player clad in a light shirt, dark shorts, and knee-high socks; the player's body staggers sharply to the viewer's right, as if he might explode off that side of the shirt at any moment. A light-colored semicircle, with the rounded side facing up, serves as a background for the top half of his figure. Inside the top left arc of the background, five blue stars are stamped in a single-file manner along the slope of the curvature, just above the player's right shoulder and outstretched right arm.**

> The writer begins description of the sweatshirt with a complex sentence containing two adverb subordinate clauses.

> An absolute phrase ending with an adjective subordinate clause

> The writer focuses on details of the monogram's design for a number of sentences.

**Assignment: "Show" a person or creature in the act of doing something distinctly ordinary**

*by Brian Costanza*

Standing naked in the middle of the master bathroom, Cameron trembles as the Hunter fan violently blows against the water residue left on his body. White goose bumps magnify as he reaches for his white cotton jockey briefs with the fingertips of his left hand. **The fringed, size thirty-three garment moving closer to his body, Cameron lifts his left leg. As the leg rises, the tendons in his toes retract like a hermit crab. Both arms gripping the elastic band, his quadriceps thrust his left appendage through the abyss of the underwear. As his leg drives its way through the warm undergarment, his shin rubs against part of the front side of the aperture. A shadow trails the underwear during its entire expedition up the hairy leg.** Cameron, who begins to air dry, elevates his right leg to a forty-five degree angle. Since he feels engulfed by ice, his right leg subtly shudders as it embarks on its path through the deep hole. When his leg touches the cold white ceramic tile floor, the hairs on his toes rise in shock. Cameron decides that he will take a stronger grip on the elastic band, which reads Jockey around its face. As he attempts to raise the underwear up his legs, the back side of the left leg hole catches itself under his left heel. Cameron releases the white cotton with his left index finger. Cameron, **clasping his left hand back on the elastic band,** exerts all of his strength and energy into the elevation of his underwear. **His forehead wrinkles like an aged prune, and his eyebrows move closer and closer until they eventually take the shape of a single brow.** As the undergarment makes its way past the knees, it violently pulls each hair that it encounters during its journey.

> The writer extensively elaborates the left leg's encounter with the jockey briefs.

> A present participial phrase located after the noun it modifies

> A compound-complex sentence, with one of its independent clauses containing an adverb subordinate clause

## THE REVISION PROCESS WHEN WRITING TO SHOW

The writer should follow these suggestions and respond to these questions:

- read the composition out loud slowly to others and to oneself.
- seek feedback from a variety of sources.
- purposely make both additions and subtractions:
  —emphasize what the person or creature is physically doing.
  —allow yourself to "re-envision" what will happen in your paper; include details you did not consider showing the first time; eliminate what does not come across well and what is unnecessary because they merely *tell.*
- make sure each sentence maintains the same focus (on a single character or single action or single object or single emotion) in every sentence.
- strive for each detail being extensively elaborated so that any reader may create a clear mental picture of the detail in all of its particulars.
- keep in mind that plurals are difficult to show or elaborate; it is the singular item, the singular event, the singular individual, the singular action that can best be elaborated extensively.

- avoid sentences that contain lists of vague or abstract adjectives; work toward concrete nouns and vivid verbs to build the showing sentence.
- create an opening sentence that truly grabs a reader's attention.
- combine sentences that entail related ideas by
    —turning one into a participial phrase and attaching it to the other;
    —turning one into a subordinate clause and attaching it to the other;
    —joining two sentences together with a semicolon only or with a correctly punctuated conjunctive adverb;
    —removing unexciting and unnecessarily repeated words from sentences and combining the crucial details that remain into one complete sentence.
- seek out the verb in each clause: Is each verb in *present* tense? Is each *vivid*?
- rework sentences by eliminating "be" verbs and substituting stronger verbs for them.
- correct misspellings, punctuation errors, run-on sentences, and any sentence fragments.

## "WRITING TO SHOW" ASSIGNMENTS AND ACTIVITIES

The following set of showing assignments helps students develop the universal writing skills they will need when crafting any type of essay:
- elaborating ideas extensively,
- using concrete details,
- focusing on the singular,
- choosing active, vivid verbs,
- controlling verb tense,
- manipulating grammatical structures, and
- grabbing the reader's attention.

Students should avoid the use of the abstract, vague, or general adjective; instead, students should build their sentences with concrete and singular nouns and active verbs, relying only on a few carefully chosen concrete adjectives.

In addition, with each assignment the teacher requires a particular grammatical structure(s) for students to highlight—present or past participial phrases, adjective or adverb clauses, absolute phrases, compound or compound-complex sentences, etc.—so that these young writers become accustomed to employing in a gradual and conscious manner syntax that increases the sophistication of their sentences. See "A Suggested Lesson Planning Sequence," p. 14, for ways of incorporation.

Finally, students should recognize that these assignments are not ultimately intended to be exercises in writing fiction. These exercises introduce students to one of the most difficult aspects of good writing: developing the ability to reflect on a topic and to choose words carefully, to choose words that are concrete and specific. In other words, they develop universal writing skills that teach students to write with language that is precise and singular. When our language laps into the vague and general, our writing becomes less meaningful.

### Writing to Show Assignment #1

**Telling Sentence:** *He is scared* or *She is scared.*

or select a different telling sentence, p. 45

**Task** Using a minimum of 15 lines (maximum 30 lines), write a composition that shows a person afraid without the reader being told that the person is afraid.

- Do not use the telling sentence, or any synonyms for it, in the composition. Therefore, *scared, frightened, horrified, terrified, fear, dread,* and the like will not be used by the writer. That would be telling the reader, instead of showing the reader, that the person is afraid.
- When students wonder, "Where do we begin?" or "How do we begin?" the most appropriate response is often *in medias res*; begin somewhere in the middle of the action. This composition's beginning is whatever the writer says it is, and since the emphasis is on showing an action, then the writer might begin with the starting point of an action.
- Show all the senses: sight, sound, touch, taste, smell.
- Show each specific movement, detailed action, as if you were filming it frame by frame; let the reader see each particular object involved in the action.
- Avoid plurals.
- Use imaginative vocabulary, vivid verbs.
- Vary the beginnings of each sentence.
- Use present tense only. (When we write about literature, we will discuss the action in the literary text in the present tense.)

### Writing to Show Assignment #2

**Telling sentence:** *The _____ is a mess* or *The _____ is old.*

or select a different telling sentence, p. 45

**Task** Fill in the blank with the name of an object—the object could be a desk, a racket, a poster, a shoe, a shelf, a drawer, a stove, a binder, a gym bag, a baseball glove, a sock, etc.. Your task is to show that the object is a mess or is old (choose one or the other) without telling the reader that it is.

- Follow all directions for Writing to Show Assignment #1 (as they are important, it is recommended that the student carefully read once again those directions); for this new assignment, also include the following changes or additions:
- Focus on specific minute details of the object. Spend many sentences—not just one sentence—on each detail before going on to the next detail.
- You must use a minimum of two present participial phrases in your composition. Highlight each of those phrases (do not highlight the entire sentence the present participial phrase is in—highlight only the phrase).
- Be sure your participial phrases are correctly punctuated. Place one of the phrases before the noun it modifies; place the other after the noun it modifies.
- Use spatial transitions to take the reader smoothly from one part of the object to another part. (Examples of some transitions: *next to, to the left of, in the right corner, underneath, adjacent to, on top of, along side of,* etc..)
- Give your piece a title.

**Telling Sentence:** *The athlete is exhausted* or
*The athlete becomes exhausted.*

or select a different
telling sentence, p. 45

**Task** The writer is to focus on one athlete performing a specific action that would lead to such exhaustion. This action may be one play in a game or one moment in an event. In a composition of 25–30 lines, the writer must thoroughly elaborate this single action from first sentence to last. Students and teacher might brainstorm possible examples of one athlete in such a specific situation. The term "athlete" may involve any activity that produces physical and/or mental exhaustion. A brainstorming list of this kind could include instances such as the following: a batter hitting a home run, a runner preparing to start a race, a swimmer on his or her final lap, a running back during one play of a game, a chess player's single movement against an opponent, a volleyball player's serve for match point.

After selecting the specific action, the writer might *think of the action as though it were happening in slow motion.* Observe exactly what is happening physically and/or mentally. Note the details, especially the subtle details, as they occur second by second.

* Follow all directions for Writing to Show Assignment #1; include the following changes or additions:
* Raise the minimum number of lines from 15 to 25.
* Continue using present tense; it's important that students maintain control of tense.
* Students are to employ two to five correctly punctuated present participial phrases, highlighting and labeling each one. (If students have studied past participial phrases, the teacher might require a combination of both present and past participial phrases. Some students will wonder *how a past participial phrase can be used when one is writing in present tense*; although the participle in a participial phrase is a verb form, the participle and its phrase are functioning as adjectives—and adjectives modify nouns or pronouns regardless of the verb tense.)
* Highlight two correctly punctuated adverb subordinate clauses.
* Employ vivid vocabulary: vibrant action verbs and precise concrete nouns.
* Give your piece a title.
* Avoid the excessive use of "be" verbs.
     —*Kiss "is" goodbye.*
     —*Make "am" into spam.*
     —*Kick "are" very far.*
     —*Turn "was" into fuzz.*
     —*And give your "were" a burr.*

## Writing to Show Assignment #4

**Task** Closely observe some person or creature in the act of doing something very ordinary. The following are merely some examples: a student in the act of taking a test, a child or select a different telling sentence, p. 45 learning to take his or her first steps, a bird leaving its nest for the first time, a child chasing a butterfly, a teenager learning to drive a car, a mosquito stinging someone, a dog gnawing on a bone, a person eating a bowl of cereal, someone washing dishes, someone washing his or her hands, the act of slicing a turkey, the act of slicing an onion, someone brushing his or her teeth.

- Follow all directions for Writing to Show Assignment #1; include the following changes or additions:
- The composition is to be 15 to 25 lines, written in present tense only.
- Every line must elaborate the one ordinary action.
- Highlight and label two of each of the following structures that you have studied up to this point. (*Note to teachers: The grammatical structures you have students highlight are dependent, of course, upon which structures you have taught up to that point.*)
    —present participial phrase
    —past participial phrase,
    —adjective subordinate clause,
    —adverb subordinate clause,
    —compound sentence with semicolon, and
    —compound sentence with a conjunctive adverb.
- Don't unnecessarily tell the reader who the person or creature is. Use suitable pronouns ("he," "she," or "it") and allow your showing to reveal to the reader who or what is performing the ordinary action. Let your word pictures reveal all.
- Give your piece a title.

## Writing to Show Assignment #5

**Task** Select a telling sentence from the "Writing to Show List of Telling Sentences," p. 45. Show what the sentence can reveal when language that employs concrete nouns and vivid verbs is used.

- Follow the directions outlined for Writing to Show Assignment #4.

## WRITING TO SHOW LIST OF TELLING SENTENCES

She (he) is very old.
It hurts.
It is the most difficult test I've ever taken.
He (she) is nervous.
I am nervous.
The car breaks down.
He (she) slips and falls.
The flower grows.
He (she) thinks he's (she's) cool.
He (she) steals second.
I am embarrassed.
The athlete is exhausted.
The baby is cute.
He got mad.
The jock thinks he's (she's) cool.
He (she) (it) moves quickly.

He (she) has never been so happy as he (she) is now.
The room is vacant.
Lunch period is too short.
She (he) has a good personality.
The party is fun.
He (she) is scared.
The pizza tastes good.
My parents seem angry.
The movie is frightening.
The _____ is a mess.
The _____ is old.
The house is falling down.
The house is haunted.
He is acting crazy.
_____ is strict.
_____ is absent-minded.

## OTHER WRITING TO SHOW ASSIGNMENTS

### Assignment: "Destroying showing writing"

**Directions** Select one of the sample "Writing to Show" exercises on pp. 42–44. Replace the concrete, singular details with plurals, vague words, abstract nouns, and weak verbs. Remove phrases or sentences where the writer has extensively elaborated.

### Assignment: Practicing extending elaboration (E3)

**Directions** Extend the elaboration of the following sentences.
1. His bony fingers brush aside the *Time* magazine.
2. Her math textbook rests along the edge of the desk.
3. Mr. McAlfiend's right hand grasps my biology final exam.
4. She reaches into the refrigerator for the gallon of 2% lowfat milk.

### Assignment: Begin with a showing image! (SH & V)

**Directions** Improve the following sentences by removing vague details and replacing them with concrete, singular ones; extend the elaboration of each detail by adding additional sentences. Show a specific object or action from the original sentence in much more detail.

Original: A nervous man with a bag walks at night toward his destination.

Revised: A man in black slithers through the shadows along the wall. He caresses the velvet bag filled with gold coins, just to assure himself of its continued existence.

1. As Mark prepares to go home, behind him his classmates make fun of him.
2. The old man is startled.
3. She drops her textbooks and quickly kneels down to gather them up.

### Assignment: Using vivid verbs ⬭

**Directions** Remove the following "be" verbs and use more active ones.
1. The face is sweaty now and his mind is screaming.
2. The overwhelming rage she felt 30 seconds ago is now replaced by the vibrations of her lower lip.
3. He has his rifle ready, and there is sweat dripping from his face. (Change "has" as it, too, is a weak verb.)
4. Her behavior was barbaric.
5. The temperature is too hot.

### Assignment: Removing vague details (V & WC)

**Directions** The following sentences contain words or phrases that are too general or abstract; work toward singular, concrete, specific detail. Fix, especially, the words or phrases in bold typeface.
1. The roof **has stains** and **has become** frail.
2. The **heavenly aroma** drifts through the kitchen.
3. He **holds** the football **with all his might**.
4. She always **wears a red cap** when she **plays tennis**.
5. Her purse **appears heavy** and **looks like it has seen better days**.

## PUBLISHING PROJECT

### The Writing to Show Anthology

After assigning four different "writing to show" compositions to his students, one of the teachers who uses these techniques has his students select one of their pieces for a thorough revision. Through peer editing activities, the composition is revised with a variety of goals in mind. Once the teacher is satisfied that the selection is publication-ready, the students prepare their final draft in a similar format (font size, spacing, titling, etc. all the same) and then the compositions are copied, collated, and published in an anthology that the students keep in their English binders throughout the year. Furthermore, the title of the anthology is created (by majority vote of the class) by students, each one having made a suggestion ahead of time, and the art for the cover (made of heavier stock) is designed by one or more of the students. The revision checklist for the second draft, p. 48, requires highlighting certain sentence structures; this highlighting will *not* be done for the final draft that is to be published. What follows is the specific procedure the teacher uses.

### Revision process for the publication of a writing to show composition
Due _____: *the second draft*   Due _____: *the published final draft*

1. A newly revised draft of the "writing to show" composition you seek to have published:
   - 25 to 50 typed lines;
   - every line pure showing, each detail extensively elaborated;
   - at least three present participial phrases used and punctuated correctly;
   - at least two past participial phrases used and punctuated correctly;
   - at least three adverb subordinate clauses used and punctuated correctly;
   - at least one solo semicolon used and punctuated correctly;
   - at least one conjunctive adverb used to join two independent clauses;
   - all verbs in present tense;
   - no more than one "be" verb allowed;
   - quality diction (dictionaries and thesauri will be used, of course);
   - concrete nouns and vivid verbs (attack weak verbs—Do not use such weak verbs as *seems, feels, gets*; do not use *have* or *has* as main verbs);
   - eliminate unnecessary repetitions;
   - avoid one-word onomatopoeia (Bang! Crunch!); instead, use as verbs;
   - no run-on sentences, comma splices, or misspellings.
2. The draft will be typed
   - double-spaced, one-inch margins; 12 pt. size; very readable font.
3. The draft must have a meaningful and creative title (do not use the original telling sentence)
   - centered at top of the page; made 24 to 36 pt. size;
   - centered underneath the title is your name in 12 pt., plain (no "by ___").
4. If you would like a small drawing to accompany text, do it in black ink.

*When you revise, follow the "Revision Process When Writing to Show," pp. 40–41, and make your revisions on the original draft itself, using a different color of ink or pencil.*

# REVISION CHECKLIST FOR THE SECOND DRAFT

**Directions** This checklist for the second draft must be completed and then attached to both the second draft and the original draft and signed by both the student and a parent.

1. The original copy should be thoroughly revised in a different color of ink or pencil. (For this assignment, telling me you did all the revisions on the computer will not be acceptable unless you computer allows you to show the specific changes as well as the original.)
   *Yes, this is done* _____ *No, this is not done* _____

2. I have highlighted three present participial phrases on the second draft. At least one of these phrases is located directly after the noun or pronoun it modifies. (Highlight the phrase, not the entire sentence.)
   *Yes, this is done* _____ *No, this is not done* _____

3. I have highlighted two past participial phrases on the second draft. At least one of these phrases is located directly after the noun or pronoun it modifies. (Highlight the phrase, not the entire sentence.)
   *Yes, this is done* _____ *No, this is not done* _____

4. I have highlighted three adverb subordinate clauses. (Highlight the clause, not the entire sentence.)
   *Yes, this is done* _____ *No, this is not done* _____

5. I have highlighted a solo semicolon that joins two independent clauses. (Highlight the semicolon, not the entire sentence.)
   *Yes, this is done* _____ *No, this is not done* _____

6. I have highlighted one conjunctive adverb that is joining together two independent clauses.
   *Yes, this is done* _____ *No, this is not done* _____

7. I have provided a key that explains the highlighting of the aforementioned sentence structures.
   *Yes, this is done* _____ *No, this is not done* _____

8. I have made substantial changes in the original draft that help to elaborate extensively details in a number of places in the composition, changes that enrich it and help the reader see more precisely what it is that I am trying to show him or her.
   *Yes, this is done* _____ *No, this is not done* _____

9. I have checked every verb and have made sure that all verbs are in present tense. (The rare exception would be a point in time when a past event is momentarily being shown.)
   *Yes, this is done* _____ *No, this is not done* _____

10. I have made sure that my verbs are vivid, the type that helps the reader to see what I'm trying to show. I have eliminated all "be" verbs (*am, is, are, was, were*) and all weak verbs such as *seem, feel, appear* and the use of *have* or *has* as main verbs.
    *Yes, this is done* _____ *No, this is not done* _____

11. I have made my opening sentence dynamic so as to grab the reader's attention.
    *Yes, this is done* _____ *No, this is not done* _____

12. I have made every effort to raise the quality of diction (word choice) in this composition in order to increase the clarity and elegance of each sentence. I have, at times, used a dictionary and/or thesaurus for the second draft.
    *Yes, this is done* _____ *No, this is not done* _____

13. I have typed the second draft as directed (12 pt., double-spaced, one-inch margins) and have produced a meaningful, creative title, centering both the title and my name as directed on the other side of this sheet.
    *Yes, this is done* _____ *No, this is not done* _____

Signature of student _____ Date _____

Signature of parent _____ Date _____

# 2

## EXPOSITORY PARAGRAPH

### DEFINITIONS

The expository paragraph is the building block of an argument, an argument for a larger paper or an argument answering an essay test question. In a larger paper, each paragraph's function, its connection to the thesis statement, should be clear. Paragraphs can be classified into three general types, according to their function:

**• One-idea paragraph**
This paragraph begins with a clear topic sentence and elaborates, or develops, a single aspect of the thesis statement, or it provides a single unified answer to an essay test question.

**• Subordinate paragraph**
This paragraph begins with a topic sentence connected to a preceding paragraph. This paragraph is an extension of the idea introduced in the previous paragraph because one plank of the thesis statement may need to be proven by more than one paragraph. For example, one may be writing about courageous characters. The initial paragraph may define courage in its topic sentence and then proceed to use one character as an example of the definition in the topic sentence. The next paragraph may provide elaboration of a second character, one who also fulfills the definition of courage stated in the preceding paragraph.

**• Glue paragraph**
This much shorter paragraph serves as a *transition* between main ideas, or topics.

# ONE-IDEA AND SUBORDINATE PARAGRAPHS: QUALITIES

### Topic sentence

A focused idea, one that supports a thesis statement or responds to an essay test question, is placed as the first sentence of a paragraph, which tells the

**Editing Symbol**

**TS**

reader the specific topic and any related issues the writer will be discussing in the paragraph. If the paragraph is part of a larger paper, the topic sentence will include two parts: *organization method + aspect of the thesis statement.* (Note: Not all skilled writers place the topic sentence as the first sentence; some place the topic sentence in the middle of the paragraph or near the end; others write paragraphs in which the topic sentence is assumed. These are skills I address individually with students as they master basic foundations of paragraphing. Beginning writers should first practice using the topic sentence as the opening for paragraphs.)

### Elaboration

An idea, a focused point, is extended and illustrated further by five types of examples:

**Editing Symbol**

**E**

• direct quotations from the text followed by the writer's commentary,
• paraphrase of details from the text and commentary,
• direct quotation blended with commentary,
• additional explanation of an idea, and
• discussion of a contemporary or literary comparison.

### Coherence

A writer ties a collection of sentences together with *word glue* and *logic glue* so that the reader understands why one sentence follows the next and how the writer organizes the evidence to support the topic sentence. The writer must continually be aware that the reader has not examined the evidence in the same manner as the writer. For this reason, the writer should use strategies of coherence to help the reader see the argument the way the writer sees it.

### Sentence variety

Varying lengths and types of sentences produce a pleasing cadence to prose. Moreover, a writer's ability to use parallel structure and modification illustrates and helps communicate more complex ideas.

### Diction

Writers should use appropriately sophisticated vocabulary, vivid verbs, and concrete nouns.

## STEPS IN CONSTRUCTING THE PARAGRAPH

### Step One: Create the topic sentence
*Write the topic sentence* in response to a test question or in support of a thesis.

### Step Two: Gather evidence supporting the topic sentence
*Gather evidence* that includes specific details (concrete showing details in the literary text) the writer may include in the paragraph. Make sure the evidence proves, or supports, the topic sentence. After evidence-gathering, the topic sentence may need revision.

Consider the following questions, *among others,* when searching for evidence:

- Where does the evidence occur in the plot or poem?
- What actions of a character support the topic? When do these actions occur? Why do they occur?
- What does a character say that supports the topic? When does the character say it? Why is it said?
- What is revealed by the narrator that provides supporting evidence?

Then, write out key passages that relate to your topic sentence.

### Step Three: Apply four strategies for drafting paragraph

### Drafting Strategy One: Organize the evidence
When writers gather concrete details to support a topic sentence, they must decide how to arrange the evidence. Clearly arranging the evidence assists the reader in understanding the writer's argument. What follows are *three* common ways of organizing evidence.

Editing Symbol

**P1**

### Organizing Method One: Time
Organize according to *chronology*—the order of the narrative's plot, for instance, or of major details in the poem.

Topic: The Sonnet as Metaphor for Brevity                    *by Frank McEachern*

*The sonnet form allows the poet to express man's ability to change.* Limited to only fourteen lines, the poem's brevity lends itself to expressing the quickness with which man moves in his thoughts. In "On His Being Arrived to the Age of Twenty-three," the author demonstrates the narrator's quick turnaround. **At first** the man feels cheated by time: "Stolen on his wing my three and twentieth year" (2), **while** "no bud or blossom show'th" (4). Also, individual words like "thief" and "stolen" are utilized to further demonstrate the narrator's despondency with his life. Then, the **last six lines** show the narrator's change as he overcomes his despondency. **Here**, he realizes that the world is a fair one in which time "shall be still in strictest measure" (10). **Next,** he analyzes his limited accomplishments, realizing that his success, "however mean or high" (11), is part of a larger plan and that he should be grateful for what he has, "so that I have the grace to use it so"(13). Therefore, as the man's thoughts change in limited time, the form is an effective tool in demonstrating the rapid change of thought in man.

### Organizing Method Two: Place

Topic: Joe Gargery as Active Servant of Community

*Pip's surrogate father, Joe, frequently safeguards Pip when he is in desperate need, demonstrating throughout the story that a servant must be an active participant in restoring community.* In the opening **kitchen** scene, for example, "gentle" Joe guards a young Pip "with his great leg" (14; ch. 2) from an enraged Mrs. Joe and her tickler. Here he actively attempts to shield Pip from being raised "by hand." In fact, Joe tells Pip he "wish there warn't no" (43; ch. 7) beatings for him. Later, at the **Christmas dinner,** Joe again alleviates the attacks on Pip from the holiday guests, who torment him and compare him to "swine." With each insult, Joe gives Pip "more gravy," demonstrating that small gestures can help ease the grief of individuals and help the community move closer toward love. Finally, **in London,** Joe helps Pip convalesce after his illness. Joe has chosen to leave the forge, his means of employment, to serve Pip, who eventually recognizes the pain he has caused both Joe and Biddy. Moreover, Pip sees Joe as the true "gentle man," the servant who has helped him become a more loving member of the community.

### Organizing Method Three: Idea

Organize according to the ideas introduced in the topic sentence. Often, these ideas are parts of a definition, an analogy, a comparison/contrast, a classification, or a cause and effect that the writer will apply to the text.

### Cause and Effect

Topic: Madame Defarge in *A Tale of Two Cities*                    *by Zachary Kettler*

*As one who refuses to be "recalled to life," Madame Defarge allows her desire for revenge to consume her memories of the past, her present life, and her future aspirations.* Her brother killed by a member of the Evremonde family, Madame Defarge **dedicates her life to the eradication** of every member of the Evremonde family, including Darnay; in fact, "it [is] nothing to her, that an innocent man [is] to die for the sins of his forefathers. She [sees], not him, but them" (281; ch.14). Seeking her revenge with **anger ascending all boundaries of moral justice,** Madame Defarge tells her husband that he can "tell the Wind and Fire where to stop…but don't tell [her]" (264; ch.12). In the end, **her desire for ultimate revenge results in her own death**—killed ironically by her own pistol. In the same manner as her brother, who is killed in the pursuit of retribution, Madame Defarge dies in **her pursuit of the extermination of Darnay's family**, her obsessive revenge paling in the presence of Miss Pross's love. Killed by Miss Pross and the "vigorous tenacity of love, always so much stronger than hate" (286; ch.14), Madame Defarge forfeits her recall to life because of her odious pursuit of retribution, a pursuit of retribution by iniquitous means leading only to a nefarious end.

## Definition

Topic: The knight's qualities in *The Canterbury Tales*

*Chaucer depicts the knight as a virtuous pilgrim, a person who fights for the Church, rejects extravagance in exchange for humility, and treats those around him with respect.* **Respecting others** means refraining from insults, a habit many others indulge. The Knight, however, "never yet a boorish thing had said / In all his life to any, come what might" (68–69). It is **this courtesy** that people from other countries recognize and revere: "He often sat at table in the chair / Of honour, above all nations, when in Prussia" (50–51). The Knight's respect is juxtaposed with **his humility,** his lack of desire to flaunt wealth extravagantly: "He possessed / Fine horses, but he was not gaily dressed" (71). In fact, not only does he avoid "fine" clothes, but he does not care about trivial aspects of his appearance, arriving at the pilgrimage "with smudges where his armour had left marks" (73). This pilgrimage ranks higher than any worldly concern. For the Knight is most concerned with his **spiritual commitment,** his obligation to the Church. He takes this duty seriously, having "done nobly in his sovereign's war / And ridden into battle" (45–46). Chaucer tells us how often the Knight has **battled successfully**: "In fifteen mortal battles he had been / And jousted for our faith at Tramissene" (60–61). Indeed, these battles, as well as his appearance and behavior toward others, earn the knight Chaucer's praise as "a most distinguished man" (70).

## Analogy

Topic: Imagery of birds in *Romeo and Juliet*                    *by Ryan Wallis*

*Shakespeare's ingenious utilization of bird imagery creates lucid pictures of man's physical and emotional qualities.* The importance of **physical appearance** quickly becomes apparent as we observe people being judged based upon their beauty or their lack of it. Soon after we learn that the maiden Rosaline will not reciprocate Romeo's love, we witness Benvolio, Romeo's companion, encouraging him to attend a party held by the Capulets, enemies of Romeo's family. Benvolio assures Romeo that **Rosaline will resemble a crow instead of a swan** when compared to "all the admired beauties of Verona" (1.2.86). Shakespeare's clever choice of a repulsive **crow** invents a vision of ugliness that contrasts with the pulchritude of a swan. Romeo, however, denies that he could ever see Rosaline as anything but the most **beautiful maiden.** Having heard Romeo's declaration of undying love, we find it surprising and a bit amusing when a fickle **Romeo views Juliet at the party and claims she is "a snowy dove** trooping with crows" (1.5.49). Selecting a **snowy dove** to portray Juliet elicits notions of pure and elegant beauty; we can just imagine her niveous complexion. Since Rosaline is now among the maidens whom Romeo considers crows, his adamantine vow to forever declare her lovely is broken. Indeed, he now thinks of her as an unsightly, vexatious bird. Later, when Friar Lawrence learns of Romeo's new love, he scolds Romeo and other young men for having love that "lies not truly in their hearts, but in their eyes" (2.3.67–68). Friar Lawrence, having lived long and learned much, considers Romeo weak since his change of heart seems to be based on Juliet's **outward appearance** rather than her inner beauty. Likewise, even in today's world, it is true that many people esteem physical attractiveness above strength of character. In addition to the artistic use of the dove and the crow to contrast the beauty and the ugliness of women, Shakespeare employs bird imagery to describe the physical attractiveness of men. Characterized by Juliet's nurse as "a lovely gentleman" (3.5.220) and having **greener, quicker, and fairer eyes than an eagle, Paris** is chosen by Lord Capulet, Juliet's father, to marry his daughter. Selecting an eagle to demonstrate the physical attributes of Paris proves successful. Undoubtedly, his eyes attract the attention of women because of their **stunning appeal.** The **eagle,** having keen sight above all birds, is a symbol of powerful beauty; Paris, having eyes more astounding than an eagle, portrays an even more exquisite image. Truly, Shakespeare includes many examples of **beauty** and its significance. Similarly, early mythological writings emphasize the merits of physical beauty. In the story of Cupid and Psyche, we behold the power of Psyche's loveliness as throngs of men worship her beauty and neglect Aphrodite, another example of literature shaping our understanding of beauty.

### Classification

Topic: The infernal marriage in *Great Expectations*                    *by Max Rosenblum*

*When the story opens, the reader encounters the first marriage, Joe and Mrs. Joe, a disconsolate marriage symbolizing the infernal level of comedy where truth and innocence are preyed upon.* In this case, the **cruel Mrs. Joe**, who "takes [Joe] by the two whiskers, [and][ knocks[s] his head for a little while against the wall behind him" (9; ch.2), **constantly dispenses blows, both physical and verbal,** to the **honest and innocent Joe**, "a mild, good-natured, sweet-tempered, easy going, foolish, dear fellow" (6; ch.2), belittling him when she complains of being "a blacksmith's wife, and (what's the same thing), a slave with her apron never off" (19; ch.3). **Mrs. Joe exhibits the selfishness** frequently found in the infernal comedy, declaring to Joe and Pip what "a precious pair [they'd] make without [her]," a statement that clearly displays her feelings of self-importance. In an extreme display of selfishness, she dresses Pip up to go off to Miss Havisham's, reminding that "he better go play there…or [she'll] make him work" (46; ch.7) and how beneficial this opportunity will be not for Pip, but "for us" (47; ch.7)—**not** exactly words of a **selfless,** nurturing mother. Even Pip shows confusion regarding Mrs. Joe's motives because he does not know "why on earth [he] was going to play at Miss Havisham's or what on earth [he] was expected to play at" (48; ch.7). Finally, **Mrs. Joe demonstrates hypocrisy,** the last mark of infernal comedy, when she hosts the Christmas party for all of her pseudo higher class acquaintances. Pip points out this quality of insincerity when he describes his sister as "unusually lively on the present occasion, and indeed…generally more gracious in the society of Mrs. Hubble than in other company" (22; ch.3).

## Comparison / Contrast

Topic: Mr. Stryver and Sydney Carton in *A Tale of Two Cities*      *by Jeff Erfe*

*The reader first meets Stryver and Carton at the first trial of Charles Darnay in the Old Bailey, an encounter in which Dickens juxtaposes both characters, revealing their true natures and opening them up for comparison.* Dickens first introduces the man with no first name, a man known simply in the business context as **Mr. Stryver, the greedy opportunist** who constantly strives to edge out the competition and climb the ladder of capitalistic success. Simultaneously funny yet disturbing, Dickens notes how Stryver has "a pushing way of shouldering himself (morally and physically) into companies and conversations" (60; bk. 2, ch. 4), and the reader witnesses this firsthand as **Stryver "shoulders" poor Mr. Lorry out of the group so he can boast** his success at acquitting Darnay. When the bloated Stryver finally leaves, in skulks Sydney Carton, and the reader is presented with glaring **contrasts** that highlight **Carton's pitiable desperation** and Stryver's worldly "success." As in his own business ventures, Carton does not "shoulder" out others from the group, but instead coolly leans "against the wall" (61; bk. 2, ch. 4) **outside the circle** "where its shadow [is] darkest" (61; bk. 2, ch. 4). Obviously, Carton represents Stryver's polar opposite: whereas Stryver jumps at the opportunity to praise himself and receive adulation, Carton **sits in the corner** and no one makes "any acknowledgement of [his] part in the day's proceedings" (60; bk. 2, ch. 4). Furthermore, he **contrasts** Stryver's previous bombastic assertions by admitting that he has "no business" (60; bk. 2, ch. 4), at least not in comparison with the great Mr. Lorry. By the end of the chapter, he has established himself as a **drunk, self-deprecating loser** for whom "no man cares" (63; bk. 2, ch. 4), the perfect **antithesis** for the haughty and unscrupulous Stryver.

### Drafting Strategy Two: Add necessary transitions

### A1 = transitions clarifying direction of paragraph

| Editing Symbol |
| --- |
| **A** |

After the initial topic sentence, further clarify and identify the path the paragraph intends to take, that is, the organization of material: time, place, idea.

#### Original

Through examples in gesture and conversation, Dickens depicts Scrooge as selfish, stubborn, and pessimistic. For example, he keeps his door "open so that he might keep an eye upon his clerk" (13; ch. 1).

#### Revision with transitional sentence added

Through examples in gesture and conversation, Dickens depicts Scrooge as selfish, stubborn, and pessimistic. **Scrooge displays his selfishness in his treatment of his employee.** For example, he keeps his door "open so that he might keep an eye upon his clerk" (13; ch. 1), a devious eye that enjoys watching his employee freeze next to a dying fire.

### Original

Dickens reveals Scrooge's rudeness and anger. For instance, approached by his nephew who wishes him "A Merry Christmas, Uncle," Scrooge rudely sputters out "Bah! Humbug!"—his temper numbing the seasonal joy.

### Revision with transitional phrases and clauses added

Dickens reveals Scrooge's rudeness and anger **towards the people around him, particularly his nephew and employee, Bob Cratchit. Such an attitude is reflected in his words and actions.** For instance, approached by his nephew who wishes him "A Merry Christmas, Uncle," Scrooge rudely sputters out "Bah! Humbug!"—his temper numbing the seasonal joy.

## A2 = Transitions defining general idea in topic sentence

Add a phrase or clause to the end of the topic sentence to further define a general word appearing in the topic sentence. Then apply definition to the text.

### Original

The Christmas dinner scene at Bob Cratchit's that Scrooge observes depicts the ideal family. Mrs. Cratchit is dressed in "ribbons, which are cheap and make a goodly show for sixpence" (77; ch.1).

### Revision with transitional phrases and clauses added

The Christmas dinner scene at Bob Cratchit's that Scrooge observes depicts the ideal family, **a family that celebrates despite ill fortune, that encourages all its members to share in responsibility, that practices acts of selflessness.** For example, **despite their poverty,** Mrs. Cratchit is dressed in "ribbons, which are cheap and make a goodly show for sixpence" (77; ch.1), **for she is able to express joy and celebration within their economic means.**

### Original

Donne uses metaphors to remind us of man's communal nature. He compares the church to one body. He needs the church, "whereof [he is] a member" (10), as a form of support, just as the head, "ingrafted into that body" (10), needs the help of the body, the larger group or structure that provides life. He compares man to a book, demonstrating that they are both "of one author" and that man naturally belongs to a community as a book belongs to a "volume."

### Revision with transitional phrases and words added

Donne uses metaphors to remind us of man's communal nature, **metaphors that reveal man's need to belong to a larger group. First**, the poet compares the church to one body. He needs the church, "whereof [he is] a member" (10), as a form of support, just as the head, "ingrafted into that body" (10), needs the help of the body, the larger group or structure that provides life. **Next,** Donne compares man to a book, demonstrating that they are both "of one author" and that man naturally belongs to a community as a book belongs to a "volume."

### Exercise: adding appropriate transitions

**Directions** Between the topic sentence and the sentence that currently follows it, create and insert either a separate transitional sentence, or a transitional clause or phrase that is attached to the topic sentence.

1. Mark is an ideal father. Last night, his eyes often drooping, he stayed up past midnight working with his daughter on a science project.
2. The public library contains reading material for every interest. A copy of *Sports Illustrated* rests on the cushioned chairs next to the magazine racks.
3. My mother demanded that I organize the mess on my desk. A petrified slice of half-eaten pizza lay atop the essay for English class I never turned in.

### Drafting Strategy Three: Maintain topic focus

Within a paragraph, a writer's sentences must focus on the topic that appears in the topic sentence. When the writer crafts a sentence that does not flow from the paragraph's stated or implied topic, such a change, or shift in topic, is likely to confuse the reader. *To prevent this problem, craft the paragraph's supporting sentences so that whatever appears at the beginning of each supporting sentence maintains the reader's focus on the paragraph's topic.* This is sometimes done by repeating the **exact topic word or words.** However, since serious writers of expository prose usually vary the beginnings of their sentences, they avoid the *monotonous usage of repetitive wording* at the beginning of supporting sentences; instead, they often use, among other connecting possibilities, **synonyms** and **pronouns** for the paragraph's topic to avoid such monotony. These writers understand, as well, that sentences do not have to start with the subject; at times, for example, their sentences open with an **introductory phrase or subordinate clause.** Regardless of the type of sentence opening, the focus of that part of the sentence ought to act as a tie, or connection, to the paragraph's topic, such connections being known as the *topic string*. The writer, then, manipulates at least four strategies to avoid monotony while creating the topic string: the occasional usage of repetitions, synonyms, pronouns, and introductory phrases or clauses.

**Editing Symbol**

**T4**

#### Original shifts in topic

In *Lord of the Flies,* **Jack's proud nature** leads to the destruction of order and authority on the island. **The conflagration, representing the boys' only hope** to leave the island, burns out due to his lack of supervision, a careless decision that commences the power struggle with Ralph. **Ralph is the elected chief** on the island and he complains about Jack hunting, even though Jack says that "we needed meat" (65; ch. 4), an action defying Ralph's authority and showing that Jack believes he knows what is best for the boys. **Later at that night's assembly, the boys** are disorderly and Ralph attempts to gain control. **He even shouts at Jack,** "You're breaking the rules!" (84; ch. 5) to which Jack responds, "Who cares?" (84; ch. 5) clearly showing his apathy towards Ralph's power and his arrogance believing that he made the right decision.

### Revision that keeps topic in focus

In *Lord of the Flies,* ***Jack's proud nature*** leads to the destruction of order and authority on the island. **Jack's pride** first manifests itself when the conflagration, representing the boys' only hope to leave the island, burns out due to his lack of supervision, a careless decision that commences the power struggle with Ralph. **In explaining his course of action, Jack** tells Ralph that "we needed meat" (65; ch. 5), an action defying Ralph's authority and showing that Jack believes he knows what is best for the boys. In response to **Jack's continued rebellion,** Ralph, at a nightly assembly, shouts at Jack, "You're breaking the rules!" (84; ch. 5) to which Jack responds, "Who cares?" (84; ch. 5) clearly showing his apathy towards Ralph's power and **his arrogance** as he believes that he made the right decision.

### Exercise: Correcting topic shifts

**Directions** In the following paragraph, what begins each supporting sentence shifts the focus away from the topic as stated in the topic sentence. Rewrite each supporting sentence so that its beginning creates a distinct tie to the topic.

*Scrooge is an inexorably bitter and greedy man,* bitter in his attitude towards the holiday season, and greedy in his refusal to share any of his wealth with people less fortunate. **In the beginning, his nephew** wishes him a Merry Christmas but Scrooge's only reply is "Bah! Humbug!" **Money** is more of a concern than responding to the kindness of his nephew. **Dickens** further shows Scrooge's cupidity with the cynical questions he later asks his nephew: "What right do you have to be merry? What reason do you have to be merry? You are poor enough" (13; ch. 1). **Christmas is a time** to be concerned with others and their needs rather than one's own needs, a point Scrooge completely disregards even though his nephew attempts to explain the holiday "as a good time; a kind, forgiving, charitable, pleasant time" (15; ch. 1).

### Drafting Strategy Four: Use word and logic glue for coherence

**Editing Symbol**

**T1**

Word and logic glue is necessary to provide coherence for a paragraph. These transitions between each sentence help the reader understand how each sentence supports the topic.

### • Word Glue

Word glue is the actual wording a writer uses to tie, or blend, two sentences together so that the reader understands the writer's thinking process.

**Key words** Literal and synonymous repetitions of words in one sentence that refer to an idea from a previous sentence

**Traditional transitional words** (see appendix for a more extensive list)

| | | | |
|---|---|---|---|
| for example | furthermore | in addition | therefore |
| to illustrate | moreover | likewise | consequently |
| next | later | finally | that is |
| as a result | even though | for this reason | first, second, etc. |

**Pronouns** Words such as *it, he, she, they, those, these, this, that* used to refer to nouns in previous sentences

### • Logic Glue

Logic glue represents the relationship between two sentences. This relationship is *implied, rather than stated with transitional words*. The following is a list of the *types* of logical relationships that occur between sentences. Although these words, or synonyms for them, do not always appear between sentences, the reader recognizes that they represent the logical relationship between them.

*and*.................continues the same idea with new facts
*but/yet*.............a change in the idea of the previous sentence
*or*....................an alternative for what is stated in the earlier sentence
*that is*..............a definition or restatement of the idea in the earlier sentence
*for example*.....an illustration of the idea in the earlier sentence
*therefore*..........a conclusion or effect based on the earlier sentence
*for*...................a reason or cause for what is stated in the earlier sentence

### More transitional words

See p. 194 for a more comprehensive listing of transitions.

### Sample paragraph examining the function of coherent language

| *Each sentence of the paragraph is numbered; the two columns to the right refer to the sentences by their numbers.* | **Word Glue** Actual words linking sentences | **Logic Glue** Implied relationship linking sentences |
|---|---|---|
| 1. Many of us in our competitive society, which emphasizes material success, do not take *personal risks*. | 1–2 personal risks | 1–2 and |
| 2. We often view *personal risks* as taking too much *time*. | | |
| 3. *For example*, some of us would find stopping in the middle of the day to discuss a friend's problem too *time*-consuming. | 2–3 time/for example | 2–3 for example |
| 4. We feel *these moments* could be spent acquiring additional *assets*, real estate investments, or stocks. | 3–4 time/these moments | 3–4 and |
| 5. For many of us, acquiring *this wealth* is an impetuous goal, for we do not often view risk-taking as a lucrative *investment*. | 4–5 assets/wealth | 4–5 and |
| 6. Unfortunately, our "lucrative *investments*" that monopolize motivations will continue to prevent risk-taking and personal growth. | 5–6 investment/ investments | 5–6 therefore |

### Exercise: *Working with transitional word and logic glue*

**Directions** Place in the blanks the word and logic glue that binds each set of two sentences together.

**Word Glue / Logic Glue**

1. Chaucer not only reveals violations of religious vows, but also violations of basic Christian theology.

2. One such character who flagrantly violates both his religious vows as well as Christian theology is the Friar.

1–2    <u>violations</u> / <u>for example</u>

3. The elitist Friar deems himself "better than lepers, beggars and that crew" (230), and, in fact, refuses to deal with such "scum."

2–3    _____ / _____

4. His refusal of service openly contradicts the most basic teachings of Jesus—to love thy neighbor as thyself and to love unconditionally.

3–4    _____ / _____

5. The Friar loves only those who have money to give, for he knows "nothing good can come of commerce / with such slum-and-gutter dwellers" (239–240).

4–5    _____ / _____

6. In fact, money dominates the life of the beggar Friar, an open violation of his vow of poverty.

5–6    _____ / _____

7. The Friar, however, is seemingly ignorant of his vows as a clergyman, particularly those of poverty and chastity: "He kept his tippet stuffed with pins for curls, / and pocket-knives, to give to pretty girls" (230–231).

6–7    _____ / _____

8. Not unlike the Friar, the Monk, too, openly violates his vow of poverty as a direct result of his affinity towards the material world.

7–8    _____ / _____

# EXAMPLE PROCESS ONE FOR CONSTRUCTING A PARAGRAPH

### Responding to an essay question

### Essay Question
What is revealed in the opening dialogue of *A Christmas Carol*?

### Step One
*Write the topic sentence/*answer the essay question.

In the opening dialogue of *A Christmas Carol*, Dickens creates Scrooge's shallow personality by the repetition of diction associated with money.

### Step Two
*Gathering evidence.*
- "You're poor enough" (13; ch. 1).
- "What's Christmas time to you but a time for paying bills without money; a time for finding yourself a year older...not an hour richer" (14; ch. 1).
- "at the ominous word 'liberality,' Scrooge frowned, and shook his head" (17; ch. 1).
- "I can't afford to make idle people merry...they cost enough" (19; ch. 1).
- "If I was to stop half-a-crown for it, you'd think yourself ill-used...and yet you don't think me ill-used, when I pay a day's wages for no work" (21; ch. 1).

### Step Three
*Organization method.*

Time: The writer follows the chronology of events in the story.

### Step Four
*Write the paragraph.*

In the opening dialogue of *A Christmas Carol*, Dickens creates Scrooge's shallow personality by the repetition of diction associated with money. ***Almost every comment Scrooge makes includes economic diction***. For example, when Scrooge's nephew **first arrives** to greet him a "Merry Christmas," Scrooge disdainfully comments about his nephew's monetary status:

> Note the transitional sentence bridging the topic sentence to the first supporting detail.

"You're poor enough" (13; ch.1), a statement that shows how Scrooge evaluates individuals by their monetary value. His nephew ignores Scrooge's remark and urges his uncle to enjoy the season. Scrooge instead sees Christmas in terms of money: "What's Christmas time to you but a time for paying bills without money; a time for finding yourself a year older, and not an hour richer" (14; ch.1). Unable to see the holiday as an opportunity for building relationships, Scrooge even disregards his nephew's new strategy of speaking with the diction of economy, stating that "I have not profited" from Christmas. Moreover, when his nephew exclaims, perhaps because he feels his uncle might be suspicious of possible monetary desire, that "I want nothing from you; I ask nothing of you" (14; ch.1),

Scrooge **ends the conversation abruptly,** indicating that since his nephew has expressed no financial motives, there exists no other reason to hold a conversation with him. This language of economy continues when **a few minutes later** two gentlemen arrive to solicit donations for the poor. Scrooge even reacts physically to the notion of parting with his money; the narrator explains that "at the ominous word 'liberality,' Scrooge frowned, and shook his head" (17; ch.1). **Later in the conversation,** he laments that "I can't afford to make idle people merry...they cost enough" (19; ch.1). Therefore, his contribution is "nothing" (18; ch.1). **Finally, Scrooge's conversation with Bob Cratchit,** his clerk, revolves around money. Scrooge moans that Bob will "want all day tomorrow, I suppose?" (21; ch.1) He continues to explain how Christmas has created an economic problem for him: "If I was to stop half-a-crown for it, you'd think yourself ill used...and yet you don't think me ill-used, when I pay a day's wages for no work" (21; ch.1). Here Scrooge demonstrates that he cannot even perceive Cratchit as a human being but as an economic possession, swindling him unfairly.

## EXAMPLE PROCESS TWO FOR CONSTRUCTING A PARAGRAPH

*Responding to a thesis statement*

### Thesis Statement
Simon possesses several characteristics of a Christ-like figure.

### Step One
*Write the topic sentence.*
First, Simon often helps those in need, paralleling Christ in his selflessness.

### Step Two
*Gathering evidence.*
- "finding for them the fruit that they could not reach, pulling off the choicest from up in the foliage" (56; ch. 3).
- "littluns cry out unintelligibly" (56; ch. 3).
- "shoving his piece of meat over the rocks to Piggy" (73; ch. 4).

### Step Three
*Organization method.*
<u>Place</u>: Where/In which places does Simon show he is selfless and helps others in need?

### Step Four
*Write the paragraph.*
First, Simon often helps those in need, paralleling Christ in his selflessness. This concern for others occurs with both the smaller children and the older ones. For example, **in the jungle** struggling to find food to preserve his own life, Simon assists the littluns by "finding for them the fruit that they could not reach, pulling off the choicest

from up in the foliage, and passing them back down to the endless, outstretched hands" (56; ch.3). Because Simon supplies nourishment for the littluns in a time of need, they "cry out unintelligibly" (56; ch.3) for him to become their provider, just as Jesus' followers intuitively sought his assistance in times of distress. In addition, **at a campfire** Simon demonstrates his willingness to put aside his own needs in order to provide for others by graciously sharing with Piggy. For instance, while Jack denies Piggy a piece of meat "as an assertion of power" (73; ch.3), Simon provides for him by "shoving his piece of meat over the rocks to Piggy" (73; ch.3). Here Simon shows his ability to put aside his needs for someone outcast, much like Christ did, serving and dining with the poor and ostracized.

## EXAMPLE PROCESS THREE FOR CONSTRUCTING A PARAGRAPH

### Responding to an essay question

### Essay Question
What is important about the escape scene in Huckleberry Finn?

### Step One
*Write the topic sentence/*answer the essay question.
Huck's escape scene reveals several characteristics about his personality.

### Step Two
*Gathering evidence.*
- "I had tried to get out of the cabin many a time, but I couldn't find no way. There warn't a window to it big enough for a dog to get through" (52; ch. 7).
- "saw a section of the big bottom log out—big enough to let me through" (54; ch. 7).
- "rid of the signs of my work and drop the blanket and hide my saw" (58; ch. 7).

### Step Three
*Organization method.*
<u>Idea</u>: Identify Huck's personality traits as they appear chronologically.

### Step Four
*Write the paragraph.*
Huck's escape scene reveals several characteristics about his personality. Aware that he's in a dangerous situation, Huck is **determined** to escape: "I had tried to get out of the cabin many a time, but I couldn't find no way. There warn't a window to it big enough for a dog to get through" (52; ch.7). This temporary setback doesn't stop him, and he **perseveres** even after hunting "the place over as much as a hundred times" (52; ch.7). Finally, Huck finds "an old rusty wood saw without any handle" (58; ch.7); he **cleverly** discovers that "under the table" he can raise the blanket and "saw a section of the big bottom log out—big enough to let me through" (54; ch.7). Not only does he devise this sagacious escape route, but also he knows he must get "rid of the

signs of my work and drop the blanket and hide my saw" (58; ch.7). This clever thinking, however, is not enough; he needs his **imagination**: "I says to myself, I can fix it now so nobody won't think of following me" (58; ch. 7). What he fixes is a feigned murder, taking "the gun and [going] up a piece into the woods" where he sees "a wild pig; so I shot this fellow and took him into camp" (58; ch. 7). Its blood spilling on the cabin floor, Huck prepares a **creative** death scene, pulling "out some of my hair, and [bloodying] the ax good,... [sticking] it on the back side, and [slinging] the ax in the corner" (58; ch. 7). When finished, his mind **still thinking**, he takes "a dipper and a tin cup, and my old saw and two blankets, and the skillet and the coffee pot" (58; ch. 7), provisions he knows he'll need later on his journey, a journey apart from the violent danger of Pap.

## REVISION PROCESS: QUESTIONS TO ASK ABOUT PARAGRAPHS

### Topic sentence
- Does each topic sentence clearly help support the argument in the thesis?
- Does the topic sentence contain more than one specific idea? Is it too broad?

### Coherence
- Is there a clear transition immediately after the topic sentence? Is it clear how the writer is going to organize the information in the paragraph?
- Is it clear what the logic glue and word glue is between each sentence?
- When the writer includes direct quotations, are these blended as if the words are part of the sentence, or is there an abrupt introduction?

### Elaboration
- Is it clear how the textual passages support the topic sentence? Does the writer explain how the reader should understand these details?
- Is the writer merely summarizing details from the story without explaining why they prove the topic sentence?
- Is it clear how each sentence helps support the topic sentence?
- Has the writer provided enough evidence to support the topic sentence?
- Are there quotations needing elaboration through commentary and analysis?

### Sentence variety
- Do some sentences need to be combined, using an absolute phrase, a participial phrase, analysis modifier, repeat word modifier, subordinate clause, infinitive phrase, gerund phrase, semicolon, conjunctive adverb?

### Diction
- Is the diction precise and concrete? Or does it contain vague and abstract ideas that may be confusing? Do wordy structures need revising?

## FIXING THE PARAGRAPH PROBLEMS

The following are examples of the editing marks, or symbols, located on the teacher's editing key listed in the appendix, pp. 196–197. The symbols are placed here in alphabetical order for ease of use. The teacher will use these marks on all student work. Students should consult this section if they are unsure how to respond to the teacher's use of a symbol.

## A = ADD A TRANSITIONAL PHRASE OR SENTENCE

**Editing Symbol**

**A**

**A1** = After the initial topic sentence, further clarify and identify the path the paragraph intends to take, that is, the organization of material: time, place, idea.

**A2** = Add a modifier to the end of the topic sentence to further define and specify a general word that appears in the topic sentence. Then apply this definition to the text.

### Original A1

Dickens reveals Scrooge's rudeness and anger. For instance, Scrooge's nephew says, "A Merry Christmas, Uncle! God save you."

### Revised

Dickens reveals Scrooge's rudeness and anger towards the people around him, **particularly his nephew and his employee Bob Cratchit. Such an attitude is reflected in his words and actions.** For instance, approached by his nephew who wishes him "A Merry Christmas, Uncle," Scrooge rudely sputters out "Bah! Humbug!"—his temper numbing the seasonal joy.

### Original A1

Through examples in gesture and conversation, Dickens depicts Scrooge as selfish, stubborn, and pessimistic. For example, he keeps his door "open so that he might keep an eye upon his clerk" (13; ch. 1).

### Revised

Through examples in gesture and conversation, Dickens depicts Scrooge as selfish, stubborn, and pessimistic. **Scrooge displays his selfishness in his treatment of his employee.** For example, he keeps his door "open so that he might keep an eye upon his clerk" (13; ch. 1), a devious eye that enjoys watching his employee freeze next to a dying fire.

### Original A1

Besides utilizing bird imagery to depict physical qualities, Shakespeare also employs such imagery to illustrate emotional characteristics of man. For example, Romeo says that "love's light wings" (2.2.67) enable him to conquer the barrier that separates them.

### Revised

Besides utilizing bird imagery to depict physical qualities, Shakespeare also employs such imagery to illustrate emotional characteristics of man. **Clearly, one recognizes the depth of Romeo's love when he scales the walls of Juliet's**

**home to testify of his love for her.** Questioned by Juliet as to how he got there, Romeo answers that "love's light wings" (2.2.67) enable him to conquer the barrier that separates them.

### Original A1

The Christmas dinner scene at Bob Cratchit's that Scrooge observes depicts the ideal family. Mrs. Cratchit is dressed in "ribbons, which are cheap and make a goodly show for sixpence" (77; ch.1).

### Revised

The Christmas dinner scene at Bob Cratchit's that Scrooge observes depicts the ideal family, **a family that celebrates despite ill fortune, that encourages all its members to share in responsibility, that practices acts of selflessness.** For example, despite their poverty, Mrs. Cratchit is dressed in "ribbons, which are cheap and make a goodly show for sixpence" (77; ch.1), for she is able to express joy and celebration within their economic means.

### Original A2

Donne uses metaphors to remind us of man's communal nature. He compares the church to one body. He needs the church, "whereof [he is] a member" (10), as a form of support just as the head, "ingrafted into that body" (10), needs the help of the body, the larger group or structure that provides life. He compares man to a book, demonstrating that they are both "of one author" and that man naturally belongs to a community as a book belongs to a "volume."

### Revised

Donne uses metaphors to remind us of man's communal nature, **metaphors that reveal man's need to belong to a larger group. First**, the poet compares the church to one body. He needs the church, "whereof [he is] a member" (10), as a form of support, just as the head, "ingrafted into that body" (10), needs the help of the body, the larger group or structure that provides life. **Next,** Donne compares man to a book, demonstrating that they are both "of one author" and that man naturally belongs to a community as a book belongs to a "volume."

> Organized by time and idea; note that, at the end of the topic sentence, the repeat word modifier serves as a transition to the first supporting detail.

### Original A1, A2

In chapter one the details and diction prepare us for a "tale of human sorrow and frailty" (38; ch.1). For example, the people gather in front of a prison, "a wooden edifice, the door of which was heavily timbered with oak and studded with iron spikes" (38; ch.1).

### Revised

In chapter one the details and diction prepare us for a "tale of human sorrow and frailty" (38; ch.1). **The details direct us to objects that evoke sorrow and depression.** For example, the people gather in front of a prison, "a wooden edifice, the door of which was heavily timbered with oak and studded with iron spikes" (39; ch.1).

> This second sentence provides a transition from the topic sentence to the first supporting detail.

### Original A1

Accepting the consequences of one's actions demonstrates courage. In *The Scarlet Letter*, the protagonist Hester Prynne has committed adultery.

### Revised

Accepting the consequences of one's actions demonstrates courage. **The hero commits a sin or violation against the community, but instead of resisting punishment, he or she acknowledges the transgression and proceeds with life.** In *The Scarlet Letter*, the protagonist Hester Prynne must face the results of her adultery everyday.

## B = BLENDING TEXTUAL SUPPORT

| Editing Symbol |
| --- |
| **B** |

**B1** = Blend text more smoothly with the analysis.

**B2** = Blend needs to be grammatically correct.

**B3** = Explain the text and include it with the writer's words, revealing why this text helps prove the point.

**B4** = Don't blend too early, without first setting up the aspect of the topic sentence the quotation is supposed to support. It is not clear how this supports the topic sentence or previous statement.

**B5** = First explain the context of the quotation.

### Three methods for blending

There are three methods to blending direct quotations in paragraphs. Ideally, the writer might use a combination of two or three of the methods.

### Method One

Blend the text as if the words were already a natural part of the sentence.

### Original B1, B2, B3

The seasonal atmosphere opens in dialogue between Scrooge quoting, "every idiot who goes about with 'Merry Christmas' on his lips should be boiled with his own pudding" (14; ch. 1), to his nephew.

### Revised

Scrooge insolently interrupts the seasonal dialogue **by exclaiming to his nephew that "every idiot who** goes about with 'Merry Christmas' on his lips should be boiled with his own pudding" (14; ch. 1).

### Original B1, B3

Another trait that exemplifies his virtue of loyalty is in a passage that states "he had done nobly in war" (11). This shows not only his physical brawn and strength, but also his loyalty and beliefs toward God by going on the crusade.

### Revised

**Not only has the Knight "done nobly in war" (11), proving his loyalty** to both God and country, but also he dispels a myth that all brawny warriors prefer killing to traveling on pilgrimages.

### Original B4, B5

Without compassion, Scrooge says, "Those who are badly off must go there." He even says, "They cost enough" (19; ch. 1).

### Revised

Without compassion, Scrooge asserts that the poor deserve their plight; **if this means living in prisons, "those who are badly off must go there."** In fact, he even appears to resent these establishments, **lamenting, "They cost enough"** (19; ch. 1).

### Original B3, B4, B5

One sees how Scrooge possesses an extreme dislike, almost hatred, for his fellow man. "'Don't be cross, Uncle,' said the nephew. 'What else can I be,' returned the uncle, 'when I live in a world of fools as this?'" (14; ch. 1).

### Revised

Scrooge's rude manner, combined with his quick, snide replies, acts as an instant indicator of Scrooge's true personality. For example, his conversation with his nephew demonstrates his disdain for others. Even Scrooge's nephew **scolds him: "Don't be cross, Uncle!"** Scrooge is inexorable, though, refusing to reflect on his own behavior and **instead blaming others "in a world of fools as this"** (14; ch. 1).

### Original B1

The Friar doesn't like to hang out with the peasants. This is shown in the quote, "nothing good can come of commerce with such slum-and-gutter dwellers" (246–47).

### Revised

Those with no gifts to give are not worthy of his eminent service, **for he knows "nothing good can come of commerce** with such slum-and-gutter dwellers" (246–47).

### Original B2, B3

"I thought it out for two or three days, and then I reckoned I would see if there was anything in it. I got an old tin lamp and an iron ring and rubbed until I sweat like a injun..." (6; ch. 1) shows us that Huck would believe anything that was told to him at first.

### Revised

In the beginning especially, Huck believes what people tell him; he believes, as Tom says, that, **if he "got an old tin lamp** and an iron ring and rubbed" (6; ch.1) it, a genie would appear. Soon, however, Huck realizes, **after he "rubbed until** I sweat like a injun" (6; ch. 1), that Tom may be full of lies.

### Original B1

The quotation "So then I judged that all that stuff was only just one of Tom Sawyer's lies. I reckon he believed in the A-rabs and elephants, but as for me, I think different" (6; ch. 1) supports this idea.

### Revised

Soon Huck begins to separate his thinking from Tom, perhaps realizing that Tom's world is not the same as his, **judging "that all that stuff was only just one of Tom Sawyer's lies"** (6; ch.1). If they are lies, according to Huck, he knows **he has the option to "think different"** (6; ch.1).

### Original B3

Like Eveline, Mrs. Kerner, in the story "Grace," becomes entrapped by an overwhelming responsibility to family life. She is married to a man and the text says "never seems to think he has a home at all" (104). Mrs. Kerner has been married for twenty-five years. "For twenty-five years…[has] kept house shrewdly." This is "irksome" and "unbearable" (105).

### Revised

Like Eveline, Mrs. Kerner, in the story "Grace," becomes entrapped by an overwhelming responsibility to family life. Married **to a man who "never seems to think he has a home at all," (104) Mrs. Kerner "for twenty-five years…[has] kept house shrewdly" in her husband's frequent absence,** an onerous burden that leads to an "irksome" and "unbearable" (105) life at home.

### Original B3, B4

Stryver tells Carton, "I want to get all the preliminaries done with." He hopes that he should give her "his hand a week or two before Michaelmas Term, or in the little Christmas vacation between it and Hilary" (108; bk. 2, ch. 12). Here he is very cold and calculating.

### Revised

Cold and calculating, Stryver treats his marriage to Lucie as a business transaction: he is concerned more about trivial preliminaries and contingency plans than he is about Lucie herself. **His first thought is to propose "to get all the preliminaries done with,"** so they **could then "arrange at their leisure whether he should give her his hand** a week or two before Michaelmas Term, or in the little Christmas vacation between it and Hilary" (108; bk. 2, ch. 12).

### Method Two

Use a colon. The sentence that precedes the colon explains the writer's point; what follows is his evidence.

#### Example

By excluding himself from humanity and working with incredible devotion, Frankenstein discovers how to generate life: "I pursued knowledge to her hiding places… [and] I became myself capable of bestowing animation upon lifeless matter" (50; ch.4).

#### Example

This violation of nature is also evident in the monster's horrible inhuman countenance: "His watery eyes seemed almost of the same colour as the dun-white sockets in which they were set…. Oh! no mortal could support the horror of that countenance" (56; ch.5).

### Method Three
Identify the speaker of the dialogue before the quotation.

#### Example
The king sadly emits, "He was my closest counselor, he was keeper of my thoughts…. Men of birth and merit all should be as Ashhere was!" (1062).

## C = COMBINE SENTENCES

Combining sentences helps eliminate wordiness, helps extend the elaboration of a single idea, and helps remove unnecessary breaks in thought. Use present

| Editing Symbol |
| :---: |
| **C** |

and past participial phrases, infinitive and gerund phrases, absolute phrases, appositive phrases, subordinate clauses, repeat word/analysis modifiers, solo semicolons, and conjunctive adverbs to make combinations.

### Original
A virtuous man exhibits high moral standards, leads an ethical life ~~and does not lose sight of life by becoming engulfed in his material possessions. In order to have high moral standards, one must~~ be truthful, possess honor, be generous ~~to those around him~~, and be courteous to all people. (50 words)

### Revised
A virtuous man exhibits high moral standards, leading an ethical life that does not lose sight of Christian values. These values demand truth, generosity, and courtesy towards all people. (29 words)

### Original
Two knobby, sand-caked digits point down toward the rust-colored clay, signaling the breaking ball. ~~Background to the sign are~~ his blue pinstripe baseball ~~pants I often focus on so intensely that I can define the middle seam of his long~~, dusty knickers. (44 words)

### Revised
Two knobby, sand-caked digits, set against dusty blue pinstripe knickers, point down toward the rust-colored clay, signaling the breaking ball. (22 words)

### Original
Driven with concentration, he pictures ~~himself reacting the fastest and diving out the farthest in the start of the race. He sees himself~~ enter the water in a tight streamline position to begin his underwater kick ~~which boosts~~ him ahead of the other swimmers. ~~Then he sees himself come up out of the water and take a powerful first stroke~~. (60 words)

### Revised
Driven with concentration, he pictures himself departing the starting block seconds before his opponents, entering the water in a tight streamline position, already set to begin his underwater kick, catapulting himself ahead of the other swimmers, and emerging to start his first stroke. (43 words)

**Original**

> He lifts his right leg to the first step. ~~He~~ proceeds with his left leg to the top of the block. ~~Then~~ his right leg rises to the top of the block. (32 words)

**Revised**

> He lifts his right leg to the first step and proceeds with his left to the top of the block, his right soon following. (24 words)

**Original**

> He turns his head back to stare at the sweatshirt ~~on the swimmer he is following. The sweatshirt's colors, reminding him of the other schools which are competing,~~ radiate green, red, and blue into his face. (36 words)

**Revised**

> He turns his head back to stare at the adversary's sweatshirt two feet in front of him, its green, red, and blue colors glaring into his face. (27 words)

## E = EXTEND YOUR ELABORATION OF IDEAS

**Editing Symbol**

**E**

E1 = The writer needs to elaborate and incorporate additional textual support.

E2 = The writer is missing some important textual examples.

E3 = The writer should extend the elaboration of details, commenting further on this point before moving to the next item.

E4 = The elaboration is vague, shallow, or merely restates the quotation.

*Extending the elaboration of ideas* is a challenging skill; it requires the writer to reflect on the evidence and to comment on aspects of the literary text that are not immediately apparent to the casual reader. This level of analysis moves beyond plot summary and is one of the defining marks of a sophisticated writer.

**Original E3**

> Consequently, Macbeth's noble image is blemished, and he intensifies the doubt about his character's true nature by showing an uncommon attachment and fondness for war when Ross refers to him as "Bellona's bridegroom"(1.2.56).

**Revised**

> Consequently, Macbeth's noble image is blemished, and he intensifies the doubt about his character's true nature by showing an uncommon attachment and fondness for war when Ross refers to him as "Bellona's bridegroom"(1.2.56). **By calling him the husband of the Roman goddess of war, Ross communicates Macbeth's true passion for war, an intimacy similar to a husband's love for his wife, an unusual and hyperbolic image that undercuts Macbeth's revered nobility, the comparison suggesting an abnormality in his character.**

### Original E3

On Juliet's balcony, Romeo says that "love's light wings" (2.2.67) enable him to conquer the barrier that separates them.

### Revised

Clearly, one recognizes the depth of Romeo's love when he scales the walls of Juliet's home to testify of his love for her. **Questioned by Juliet as to how he got there**, Romeo answers that "love's light wings" (2.2.67) enable him to conquer the barrier that separates them. **This image of a bird's flight reinforces the idea that Romeo's love is invincible and unfettered, a love soaring beyond all limitations.**

Past participial phrase

### Original E4

In response to his nephew's felicitous greeting, Scrooge retorts, "What reason have you to be merry? You're poor enough" (13; ch. 1), a statement that shows how Scrooge points out that his nephew is poor.

### Revised

In response to his nephew's felicitous greeting, Scrooge retorts, "What reason have you to be merry? You're poor enough" (13; ch. 1), **a response showing how Scrooge thinks happiness can be measured by monetary wealth.** Ironically, Scrooge demonstrates the opposite because he is wealthy and not happy.

Absolute phrase

### Original E4

To his nephew, he exclaims of Christmas, "much good it may do to you! Much good it has ever done you!" (14; ch. 1). His view of Christmas remains warped, and he refuses to acknowledge the spirit of the season.

### Revised

To his nephew, he exclaims of Christmas, "much good it may do to you! Much good it has ever done you!" (14; ch. 1). Once again, Scrooge sees the season as devoid of tangible value, **a view of the world that is base and political**. Moreover, his cynicism thwarts a relationship with his nephew.

Analysis modifier

### Original E3, E4

Again, this self-centered side of his character becomes extremely obvious when he concludes, "I wish to be left alone" (19; ch. 1), and ushers them out with another "Good afternoon, Gentlemen." Scrooge acts with no concern for others and does so in a manner that ruins other people's good cheer, making himself look glum.

### Revised

Again, this self-centered side of his character becomes extremely obvious when he insists, "I wish to be left alone" (19; ch. 1), and ushers them out with another "Good afternoon, Gentlemen." **These statements emphasize Scrooge's desire to isolate himself from society, not simply physically, but emotionally and socially, refusing to recognize any communal responsibility for those less fortunate.**

### Original E3

In a fit of anger and grief, Juliet declares that Romeo is "a dove-feathered raven" (3.2.74). Certainly, Shakespeare masterfully applies bird imagery to demonstrate the emotional complexities of man.

### Revised

In a fit of anger and grief, Juliet declares that Romeo is "a dove-feathered raven" (3.2.74). **This image reflects Juliet's feelings of betrayal by Romeo, a man who on the outside seems honorable but on the inside is despicable; however, Juliet's unending love calms her tumultuous emotions, and she forgives the sin of Romeo. Without a doubt, human emotions of the sixteenth century were as volatile and unpredictable as they are today.** Certainly, Shakespeare masterfully applies bird imagery to demonstrate the emotional complexities of man.

### Original E2

"I shall help you" (68), Wyglaf yells as he goes to help defend Beowulf's life in the battle of the dragon. He fights "alongside the king, the brave soldier" (68).

### Revised

Wyglaf rushes to defend Beowulf's life in the battle against the dragon as he shouts, "I shall help you" (68). **Risking his own life, Wyglaf "fights along-side the king" (68), and through their combined effort, "they had downed their foe by common action, the atheling pair." Only with the aid of Wyglaf is Beowulf able to achieve "the last victory in the list of his deeds and works in the world" (69).**

### Original E3, E1

For example, "she had little dogs" she would be feeding with roasted flesh, or milk, or fine white bread. Furthermore, she has a cloak with a "graceful charm" and "[wears] a coral trinket on her arm, / a set of beads, the gaudies tucked in green," and a "golden broach of brightest sheen" (153–155).

### Revised

For example, she **has** little dogs **she feeds** with roasted flesh, or milk, or fine white bread, **an abhorrent ownership that shows her lack of consideration for the starving people of this epoch.** Furthermore, **for one who should be living a simple life as a nun,** she has a cloak with a "graceful charm," and "[wears] a coral trinket on her arm, / a set of beads, the gaudies tucked in green," and a "golden broach of brightest sheen" (153–155).

### Original E3, E2

Another vice Chaucer illustrates is greed. Chaucer begins his description of the doctor as a man who "had a special love of gold" (426). Rather than serve the individual, the doctor has forgotten his oath and pursues his work with an ardent desire for material wealth. He takes advantage of those in need of his services and works with the apothecary.

### Revised

Another vice Chaucer illustrates is greed. Chaucer begins his description of the doctor as a man who "had a special love of gold" (426). Rather than serve the individual, the doctor has forgotten his oath and pursues his work with an ardent desire for material wealth. **Knowing "no one alive could talk as well as he did / on points of medicine and of surgery" (400–401),** he takes advantage of those in need of his services. Manipulating his position, **he "made money from other's** [apothecaries with whom he dealt] **guile," never forgetting that "gold stimulates the heart"** (415–416).

### Original E3, E2

Even when her husband does come home, he returns drunk after spending the "money in his pocket" (104) at the local tavern, irresponsible behavior that creates many problems for Mrs. Kerner. She has to take care of her kids alone and she has to take care of her husband when he's sick. He's little help to her.

### Revised

Even when her husband does come home, he returns drunk after spending the "money in his pocket" (104) at the local tavern, irresponsible behavior **that presents Mrs. Kerner with two problems. First, she alone must deal with the pressures of mature life, pressures caused by the adult responsibility of making sure that the human necessities of nutrition and shelter are fulfilled, both of which are provided by finances. Because her husband spends some of the family income on alcohol, Mrs. Kerner obviously must worry that her family may not receive what they need and, therefore, must work harder in order to ensure that this does not occur. Second, she must heal her husband "dutifully whenever he [is] sick" (105) while simultaneously watching over "two girls and a boy" (104) and, previously, "her two eldest sons" (105), a handful of children that obviously presents her with the arduous task of raising them also. Furthermore, because she does not receive any help from her husband, Mrs. Kerner must raise the children as both their mother and father, a strong indication that all her time and efforts are restricted to her family.**

## L = LISTING PLOT DETAILS

The student is merely listing details without elaborating or explaining why

| Editing Symbol |
|:---:|
| **L** |

these details or quotations provide support for the topic sentence. The writer, in this case, is forgetting about the reader, who has not viewed the evidence in the same manner or to the same degree of reflection that the writer has.

### Original

"What right have you to be dismal? What reason do you have to be morose? You're rich enough" (14; ch. 1), says the nephew. Scrooge replies with a remark saying, "Humbug." Scrooge even refuses to help the needy. "At this festive time of the year, Mr. Scrooge, it is more than desirable that we should make some slight provision for the poor and destitute, who suffer greatly at the present time" (17; ch. 1). Mr. Scrooge blatantly and bluntly says no and shows them out.

### Revised

**Scrooge attempts to lower the spirits of his nephew by asking, "What right have you to be merry? You're poor enough" (14; ch. 1). His attempts to deride his nephew fail, for the nephew quickly retorts,** "What reason do you have to be morose? You're rich enough" (14; ch. 1), **an attempt to make Scrooge confront his own logic. Unfortunately,** Scrooge's "Humbug" reply **not only demonstrates his unwillingness to engage in a logical debate but also demonstrates another example of his desire to isolate himself. In a similar manner, Scrooge seeks to separate himself from the social obligation to donate to those less fortunate. For example,** two men approach Scrooge requesting "some slight provision for the poor and destitute" (19; ch.1).

### Original

Besides utilizing bird imagery to depict physical qualities, Shakespeare also employs such imagery to illustrate emotional characteristics of man. Climbing up to Juliet's balcony, Romeo answers that "love's light wings" (2.2.67) enable him to conquer the barrier that separates them. Along with the stirring picture of Romeo's desire, one observes the passion of Juliet in the balcony as she compares herself to a spoiled child who refuses to release a bird. She says, "I would have thee gone— / And yet no farther than a wanton's bird, / That lets it hop a little from his hand" (2.1.221–223) and then plucking it back again. Again, in her room, Juliet's mercurial emotions are vividly demonstrated with bird imagery; we feel Juliet's turmoil as she discovers that Romeo has killed her cousin Tybalt. In a fit of anger and grief, Juliet declares that Romeo is "a dove-feathered raven" (3.2.74).

### Revised

Besides utilizing bird imagery to depict physical qualities, Shakespeare also employs such imagery to illustrate emotional characteristics of man. **Clearly, one recognizes the depth of Romeo's love when he scales the walls of Juliet's home to testify of his love for her. Questioned by Juliet as to how he got there, Romeo answers that "love's light wings" (2.2.67) enable him to conquer the barrier that separates them. This image of a bird's flight reinforces the idea that Romeo's love is invincible and unfettered, a love soaring beyond all limitations.** Along with the stirring picture of Romeo's desire, one observes the passion of Juliet in the balcony as she compares herself to a spoiled child who refuses to release a bird. **The image shows a small bird in captivity, while a young child holds tightly to the beloved** possession, letting "it hop a little from his hand," (2.2.179) and then plucking it back again. **Likewise, Juliet protests the release of Romeo but later relents and frees him because she realizes that her grasp will kill him if he stays.** Again, in her room, Juliet's mercurial emotions are vividly demonstrated with bird imagery; we feel Juliet's turmoil as she discovers that Romeo has killed her cousin Tybalt. In a fit of anger and grief, Juliet declares that Romeo is "a dove-feathered raven" (3.2.74). **This image reflects Juliet's feelings of betrayal by Romeo, a man who on the outside seems honorable but on the inside is despicable; however, Juliet's unending love calms her tumultuous emotions, and she forgives the sin of Romeo. Without a doubt, human emotions of the sixteenth century were as volatile and unpredictable as they are today. Certainly, Shakespeare masterfully applies bird imagery to demonstrate the emotional complexities of man.**

### Original

The narrator in "To His Coy Mistress" demonstrates a keen knowledge of persuasion. He uses this knowledge to convince his mistress to consummate their relationship. To achieve this goal, he uses many methods: speaking about her beauty, mentioning that he may die soon, and saying that they must seize the day. First, he mentions her appearance: "Thine eyes, and on thy forehead gaze / Two hundred to adore each breast" (12–13). Moreover, if there were enough time, he says, he would spend "an age, at least, to every part" (16), for she "deserve[s] this state" (17). Unfortunately, he does not have time for such adoration, nor does she, for "at my back, I always hear / Time's winged chariot hurrying near" (19–20). With death's imminent arrival comes additional fears: If she dies tomorrow, "Thy beauty shall no more be found" (23). She will be found alone, he tells her, without his love, without his "echoing song"—alone in that "private place / But none, I think, do there embrace" (29–30). Once finished with these potential scenarios, he beseeches her to seize the day, carpe diem: "while the youthful hue / sits on thy skin like morning glow... / Now let us sport us while we may" (31–33). He hopes that after this begging, they will "roll all our strength, and all / our sweetness, up into one ball" (34–35).

> The student is merely summarizing and listing the details of the poem, not explaining what's persuasive about them.

### Revised

The narrator in "To His Coy Mistress" demonstrates a keen knowledge of persuasion, a carefully plotted strategy of seduction: first, secure trust; second, create discomfort; and third, provide relief. **He begins with flattery, necessary to gain trust and to prove his devotion, not simply to her physical appearance**—"Thine eyes, and on thy forehead gaze / Two hundred to adore each breast" (12–13)—**but to her spiritual appearance as well**—"And the last age should show your heart / For, Lady, you deserve this state" (16–17). **Here the narrator highlights a love that transcends the mere physical and reaches the spiritual. Once she trusts these intentions, the narrator begins to create discomfort:** "But, at my back, I always hear / time's winged chariot hurrying near / And yonder, all before us lie /

> Notice the change. The writer explains the persuasive technique of flattery; what follows is text to support this claim. After going further to point out two types of flattery—physical and spiritual—the writer continues beyond summary to provide his analysis of the details.

deserts of vast eternity" (19–22). **He goes beyond this imminence of death to list specific possibilities, scenarios especially disconcerting to a woman: first,** "thy beauty shall no more be found" (23); **second, she'll die a virgin and be subject to the** "worms [that] shall try that long preserved virginity" (26); third, she'll be alone, for "the grave's a fine and private place, / But none, I think, do there embrace" (29–30). **The narrator quickly leaves these ghastly images, and he introduces relief, a solution much more pleasant, one that will eliminate this fear of potential waste of beauty and purity. His mistress only needs to act now** "While the youthful hue / sits on thy skin like morning glow" (31–32). **If she acts now, the two of them can enjoy their youth,** "like amorous birds of prey, / rather at once our time devour, / than languish in his slow-chapped power" (36–38). **Now with his plot complete, the narrator is ready to** "tear our pleasures, with rough strife, / through the iron gates of life" (41–42).

### Original

He rests himself on a Disney World t-shirt and stares into Mickey Mouse's eyes. He sees a yellow Penn 6 tennis ball peeking around the side of the Snoopy wastepaper basket. Next to the basket sits a half-eaten slice of pepperoni pizza with ten ants running along the burnt crust.

### Revised

He rests himself on a Disney World t-shirt and stares into Mickey Mouse's eyes. Intimidated **by Mickey's grin, Bernie begins to swipe him with his black furry paw. After ten swipes, Bernie, realizing Mickey** poses no further threat, yawns, rests his left cheek on his two front legs, closes his eyes, and falls asleep.

### Original

Peering into the tight, dark closet, my nose, prying for clues, searches the room as it vacuums the air. My left hand reaches out and touches a suede suit. Next, I touch a cold aluminum baseball bat, the rubber part frayed.

### Revised

Peering into the tight, dark closet, my nose, prying for clues, searches the room. **As it vacuums the air, sniffing left and right, a pungent odor reaches its attention. Cringing itself upwards, the nose attempts** to hide from this smell as I retreat quickly because of my sudden antipathy for this place.

### Original

Finding evidence of gluttony one could point out, "He was a fat and personable priest," and "He liked a fat swan best, and roasted whole" (200–202).

### Revised

At a time when food was scarce for many medieval people, Chaucer portrays a "fat and personable priest...[who] liked a fat swan best and roast whole" (200–202), a religious who clearly demonstrates gluttony as a mortal sin.

## O = OFF-TOPIC

**Editing Symbol**

O1 = This evidence doesn't support the topic sentence.
O2 = Not completely off-topic, but the writer is either slipping into plot summary or failing to explain adequately how the evidence supports the topic sentence.

### Original O1

In the opening dialogue of *A Christmas Carol*, Dickens creates Scrooge's shallow personality through the repetition of diction associated with money. Almost every comment Scrooge makes includes economic diction. For example, Scrooge's nephew first arrives and says, "A Merry Christmas, Uncle" (13; ch.1). The narrator describes his nephew as "all in a glow; his face was ruddy and handsome; his eyes sparkled" (13; ch.1).

### Revised

In the opening dialogue of *A Christmas Carol*, Dickens creates Scrooge's shallow personality through the repetition of diction associated with money. Almost every comment Scrooge makes includes economic diction. For example, when Scrooge's nephew first arrives to greet him a "Merry Christmas," **he disdainfully comments about his nephew's monetary status. "You're poor enough" (13; ch.1), he retorts, a statement that shows how Scrooge evaluates individuals by their monetary value.**

### Original O2

[Topic sentence: In the opening dialogue of *A Christmas Carol*, Dickens creates Scrooge's shallow personality through the repetition of diction associated with money.]

Finally, Scrooge says to his clerk that he will "want all day tomorrow, I suppose?" (21; ch.1). He then says, "If I was to stop half-a-crown for it, you'd think yourself ill used...and yet you don't think me ill-used, when I pay a day's wages for no work" (21; ch.1).

### Revised

Finally, Scrooge's conversation with Bob Cratchit, his clerk, **revolves around money. Scrooge moans that Bob will** "want all day tomorrow, I suppose?" (21; ch.1). **He continues to explain how Christmas has created an economic problem for him**: "If I was to stop half-a-crown for it, you'd think yourself ill used...and yet you don't think me ill-used, when I pay a day's wages for no work" (21; ch.1). **Here Scrooge demonstrates that he cannot even perceive Cratchit as a human being but as an economic possession, swindling him unfairly.**

### Original O2

In "Sonnet 29," William Shakespeare uses many images that illustrate love is the power that helps man move out of his despondency. The character says, "outcast state" (2). Next, he says he wants to be like "one more rich in hope / featured like him with friends possessed" (5–6). He has antipathy for his life because he isn't as fortunate as others. Then "haply I think on thee, and then my state / like to the lark at break of day arising from sullen earth" (10–11). He finally says, "That then I scorn to change my state with kings" (14).

> Writer must explain how these details support the topic sentence.

### Revised

In his "Sonnet 29," William Shakespeare uses many images that illustrate love is the power that helps man move out of his despondency. **Feeling melancholy, the character disdains his "outcast state" (2), a state he curses because he cannot** be like "one more rich in hope / featured like him with friends possessed" (5–6). He has antipathy for his life because he isn't as fortunate as others. **However, his despondency—his "self almost despising" (9)—is ephemeral, for another person's "sweet love" (13) brings him from despair into a new day, a day in which he sees the value of his life and knows the power of love. He now is like "the lark at break of day arising / from sullen earth" (11–12), a man who can arise and sing with contentment despite any troubles. Furthermore, he realizes that love is more valuable than changing his "state with kings" (14).**

### Original O1

Though the Victorian Age is filled with potential, many poets recognized that all is not well with society, for society may appear, as the sea, "calm tonight" (1), but if one "listen[s] you hear the grating roar" (9). The roar comes from a people with confused values and unmet spiritual needs, a people who lost "the sea of Faith," faith in a God, faith in human relationship. In Browning's "My Last Duchess," the Duke calls the portrait of his wife a "piece of wonder" (3). In addition, Arnold's narrator says, "ah, love, let us be true" (29). Arnold recognizes that it is only this love that will battle against the "ignorant armies [that] clash by night" (37). By contrast, Housman says, "smart lad, to slip betimes away" (9), the lad who still has his "defended challenge cup" (24). It is this culture that says "I shot him dead because— / because he was my foe" (9–10), a culture that does not value the potential for human love, but a culture that values a push to "strive, to seek, to find, and not to yield" (70).

> Confusing details. Not clear how they are on topic.

### Revised

Though the Victorian Age is filled with potential, many poets recognized that all is not well with society, for society may appear, as the sea, "calm tonight" (1), but if one "listen[s] you hear the grating roar" (9). The roar comes from a people with confused values and unmet spiritual needs, a people who lost "the sea of Faith," faith in a God, faith in human relationship. **Their faith, rather, is in material—superficial—accomplishments; art, for example, is a "piece of wonder" (3), says the Duke in Browning's "My Last Duchess."** The genuine wonder, **however, is man and his power to form relationships: "Ah, love, let us be true" (29). Here, in Arnold's "Dover Beach," the narrator recognizes that it is only this love that will battle against the "ignorant armies [that] clash by night" (37). Rather, this culture cares more, as Housman says, about the "smart lad, to slip betimes away" (9), the lad who still has his "defended challenge cup" (24).** It is this culture that says "I shot him dead because— / because he was my foe" (9–10), a culture that does not value the potential for human love, but a culture, as Tennyson says, that values a push to "strive, to seek, to find, and not to yield" (70).

### Original O2

In chapter one, the details and diction prepare us for a "tale of human sorrow and frailty" (38; ch. 1). The details direct us to objects that evoke sorrow and depression. For example, the people gather in front of a prison, "a wooden edifice, the door of which was heavily timbered with oak and studded with iron spikes" (38; ch. 1). Revealing an aspect of humanity that often brings suffering to the community, this "prison house somewhere in the vicinity of Cornhill" (38; ch. 1) reminds us of the consequence of our sinful nature. Moreover, there is a "grass plot, much overgrown with burdock, pigweed, apple peru, and such unsightly vegetation" (38; ch. 1). Near this prison rests "a portion of the virgin soil...a cemetery" (38; ch. 1). In addition to these gloomy details, the diction adds to the despondency of the setting, providing words that remove life and energy from this environment. For example, the "gray, steeple-crowned hats," the prison "with weather stains [and its] beetle-browed and gloomy front," and "the black flower of civilized society" (38; ch. 1) Along with the absence of color, visually suggesting sorrow, there are the objects of touch, such as the door "heavily timbered with oak and...iron spikes" and the "rust on the ponderous iron-work" (38; ch. 1).

> How do these details support the topic sentence?

### Revised

In chapter one, the details and diction prepare us for a "tale of human sorrow and frailty" (38; ch.1) The details direct us to objects that evoke sorrow and depression. For example, the people gather in front of a prison, "a wooden edifice, the door of which was heavily timbered with oak and studded with iron spikes" (38; ch.1). Revealing an aspect of humanity that often brings suffering to the community, this "prison house somewhere in the vicinity of Cornhill" (38; ch. 1) reminds us of the consequence of our sinful nature. **Moreover, a "grass plot, much overgrown with burdock, pigweed, apple peru, and such unsightly vegetation" (38; ch. 1), creating a place few would find inviting, suggests that there is little beauty to be seen. Near this prison rests "a portion of the virgin soil...a cemetery" (38; ch. 1), reminding the reader that death, a sorrowful event, will soon affect this community.** In addition to these gloomy details, the diction adds to the despondency of the setting, providing words that remove life and energy from this environment. For example, **dark colors dominate the chapter:** the "gray, steeple-crowned hats," the prison "with weather stains [and its] beetle-browed and gloomy front," and "the black flower of civilized society" (38; ch. 1). Along with the absence of color, visually suggesting sorrow, the objects of touch, such as the door "heavily timbered with oak and...iron spikes" and the "rust on the ponderous iron-work" (38; ch. 1), **reveal the hardness and coldness that often accompanies a mood of sorrow and frailty.**

# P = PARAGRAPH NEEDS REVISION

**Editing Symbol**

**P**

**P1** = The organization (time, place, idea) of main points that support the topic sentence needs to be identified or emphasized more clearly.

**P2** = This collection of sentences doesn't provide complete coherence; check logic and word glue, and topic string.

**P3** = Paragraph could use more textual support and analysis; look for additional examples.

**P4** = Tie to thesis needs to be stronger.

### Original P1, P2, P3

Scrooge and his nephew have an interesting discussion in chapter one. His nephew greets his uncle, but Scrooge only says, "Bah Humbug!" (13; ch. 1). The narrator describes the nephew as very jovial. Even Scrooge recognizes his nephew's ebullient appearance as he wonders, "What reason have you to be merry?" (13; ch. 1). Scrooge asks, "What right have you to be dismal? What reason have you to be morose?" (14; ch. 1). Scrooge thinks money governs everything, "bills without money...a time for finding yourself a year older, and not an hour richer" (14; ch. 1). His nephew, however, admits that he has 'not profited" from Christmas but describes it as "a kind, forgiving, charitable, pleasant time...when men and women seem by one consent to open their shut-up hearts freely, and to think of people below them as if they really were fellow passengers to the grave" (15; ch. 1). His nephew pleads, "Why cannot we be friends?" and Scrooge ignores the request for relationship and dismisses him with "Good Afternoon" (16; ch. 1). When men come to solicit money, Scrooge says, "It's enough for a man to understand his own business, and not to interfere with other people's. Mine occupies me constantly" (19; ch. 1). Scrooge's repetition of "own," "mine," and "me" shows his interest in withdrawing from society rather than joining it.

> Topic sentence needs to be more precise.

> It is unclear how the writer is organizing the textual support. The writer is summarizing.

### Revised

**Scrooge's nephew is his uncle's foil, a character whose qualities contrast with the qualities of another character. First, unlike Scrooge, his nephew uses language and is described by the narrator with language that is sociable and friendly. For example, after his initial greeting to his uncle,** the narrator describes the nephew's voice as "cheerful." **This diction is immediately opposite to Scrooge's** response, "Bah Humbug!" (13; ch.1). **The narrator continues to use diction and imagery of friendliness, describing the nephew** as "all in a glow," with a face "ruddy and handsome," with eyes that "sparkled" (13; ch.1). **Even Scrooge recognizes his nephew's ebullient appearance** as he wonders, "What reason have you to be merry?" (13; ch.1). Scrooge, however, is described with diction of harshness and unsociability, his nephew asking, "What right have you to be dismal? What reason have you to be morose?" (14; ch.1). **Second, Scrooge defines wealth in life as monetary accumulation, whereas his nephew defines wealth in terms of relationship.** For example,

> Paragraph is organized by idea—contrast. Note the second sentence as transitional **A1**.

> Notice that the writer explains how the quoted material supports the topic sentence.

Scrooge sees Christmas as a time when others pay "bills without money...a time for finding yourself a year older, and not an hour richer" (14; ch.1). His nephew, however, admits that he has "not profited" from Christmas but describes it as "a kind, forgiving, charitable, pleasant time...when men and women seem by one consent to open their shut-up hearts freely, and to think of people below them as if they really were fellow passengers to the grave" (15; ch.1). **Here his nephew views life's wealth as developing relationships rather than developing economic riches. This contrast occurs again with Scrooge's language of selfishness as opposed to his nephew's language of invitation. Whereas his nephew pleads**, "Why cannot we be friends?" Scrooge ignores the request for relationship and dismisses him with "Good Afternoon" (16; ch.1). **Scrooge's isolation appears later when he turns away the two gentlemen** who are soliciting funds for the poor; Ebenezer uses language of the self. He says "it's enough for a man to understand his own business, and not to interfere with other people's. Mine occupies me constantly" (19; ch.1). **Scrooge's repetition of "own," "mine," and "me" shows his interest in withdrawing from society rather than joining it.**

### Original P3

Many characters are loving. In *Beowulf*, Wiglaf washes the hero after he kills the dragon. "Then that excellent thane with his own hands washed his battle-bloodied prince, bathed with water the famous leader, his friend and lord" 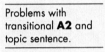 Problems with transitional **A2** and topic sentence.
(120). The prologue of *The Canterbury Tales* has loving characters, too. The parson, for example, "was a good man of the priest's vocation" (120). The parson also has a large parish that covers several miles. "Wide was his parish, with houses far asunder, / but he would not be kept by rain or thunder, / if any had suffered a sickness or a blow, from visiting" (121–23). He visits his parishioners even in bad weather.

### Revised

The comic and epic worlds depict characters who demonstrate **an ability to love others, to "move beyond self-interest" (120), and to serve their fellow man.** In *Beowulf*, Wiglaf places his king's needs before his own, taking "that excellent thane with his own hands" and washing "his battle-bloodied prince" (120), preparing the king for a dignified death. Here Wiglaf stands in contrast to the selfish thanes who previously fled from the flames of the dragon. Likewise, Chaucer's parson equally acts to help **serve others'** needs before his own. This "good man of the priest's vocation" ignores the  Writer will apply this expanded definition of love to his examples.

Notice words from topic sentence.
difficulties of his job, serving a parish "with houses far asunder" (120–121). More important than distance is his desire to help those who "had suffered a sickness or a blow"; for them "he would not be kept by rain or thunder" (125–126).

### Original P1, P2, P3

The comic and tragic worlds have characters who have an appetite for knowledge. In Chaucer's prologue, the Oxford cleric says "he much preferred to have beside his bed / his twenty volumes bound in black or red" (210–11). In addition, "For though he knew what learning had to offer, / there was little coin to jingle in his coffer. / On books and learning he would promptly spend" (298–300). He says that "his scholarship was what he truly heeded" (229). His dress is reflected by this knowledge: "He rode a mount as skinny as a rake, / and he was hardly fat. / He wore an outer cloak of threadbare stuff" (224–26). In addition to the comic world, the tragic world has characters who illustrate this point. Victor Frankenstein says he "explore[s] unknown powers, and unfold[s] to the world the deepest mysteries of creation" (39; ch. 2). His friend Henry says, "How very ill you appear; so thin and pale; and look as if you had been watching for several nights" (60; ch. 5). Henry thinks Victor looks sick. Often, Victor "nearly sank to the ground through languor and extreme weakness" (54; ch. 4), but his desire "could not tear my thoughts from my employment, loathsome in itself, but which had taken an irresistible hold of my imagination" (56; ch. 4). Victor admits that he has an appetite: "If the study to which you apply yourself has a tendency to weaken your affections, and to destroy your taste for those simple pleasures in which no alloy can possibly mix, then that study is... not befitting the human mind" (41; ch. 3). This is what is important about Walton. He also is an example of a person who has an appetite for knowledge. He is interested in "the marvelous, a belief in the marvelous, intertwined in all my projects" (42; ch. 3), a life shaped by "a steady purpose, a point on which the soul may fix its intellectual eye" (42; ch. 3).

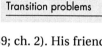

What are the main points that support **TS?**

Transition problems

Writer listing, summarizing

### Revised

Both the comic and tragic worlds depict characters whose appetite for knowledge **becomes obsessive**. In Chaucer's prologue, the Oxford cleric's **pursuit of knowledge, his desire "to have beside his bed / his twenty volumes bound in black or red"** (210–211), demonstrates an imbalance, a lack of restraint that is reflected in his physical form, a young man "hardly fat.... He wore an outer cloak of threadbare stuff" (220, 226). Instead of attending to his physical needs, he would "for learning's sake, let himself look hollow and sober enough" (228), preferring "his scholarship, [which] was what he truly heeded" (229). **This physical decay occurs in Victor Frankenstein, who, like the cleric, seeks to** "explore unknown powers, and unfold to the world the deepest mysteries of creation" (39; ch. 2). **He pursues these intellectual goals impetuously, paying the price physically. Even Clerval notices** "how very ill you appear; so thin and pale; and look as if you had been watching for several nights" (60; ch. 5). **Unfortunately, even though Victor, at one point,** "nearly sank to the ground through languor and extreme weakness" (54: ch. 4), **his deleterious desire "could not tear** my thoughts from my employment, loathsome in itself, but which had taken an irresistible hold of my imagination" (56; ch. 4). Victor justifies this obsession for knowledge, since often "we [are] upon the brink of becoming acquainted" with a discovery, but our "cowardice or

Writer makes the topic sentence more specific.

carelessness" restrains "our enquiries" (42; ch. 3). Later, when Victor meets Walton, he sees that Walton, too, craves "the marvellous, a belief in the marvellous, intertwined in all my projects," a life shaped by "a steady purpose, a point on which the soul may fix its intellectual eye" (42; ch. 3).

## S = SUMMARIZING PLOT

Summarizing here rather than explaining how these details support the topic. This problem is similar to listing (**L**). See those examples, pp. 75–77.

## SH = SHOW CONCRETE IMAGES

**Editing Symbol**

**SH**

*Show* rather than *tell* these details. The reader can't see any images. Showing text includes direct excerpts—quotation, paraphrase, etc.—from the literary text, along with the writer's commentary. See pp. 35–36 for more examples.

### Original

My room has so much junk in it I can barely move.

### Revised

Pushing open my bedroom door, I kick aside the stack of dirty underwear, which soon covers my copies of *Hamlet*, *Macbeth*, and *Othello*, their pages open from last night's comparative reading.

### Original

When Hester **leaves prison, she faces harassment** from the town, but she does not run away.

### Revised

From the moment she exits from behind the prison door, Hester, **holding her head high, confronts the accusing eyes of the community,** all of whom, including at times her daughter Pearl, serve as the agents for her punishment. **Forced to wear a scarlet letter "A" upon her chest, Hester does not flee from the town that has so harshly judged her; rather, she chooses to remain close to the community, living in a small cottage just outside the town limits.**

### Original

During the feasts, the scop tells **important stories** that affect his audience.

### Revised

The feast also allows the scop to tell important tribal stories—tales of heroic idealism, such as that of **Sigemund and Fitela, and tales of warning, such as that of Heremod and his greed**.

### Original

The knight is a very humble person; **he doesn't wear fancy clothes.**

**Revised**

Chaucer illustrates the knight's humility through his appearance: **"He possessed / fine horses, but he was not gaily dressed" (24–25).** In fact, not only does he avoid "fine" clothes, but he does not care about trivial aspects of his appearance, arriving at the pilgrimage **"with smudges where his armour had left mark" (30).**

**Original**

The Parson lives **a simple life and tries to share with others.**

**Revised**

The Parson goes beyond his individual poverty, **living simply, by sharing his own paltry resources, "giving to poor parishioners both from Church offerings and his property" (60).**

**Original**

The monk loves the **pleasures of the material world.**

**Revised**

This material world beckons the monk with its offerings of **fashionable gold, fine clothing, food, and beer.**

**Original**

The Friar only loves to hang around people who are rich.

**Revised**

The Friar loves only those who have money to give, **for he knows "nothing good can come of commerce with such slum-and-gutter dwellers" (75).**

## T = TRANSITIONS ARE WEAK

| Editing Symbol | **T1** = Check word glue and logic glue between each sentence. |
| --- | --- |
| **T** | **T2** = Revise transition so there is a closer link between these two sentences. |
| | **T3** = The transition could be less wordy. |

**T4** = Maintain topic focus.

There must be a transition between the quotation and the previous sentence; otherwise, the reader does not understand why the writer has presented the quotation. Therefore, the writer should not begin a sentence with a quotation because this could confuse the reader.

**Original *T2 T4***

Scrooge deals with a great deal of money that he is unwilling to give away. Two gentlemen come to ask for donations for the "poor and destitute."

**Revised**

Scrooge deals with large amounts of money that he is unwilling to give away. **For example, he refuses to donate money** to the "poor and destitute" despite the pleas of two gentlemen.

### Original T1

To keep his minimalist ways, "Scrooge kept the coal-box in his own room" (13; ch. 1) to ensure that his clerk cannot replenish his single ember should it burn out. Dickens illustrates Scrooge's attitude towards his nephew's financial situation when he responds to a comment from his nephew.

### Revised

To keep his minimalist ways, "Scrooge kept the coal-box in his own room" (13; ch. 1) to ensure that his clerk cannot replenish his single ember should it burn out. **Scrooge is also conservative** with his speech, as illustrated in his terse conversation with his nephew.

### Original T2, T4

Huck is resourceful, an ability to look around and use everything he has to complete **tasks. "An old rusty** saw without any handle; it was laid in between a rafter and the clapboards of the roof" (33; ch. 7). This is a good example of resourcefulness.

### Revised

Huck is resourceful, an ability to look around and use everything he has to complete tasks. **For example, when Huck is locked up in his one-room shack, wondering if his father has left for good, he cannot find a way out until he looks closer at the wall and finds "an old** rusty saw without any handle; it was laid in between a rafter and the clapboards of the roof" (33; ch.7). **Here Huck uses his keen sense of survival, his ability to find a way out of the house, to create a plan to fake his death to get away from his father.**

### Original T1

Dimmesdale, carrying the burden of his ignominious sin within his heart, has suffered for seven years. He often beats himself "with a bloody scourge [which he] had plied...on his own shoulders" (141; ch. 11). On Sundays, he tells his parishioners that he is "utterly a pollution and a lie!" (140; ch. 11). Chillingworth is "a chief actor in the poor minister's interior world," one who could "arouse him with a throb of agony" (137; ch. 11). The narrator says Dimmesdale is "looking like pure fallen snow" before his parishioners, men and women who label him "the saint on earth" (140; ch. 11). Dimmesdale says his heart is "all speckled and spotted with iniquity" (130; ch. 11).

> Transitional glue is missing, and the Chillingworth example is off-topic.

### Revised

Dimmesdale, carrying the burden of his ignominious sin within his heart, has *suffered* for seven years. **He, more than anyone, knows that he is guilty of a crime,** *punishing* himself physically "with a bloody scourge [which he] had plied...on his own shoulders" (141; ch. 11) **and mentally** with his Sunday reproach: "I, your pastor, whom you so reverence and trust, am utterly a pollution and a lie!" (140; ch. 11). **Adding to this self-inflicted** *torture*, Dimmesdale battles Chillingworth, not simply a physician helping to abate Dimmesdale's pain but "a chief actor in the poor minister's interior world," one who could "arouse him with a throb of

> The words in italics are transitional word glue—repeating the idea of suffering established in the topic sentence.

agony" (137; ch. 11). **Even beyond these forces,** Dimmesdale **must face an** *agonizing* **duplicity**—"looking like pure fallen snow" before his parishioners, men and women who label him "the saint on earth," (140; ch. 11) and knowing that his heart is "all speckled and spotted with *iniquity*" (130; ch. 11). **His soul** *besieged* **by forces on every side,** Dimmesdale cannot hide the truth from Hester; she recognizes that he stands "on the verge of lunacy," that "a *deadlier* venom [has] been infused into him by the hand that proffered relief" (160; ch. 13).

### Original T2 T4

The second and, perhaps, most vital event that marks Roger's descent to savagery is his abdication of order and logic for acts of evil. Piggy, the remnants of the old society, "the rational mind opposed to intuition and insight" (Delbaere-Garant 190) is killed by Roger who frees himself through the act.

### Revised

The second and, perhaps, most vital event that marks Roger's descent to savagery is his abdication of order and logic for acts of evil. **Here, Roger** frees himself of the remnants of the old society through the killing of Piggy, who exists as "the rational mind opposed to intuition and insight" (Delbaere-Garant 190).

### Original T3

When the narrator describes her smell, he first allows us to dream of the sweet scent of perfume, but then surprisingly emphasizes how his mistress' breath "reeks." **Disgusted by her visage and scent that smells so bad,** the reader then reads about the voice of the narrator's mistress as he wonders if she could be decent in any way.

### Revised

When the narrator describes her smell, he first allows us to dream of the sweet scent of perfume, but then surprisingly emphasizes how his mistress' breath "reeks." **The reader disgusted,** he then reads about the voice of the narrator's mistress as the reader wonders if she could be decent in any way.

### Original T2

One will regret and "forever tarry" (17) once one is old because there is not enough time to go out and do what one has already passed up. In addition, Herrick says, "Old Time is still a-flying" (3); time keeps on going whether you want it to or not.

### Revised

One will regret and "forever tarry" (17) once one is old because there is not enough time to go out and do what has already been passed up. **For time, as Herrick reminds, does not exhibit this lethargy but is always "still a-flying" (3).**

### Original T2

His professor, M.Waldman, gives him many scientific books, all of which Frankenstein "read with ardour" (44; ch. 3). Frankenstein's obsessive work habits keep him "engaged in [his] laboratory" for such long periods of time that "the stars often disappeared in the light of morning" (52; ch. 4).

### Revised

His professor, M.Waldman, gives him many scientific books, all of which Frankenstein "read with ardour" (44; ch. 3). **This ardour quickly becomes obsessive** as Victor is "engaged in [his] laboratory" for such long periods of time that "the stars often disappeared in the light of morning" (52; ch. 4).

## TS = REVISE THE TOPIC SENTENCE

| Editing Symbol |
|:---:|
| **TS** |

**TS1** = Need a stronger focus so that all sentences can clearly connect to this main sentence; this will help coherence.

**TS2** = Topic sentence contains an example, that is, a plot detail rather than an organizing idea + aspect of thesis.

**TS3** = Connect the topic sentence to thesis more clearly, perhaps adding actual words or synonyms from the thesis.

**TS4** = This might be too broad or vague—not sure the reader will understand what is meant.

**TS5** = The diction is imprecise.

*Note: The examples that follow are only partial paragraphs.*

### Original TS4, TS5

Dickens is showing Scrooge's absolute cold heart.

### Revised

Dickens **shows** Scrooge's **unsympathetic and selfish heart.**

### Original TS4, TS5

Scrooge's nephew is not like his uncle.

### Revised

Scrooge's nephew is his uncle's **foil, a character whose qualities contrast with the qualities of another character.**

### Original TS4, TS5

Shakespeare has a lot of bird imagery, and it means various things.

### Revised

Shakespeare uses bird imagery **to create portraits of man's physical and emotional qualities**.

### Original TS2

**The knight has decided to go immediately from the battlefield to the journey toward Canterbury.** Even his tunic is still dirty; he doesn't bother to look good. Later, we meet the parson who also, we know through the narrator, will put service ahead of his needs.

### Revised

**The first class deals with the "most holy" people, those who put the Lord as well as their fellow man in front of their own needs and desires, men and women who possess many of the qualities of Christ.** For example, the knight, uninterested in resting after fighting in the Crusades, immediately joins the pilgrimage to worship his God.

> This category is defined in the topic sentence. The student will then apply this definition to the characters he uses as examples.

**Thesis** Just as Jesus taught us to serve others, Charles Dickens, in *Great Expectations*, reveals that, through the caring example of a fallen community's servants, the community can be restored to a state of love.

### Original TS3, TS2

During the Christmas dinner, Joe gives Pip gravy and throughout the book does things like this.

### Revised

Finally, Pip's surrogate father, Joe, frequently safeguards Pip when Pip is in desperate need, demonstrating that a servant must be an active participant in restoring community.

### Original TS4, TS5

Some characters are greedy.

### Revised

Some of the minor characters in *Great Expectations*, people who devote their lives procuring a higher social status and acquiring material wealth, illustrate the greed and hypocrisy inherent in infernal comedy.

### Original TS1, TS5

Some characters are honorable.

### Revised

While such vices, however, are the prevailing forces of infernal comedy, not everyone is so despicable and odious; we see characters who represent the virtues of honor and integrity, characters who help to push the novel towards community.

### Original TS2, TS3

Pip begins to hate life at the forge after he visits Miss Havisham and Estella.

### Revised

Shortly after early childhood, Pip begins to grow into the more contemplative stage of preadolescence, a stage in which he begins to question his surroundings as well as draw conclusions about them.

### Original TS2, TS3

The poem opens with the narrator standing before the ocean.

### Revised

The sea depresses the narrator into a cheerless mood of isolation.

### Original TS4

The narrator remembers the faith of the Greeks.

### Revised

Arnold changes the speaker's concentration from the physical sea to the metaphorical sea to reflect on the condition of humanity's spiritual faith.

### Original TS2

Love is the answer.

### Revised

The isolation and loss of faith compel the author even more to move toward personal love.

### Original TS2

The mariner attempts reconciliation right after shooting the albatross.

### Revised

Man's first step after sin is to move toward reconciliation.

### Original TS2

The mariner's misfortunes begin by abruptly and without cause killing the albatross.

### Revised

Since the Fall, man often discovers himself sinning without cause and sometimes without explanation.

### Original TS2

The narrator learns that the mariner must now tell his tale.

### Revised

With reconciliation comes penance, another stage on the path to forgiveness.

# TH = THESIS PROBLEMS

**Editing Symbol**

**TH**

**TH1** = Make minor adjustments in style and clarity.
**TH2** = Thesis contains only a subject, not an opinion.
**TH3** = The idea in the thesis is unclear.

### Original TH2, TH3

Scrooge has to encounter three ghosts who make him confront issues of his past, finally resulting in Scrooge attending his nephew's Christmas dinner.

### Revised

Scrooge's encounter and journey with the three ghosts depicts the requirements necessary for spiritual growth.

### Original TH1 TH2

Athena has Telemachos visit Menelaos because she knows this king can be helpful and is impressive.

### Revised

Menelaos represents the ideal balance between the spiritual concepts of the yang and the yin.

### Original TH3

Minor characters help the theme of the infernal realm in *Great Expectations*.

### Revised

In *Great Expectations* we meet many minor characters whose parts in the story are rather transitory, but who play a major role in the thematic development of the novel, personifying the virtues and vices of infernal comedy.

### Original TH2

Dickens repeats images of "hands" throughout the novel.

### Revised

In *Great Expectations* the motif of the hands indicates Pip's location in the journey toward maturity.

### Original TH3

Matthew Arnold's sea metaphor plays a significant role in the poem.

### Revised

Matthew Arnold's sea metaphor allows him to complete a political commentary on the Victorian Age, a time in which man is isolated and void of religious conviction, a situation that can only be rectified by human love.

### Original TH2

The narrator in Coleridge's "Rime of the Ancient Mariner" must tell his tale of sin to everyone he meets.

### Revised

Coleridge's "Rime of the Ancient Mariner" illustrates man's proclivity, since the Fall, to sin without cause, to possess the opportunity of reconciliation, and to have the option to do penance, all in hopes of receiving forgiveness.

### Original TH1

The images in "Kubla Khan" are very significant and tell us something about Coleridge.

### Revised

The imagery in "Kubla Khan" represents Coleridge's vision of conceiving and writing poetry.

### Original TH1

When Mary Shelley creates her monster and Victor Frankenstein, she is influenced by Milton's Satan and God and uses their characteristics.

### Revised

In creating the monster and Victor, Mary Shelley borrows from Milton's *Paradise Lost*, using aspects of both Satan and God interchangeably.

## V = VAGUE DETAILS

| Editing Symbol | **V1** = This comment needs to be more specific, precise; avoid |
|---|---|
| **V** | plurals. |
| | **V2** = This comment does not really say anything. |

### Original V2

In response to his nephew's felicitous greeting, Scrooge retorts, "What reason have you to be merry? You're poor enough" (13; ch. 1), a response that shows the cold-heartedness of Scrooge.

### Revised

In response to his nephew's felicitous greeting, Scrooge retorts, "What reason have you to be merry? You're poor enough" (13; ch. 1), **a response showing Scrooge thinks happiness is measured by monetary wealth.**

### Original V1

Scrooge rejects his invitation and shows he is not a very festive person.

### Revised

Scrooge rejects his invitation and reveals his desire to **isolate himself from situations that would require not only monetary generosity but also spiritual.**

***Original V2***

The nephew displays kindness toward his cruel uncle and invites him to Christmas dinner: "Dine with us tomorrow. I want nothing from you" (15; ch. 1), an example of his unselfish deeds that he performs towards his uncle.

***Revised***

The nephew displays kindness toward his cruel uncle and invites him to Christmas dinner: "Dine with us tomorrow. I want nothing from you" (15; ch. 1), **an invitation that not only attempts to use the power of community to change Scrooge, but also anticipates Scrooge's suspicion of his nephew's possible monetary motives.**

***Original V2***

The king and his warriors are brought together in a **friendly atmosphere,** where a spiritual connection known as *comitatus* is formed.

***Revised***

**Feasting** helps bring the community closer together. **Hrothgar** knowing this, he commands the **construction of Heorot** so that he may **"share the gifts God had bestowed on him upon its floor with folk young and old"** (67).

***Original V1***

Feasting, one of the most recurrent themes in *Beowulf,* helps the reader understand the significant elements of the Anglo-Saxon culture. One such element is gift-giving, which is an example of *comitatus.* For example, Hrothgar gives Beowulf many gifts. In addition, Wealhtheow, the queen and Hrothgar's wife, also gives presents to Beowulf .

***Revised***

Feasting, one of the most recurrent themes in *Beowulf,* helps the reader understand the significant elements of the Anglo-Saxon culture. <u>One significant element</u> is **gift-giving**, not simply a sign of monetary remuneration but a spiritual symbol of appreciation and fulfillment of the sacred *comitatus* bond that maintains order in the tribe. <u>For example,</u> Hrothgar **bestows "on Beowulf a standard worked in gold, a figured battle-banner, breast and head armour"** (69). <u>In addition,</u> Wealhtheow, the queen and Hrothgar's wife, also presents to **Beowulf "two arm-wreaths, with robes and rings also, and the richest collar the monk has ever heard of in all the world"** (69).

> Note the underlined transitions.

***Original V1***

Dimmesdale, carrying the burden of his ignominious sin within his heart, has suffered for seven years. He frequently **beats himself** and even **tells his parishioners, amazingly, the truth,** but they don't believe it.

***Revised***

Dimmesdale, carrying the burden of his ignominious sin within his heart, has suffered for seven years. He, more than anyone, knows that he is guilty of a crime, for he punishes himself **physically "with a bloody scourge [which he] had plied...on his own shoulders" (141; ch. 27) and mentally with his Sunday reproach: "I, your pastor, whom you so reverence and trust, am utterly a pollution and a lie!" (140; ch. 27).**

# W = WORDY STRUCTURES

**W1** = This phrase is unnecessary. Do not write, "In chapter one it says, 'Hester walked down the path.'" Instead, blend text with the writer's analysis. See B1.

**W2** = Use fewer words: transform longer phrases into single concrete words; turn prepositional phrases into single adjectives.

**W3** = Be careful about piling adjectives or adjective phrases one after another; this slows down the rhythm of the sentence. Either eliminate unnecessary adjectives or reposition some in participial phrases.

**W4** = Remove redundant words within the sentence.

**W5** = Do not make sentence glue unnecessarily long; use synonyms or pronouns, where possible.

### Original W2

The reader could possibly argue here that Scrooge is unaware ~~of the uncomfortable state of his employee~~; however, the text ~~goes on to show how little care Scrooge does have for the well being of~~ his employee. (37 words)

### Revised

The reader could possibly argue here that Scrooge is unaware of **Cratchit's discomfort**; however, the text provides more evidence of **Scrooge's lack of concern** for his employee. (27 words)

### Original W1

~~In further~~ expression of his lust for money, ~~the Pardoner goes on to say~~, "But let me briefly make my purpose plain; / I preach for nothing but for greed of gain" (4–5). (31 words)

### Revised

The Pardoner again states his lust for money: "But let me briefly make my purpose plain; / I preach for nothing but for greed of gain" (4–5). (25 words)

### Original W2

Furthermore, the Friar ~~was a man who~~ put money ahead ~~of anything else in his life, who did not work~~ for the poor, ~~but only the rich~~; he didn't even go into areas that were inhabited by poor people. (39 words)

### Revised

Furthermore, the Friar puts money ahead of his religious obligation, helping the poor. In fact, he makes a deliberate point not to enter impoverished neighborhoods, but only those of the rich. (31 words)

### Original W2

Keeping the sock company ~~from their vantage point several~~ inches away near the closet door, two ~~dilapidated~~ gray Nike track spikes smell of the trials and tribulations of a long, full athletic career. (33 words)

### Revised

Keeping the sock company, two Nike track spikes, inches away near the closet door **and dappled with mud streaks and gashes in the faded leather,** smell of sweat and dried grass. (31 words)

### Original W2

As I hastily walk down the hall, ~~I see some~~ gray ~~shirts that have turned almost completely white after several~~ bleachings creeping out of my doorway; ~~one shirt in particular looks like~~ a Dalmation except it is gray with white spots instead of white with black spots. (47 words)

### Revised

As I hastily walk down the hall, a gray shirt, spotted with bleach stains like a Dalmation's coat, creeps out of my doorway. (23 words)

### Original W3

He adjusts his red and white-billed helmet with his ~~left black~~ Reebok batting ~~glove-clad hand.~~ (17 words)

### Revised

**With his left hand**, covered by a Reebok batting glove, he adjusts his red and white-billed helmet. (18 words)

### Original W2 / W4

Its **movement journeys toward a recapturing of** virtue.

### Revised

It seeks to recapture virtue.

### Original W5

Unfortunately, Scrooge's "Humbug" reply not only demonstrates his unwillingness to engage in a logical debate but also demonstrates **another example of his desire to isolate himself. In another example of his desire to isolate himself,** Scrooge seeks to separate himself from the social obligation to donate to those less fortunate.

### Revised

Unfortunately, Scrooge's "Humbug" reply not only demonstrates his unwillingness to engage in a logical debate but also demonstrates **another example of his desire to isolate himself. In a similar manner,** Scrooge seeks to separate himself from the social obligation to donate to those less fortunate.

## [ ] = VARY YOUR SENTENCE BEGINNINGS

**Editing Symbol**

**[ ]**

Vary some of these sentence beginnings. Use adverb or noun subordinate clauses; absolute phrases; adverb or noun infinitive phrases; present and past participial phrases; prepositional phrases; gerund phrases, etc.

### Original

**Hector**, likewise, **is** lauded for his bountiful skills in military leadership. **Hector has** no love for war, which is different from Achilles. Achilles fought ferociously. **He does** it out of a sense of responsibility to his community. Furthermore, **he is** noted for his compassion and gentleness, which we witness when we observe his loving farewells to his wife and baby son prior to his departure for the final battle. **He earns** the esteem not only of the men under his command, because he is the leader of all the Trojan armies, but also of his adversaries; nevertheless, no one mistakes him for Achilles.

### Revised

Hector, likewise, is lauded for his bountiful skills in military leadership. **Unlike Achilles,** Hector has no love for war. **While he fights ferociously,** he does it out of a sense of responsibility to his community. Furthermore, he is noted for his compassion and gentleness, which we witness when we observe his loving farewells to his wife and baby son prior to his departure for the final battle. **Being leader of all the Trojan armies,** he earns the esteem not only of the men under his command but also of his adversaries; nevertheless, no one mistakes him for Achilles.

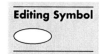 **= VIVID VERB USAGE**

| **Editing Symbol** | ⬭ **1** = Revise this "be" verb with a more vivid, active verb. |
| | ⬭ **2** = Avoid the passive verb in this context. (p. 149) |

**Original 2**

The next example of selfishness is shown towards Scrooge's clerk.

**Revised**

The next example of selfishness **occurs** towards Scrooge's clerk. *Or recast the sentence:* Scrooge **aims** his next act of selfishness at his clerk.

**Original 2**

Instead of being kind and caring towards his fellow man in this season, all of his feelings during Christmas are directed towards money. This is shown when he is speaking to his nephew about the wonderful events of Christmas.

**Revised**

Instead of being kind and caring towards his fellow man in this season, Scrooge **focuses** on money. For example, when he **speaks** to his nephew about Christmas, Scrooge **insists**, "It is a time for paying bills without money" (14; ch. 1).

**Original 2**

The scene is opened with a great look at the coldness of Scrooge.

**Revised**

The scene **opens** with an image of Scrooge's lack of compassion for others.

**Original 1**

In not sharing his coal with others, he is symbolically not sharing the warmth that he has inside of him, warmth that everyone is capable of sharing.

**Revised**

In not sharing his coal with others, Scrooge symbolically **imprisons** the warmth he has inside, warmth each person's soul possesses.

**Original 1**

His hands are massaging Johnny's aching back muscles. The fingers are dancing nimbly, and they are digging into the quivering brawn and kneading the soft white dough.

**Revised**

Strong hands violently **massage** Johnny's aching back muscles. Ebony fingers, **dancing nimbly, dig** into the quivering brawn and **knead** the soft white dough.

The following paragraphs have gone through various stages of the revision process. The teacher may use these examples for general class discussion. As these passages contain annotations pointing out the skills discussed throughout this text, the teacher may find that some paragraphs may be used for imitation or modeling exercises, or as "worksheets" for students to identify the qualities of effective writing.

**Note** Where some of the following paragraphs have been written by an individual student, that student's name is listed above the paragraph. Other paragraphs contain a combination of various students' work so, instead of a single author, I have listed only the general subject of the paragraph on the first line.

**Topic: *Biddy and Pip* in Great Expectations**                    *by Tyler Green*

Biddy is an ignoble country girl who represents Pip's loving side that cares about other people. Despite being plain and common, Biddy is a loving and devoted person. She works hard as a servant for Mrs. Joe and also manages to be a loyal friend to Pip. Biddy also teaches him, takes care of his family, and listens to his personal problems. Unlike Estella, "Biddy was never insulting, or capricious, or Biddy today and somebody else tomorrow" (122; ch. 17). She likes Pip for who he is and "only wants [him] to do well, and be comfortable" (120; ch. 17), not minding of his social status. Pip can also be selfless like Biddy, such as when he helps Magwitch both on the marshes and in London. **Obligated by his sense of duty to his benefactor,** Pip puts himself into danger on Magwitch's behalf. **Pip's mind, "wholly set on Provis's safety" (404; ch. 54), forgets the risk involved to his own self and reputation.** Pip also helps his friend Herbert, secretly setting him up with a profitable partnership, using his own money to finance his less fortunate friend. Pip acts like Biddy in these situations by putting the well being of others ahead of his own, **a trait that he had inherently as a boy but needed to learn again as he matured.** Biddy is the embodiment of this inherent good and is the companion Pip would have had if he stayed and worked at the forge. Her character represents the hard, honest, happy life.

*[Annotation: Introductory past participial phrase adds variety to sentence beginnings.]*

*[Annotation: Writer effectively blends Dickens' words with his own.]*

*[Annotation: Analysis modifier extends elaboration.]*

**Topic: *Feasting as a cultural totem in* Beowulf**

Feasting, one of the most recurrent themes in *Beowulf*, helps the reader understand <u>the significant elements of the Anglo-Saxon culture</u>. <u>One significant element</u> is gift-giving, not simply a sign of monetary remuneration but a spiritual symbol of appreciation and fulfillment of the sacred *comitatus* bond that maintains order in the tribe. <u>For example</u>, Hrothgar bestows "on Beowulf a standard worked in gold, a figured battle-banner, breast and head armour" (83). <u>In addition</u>, Wealhtheow, the queen and Hrothgar's wife, also <u>presents</u> to Beowulf "two arm-wreaths, with robes and rings also, and the richest collar the monk has ever heard of in all the world" (83). <u>These gifts</u> represent Hrothgar and Wealhtheow's gratitude towards Beowulf for killing the notorious, malicious Grendel, cleansing their community of evil. Moreover, a warrior's gifts, their quality and quantity, indicate the degree of his heroism. <u>Feasting provides not only gifts and honor</u>, but entertainment as well, a spirit of festivity. In Heorot, "the hall [fills] with loud amusement; there [is] the music of the harp," while Hrothgar "[gives] out rings, arm-bands at the banquet," and the "men [drink] their wine" (86), activities that allow the community to forget the conflicts that may plague their lives outside the hall. <u>Finally</u>, the feast provides warnings to heroes, tales of past failures. <u>The story of Heremod</u>, a figure called to "assume the kingdom, the care of his people, the hoard and the stronghold, the Scylding homeland" (87), serves to <u>warn</u> Beowulf about the darker side of man's heart, the evil that had seduced Heremod, who became "a deadly grief to his people and the princes of his land" (89). Instead, Hrothgar <u>cautions</u> Beowulf to "put away arrogance" (90) and to know that he has to act justly and morally throughout his life. <u>By contrast, stories</u> praise virtuous action. <u>For instance</u>, the scop tells of Sigemund, **"who had slain the dragon" and killed a serpent with the "best of swords" (87),** to compare Beowulf's deeds with past Danish warriors, Beowulf's *kleos* now secured in the legends of the Danes. <u>Not only does Beowulf</u> leave the feast refreshed and <u>honored</u>, but all members of the court also reap the benefits of this cultural exercise, for these hours contain the energy of *communitas*, **that human phenomenon binding people together for a unified purpose, reminding them of their shared values**; this provides the stamina needed to return to previous roles and to maintain order in their lives.

*[Margin annotations:]*

Topic sentence identifies a focus for the paragraph and suggests a way to organize.

Writer explains context before incorporating direct quotation.

Underlined words are key words that glue each sentence together. Notice how new information appears at the end of the sentence—old at the beginning.

Adjective clause extends information about Sigemund.

Absolute phrase

### Topic: Time as a tool in "To His Coy Mistress"  *by Robby Markose*

In Andrew Marvell's "To His Coy Mistress," the speaker utilizes the aspect of time to influence his mistress's decision about having a sexual relationship with him. In the first stanza, the narrator uses the concept of time to comfort his mistress. He begins by stating that if he "had but world enough and time" (1), he would cherish her even more than he already does. He believes that if they could control time, he would spend a hundred years "to adore each breast" (13) and maybe even "thirty thousand" (14) more years to adore the rest of her body. By asserting this, the narrator convinces his mistress that time is the reason why he cannot satiate all of her needs; this idea also allows her to believe that the narrator really does love her but consequently faces time as an opponent. In the second and third stanza, the narrator uses time to manipulate his mistress's emotions; he places her in a state of fear and discomfort. **Although the narrator tells his mistress that his love for her remains strong,** he feels that "time's winged chariot [hurries] near" (20). He reveals this in hope that the image of this chase scene will serve as a catalyst to speed up her decision in shifting their relationship to a physical level. **Trying to discomfort her once more**, the narrator uses a morose image to describe the effects of time as he tells his mistress worms will be the first to pleasure her "long preserved" (26) virginity. The narrator, **using this image**, hopes the mistress will want him, instead, to be the first lover to share this experience. Also in the second and third stanza, he tells his mistress that time will strip away her beauty if she continues to allow her "youthful hue / [to sit on] thy skin like morning glow" (33–34). **Since the morning dew evaporates as the day passes**, the narrator warns his mistress she, too, will grow old and die. In these last two stanzas, the narrator hopes that, by scaring his mistress, she will more easily submit to his request. He tells her that we should "rather at-once our time devour, / than languish in his slow-chapped power" (39–40). He believes they should be in a sexual relationship, immediately, before time becomes the reason that forbids them from doing so.

> The writer repeats the word "time" throughout the paragraph to maintain clarity and coherence.

> The writer employs adverb clauses, participial phrases, and semicolons for sentence structure variety.

### Topic: The Yin of Joe Gargery in Great Expectations  *by Juan Salazar*

Throughout *Great Expectations*, Dickens develops Joe's *yin* characteristics, those traditionally associated with the feminine, causing us to rethink our stereotype of the father. Joe Gargery's semblance of "a muscular blacksmith, [with a] broad chest" (6; ch. 2), connotes stereotypical masculine imagery, though Pip later contradicts this imagery. **As a mother protects her offspring from danger, Joe, too, assumes this task at the dinner table on Christmas Eve.** Hearing Pip being battered by the family, Joe extends his "restoring touch" unto Pip, "aiding and comforting [him]…by giving [Pip] gravy" (23; ch. 4), **a benevolent deed that demonstrates not just his concern for Pip, but his willingness to help and care for him;** in fact, Joe, instead of seeing Pip suffer, would "wish to take it [the Tickler] on himself" (43; ch. 7),

> Writer proceeds to show and extend elaboration of Joe's feminine qualities.

> Analysis modifier (p. 160) inside a compound-complex sentence whose independent clauses are joined by a conjunctive adverb

showing his legitimate concern for Pip's well-being. Apart from his concern for Pip, Joe also desires the unification of the household, his concern for the *oikos*, an important *yin* characteristic. For example, Joe avoids confrontations with Mrs. Gargery when she "is in a cross temper," and gives Pip "encouraging...pieces of wisdom" (64; ch. 9) that help him alleviate his painful feelings of being "common...and wishing that he was not common." In addition, the conflict between Mrs. Joe and Orlick having been suppressed, Joe demonstrates his desire to maintain tranquility in the household. To Pip, Joe's arm is "an angel's wing" (431; ch. 57), a description that identifies Joe as being more than just the male, but the protector of the household.

> Writer effectively blends direct quotations into sentences.

### Topic: Roger unrestrained in Lord of the Flies            *by Neal Talreja*

Roger represents the intentionally cruel human being whose evil nature emerges once civilized restraints are stripped away. Throughout the novel, Roger demonstrates his cruelty in several scenes. First, while the littluns play on the beach, Roger gathers "a handful of stones and [begins] to throw them" (62; ch. 4) near the children; however, he does not throw the stones directly at them because his "arm [is] conditioned by a civilization" (62; ch. 4). As a young British boy, Roger has grown up in a civilized society where "parents and school and policemen and the law" (62; ch. 4) have instructed him to be kind to others, to become educated, and to follow the laws; however, stranded on an island, the people who enforce these fetters are not present, **an absence of authority that enables "some source of power to pulse in [his] body" (175; ch. 11), a power, or evil nature, that obliterates common sense as well as care for the rules and customs of society.** Roger's destruction of reason and order enables him to abandon his previous life and, consequently, to succumb to the primitive impulses of hunting and killing. These impelling forces appear later in the forest where the boys kill a sow, **Roger prodding "with his spear whenever pig flesh" appears, finding "a lodgment for his point . . . to push" (135; ch. 8),** *actions that show his ability to harm a living creature.* Moreover, when the boys reenact the hunt after performing this gruesome act, Roger demonstrates the intentional cruelty used to kill the sow when he becomes "the pig, grunting and charging. . . [and mimicking] the terror of the pig" (151; ch. 9). The fact that Roger can kill a living creature, then mimic the terror he inflicts upon it, shows how he is aware of the evil of his actions but does not care. Later, on Castle Rock, his incapacity to care advances him to a more homicidal level of cruelty when he, "with a sense of delirious abandonment, [leans] all his weight on the lever" (180; ch. 11), releasing the giant rock that kills Piggy, **who was merely addressing the savages about the need for reason and order on the island prior to his execution.** The fact that Roger kills a fellow human being, particularly the only human being on the island with reason and intellect, shows how he only cares

> An analysis modifier followed by a repeat word modifier, both of which extend the elaboration of the writer's idea regarding the abandonment of civilized restraints.

> An absolute phrase extends elaboration, as does the analysis modifier (in italics) that ends the sentence.

> Writer extends elaboration with an adjective clause noting the irony involved in the situation leading to Piggy's murder.

to do what is cruel as opposed to do what is reasonable. This lack of conscience leads to more barbarous behavior on Castle Rock. For example, when Sam and Eric refuse to join the tribe, he threatens to torture them by advancing "upon them as one wielding a nameless authority" (182; ch. 11), a "nameless authority" that once more shows how he has lost his previous identity as a civilized boy due to the truculent nature within. **The deeds of killing a human being and torturing others accomplished,** he concludes his sadistic rampage when he sharpens "a stick at both ends" (190; ch. 12) and saunters through the jungle, hunting for Ralph. Like the stick whetted at both ends, Roger has no kind and civilized side, for his cruel nature has cast him into a domain of evil.

> Writer employs an absolute phrase to sum up Roger's descent into barbarity as he concludes the paragraph with the image of the stick sharpened at both ends.

### Topic: Forming community in Donne's "Meditation 17" *by Young Cho*

Donne uses **metaphors** to remind us of man's communal nature, **metaphors** that reveal man's need to belong to a larger group. First, Donne compares the church to one body. Donne needs the church "whereof (he is) a member" (10), as a form of support, just as the head, "engrafted into that body" (10), needs the help of the body, the larger group or structure that provides life. Next, Donne compares man to a book, demonstrating they are both "of one author" and that man naturally belongs to a community as a book belongs to a "volume." This community is so important to mankind that even after some process of transformation such as death, where one sheds his physical element, thus gaining a more spiritual character, the one aspect that he does not change is that he is still part of a **community, a community now actually better than the first—the kingdom of heaven.** Likewise, a book, after being "translated into a better language," is still part of that "library where every book shall lie open to one another" (11). Similarly, a piece of land serves as a metaphor to man; however, this metaphor reveals how the community also needs man. Donne says that no piece of land should be "an island entire to itself" (11), deserted, neglected, its environment void of any other lands, a melancholy situation man should similarly avoid. Instead, this piece of land should be "a piece of a continent, a part of the main" (11), as man needs community, and if this piece of land happens to "be washed away by the sea" (11), its continent becomes "the less," meaning it experiences a loss in size, paralleling a community's disappointment and the loss when one of its members dies. Donne, through use of his metaphors, visually portrays to the reader the relationship between man and community, demonstrating how man is isolated without community and the community "diminished" without man.

> Repeat word modifier

> Repeat word modifier extends elaboration.

**_Topic: Avarice in_ Great Expectations**              _by Damian Smith_

Some of the minor characters in _Great Expectations_, **people who devote their lives procuring a higher social status and acquiring material wealth, illustrate the greed and hypocrisy inherent in infernal comedy.** Pumblechook represents the acme of hypocrisy, a fearful imposter who presents himself as a venerable aristocrat. Yet, his prodigious lies about his knowledge of Miss Havisham reveal him to be a deceitful person, a man of guile rather than veneration. Furthermore, his nauseating "May I's" to Pip, in order to gain his favor after Pip has acquired money, only cause the reader to disdain him even more. Another character similar to Pumblechook in her snobbish pretensions is Mrs. Belinda Pocket; however, while Pumblechook merely desires to become part of the aristocracy, she already believes that, being the daughter of an alleged knight, she is. As she is to be guarded from the acquisition of plebeian domestic knowledge, she knows very little about the care of her own children, consequently allowing one child to nearly kill itself with a nutcracker and spurning another child for trying to prevent it, an act of opprobrium revealing not only her stubborn and impetuous mien, but also the absurdity and imprudence of the people she represents. She is a wife and mother, yet she rejects the virtues of a wife and mother, her role as protector and nurturer of her family. In addition, Compeyson, Miss Havisham's ex-lover, is seen as devoting himself to material self-interest, but he represents a more sinister and vile side. One first views him as a perfect gentleman, a smooth one to talk, with his curly hair, and his black clothes and his white pocket handkerchief, but in reality, his business is swindling, handwriting, forging, and stolen banknote passing. As well, he is a man without a heart, cold as death and with the head of the devil, having pity on nothing and nobody. According to George R. Thomas, Compeyson demonstrates the basic unreality of Magwitch's assumption that being a gentleman is one of the best blessings he can bestow on Pip (34). Magwitch's reaction to finally seeing his creation leads one to ascertain that he has given Pip a gift, yet through Compeyson we learn that being a gentleman is not as fantastic as it seems.

Writer will apply this definition to examples.

Writer extends elaboration of Pumblechook.

Note the concrete detail about Mrs. Pocket.

**Before Dickens places Carton into his Passion Story,** he first gives the reader images of Carton's similarities to Christ. Dickens accomplishes this through a comparison of the characters' common traits. The author commences this imagery by describing Carton as "wearing the white riding-coat and top boots, then in vogue, and the light of the fires touching the light surfaces of his face made him look very pale, with long brown hair, all untrimmed, hanging loose about him" (240; bk. 3, ch. 9). In this description, Dickens compares both the physical and metaphysical traits the two have in common. First, Dickens' description of Carton shows the physical features he has in common with Christ. Carton displays the pale face and long brown hair **depicted in the classic European artwork done of Christ.** Dickens begins his metaphysical comparison through color archetypes. Carton wears a white riding-coat, **associating him with the color white,** a color of purity. By linking Carton with white, Dickens connects him to a trait commonly associated with Christ, purity. **To advance the metaphysical comparison between Carton and Christ as the novel continues,** Dickens uses a second archetype. He gives the reader an image of "the light of the fires touching the light surfaces [of Carton]." The repetition of the word "light" in this image forces the reader to connect Carton with light, **an archetype of life,** which is an association that also takes place in the Bible with Christ. For example, in John's gospel, the Bible tells the reader, "What came to be through him was life, and this light was the light of the human race; the light shines in the darkness, and the darkness has not overcome it" (John 1.5). Dickens extends his comparison between Jesus and Carton through imagery showing how Carton's actions bring about "light that shines in the darkness," just as John informs us that Jesus' actions did in the passage above. Directly after Carton's decision to die for Darnay, Dickens says, "Then, the night, with the moon and the stars, turned pale and died, and for a little while it seemed as if creation were delivered over to Death's dominion. But the glorious sun, rising, seemed to strike those words, that burden of the night, straight and warm to his heart in its long bright rays" (294; bk. 3, ch. 9). Dickens' decision to show this specific change in nature, directly after Carton's decision to die for another, forces the reader to connect Carton's actions with the sun, which brings light. This image clearly shows that Carton's actions bring light, or life, just as Jesus' actions did.

> Writer employs a variety of structures, including the introductory adverb clause, both the past and present participial phrase, the introductory infinitive phrase, and the appositive phrase.

## ASSIGNMENT #1: PUTTING A PARAGRAPH TOGETHER

An explanation of this first assignment, which is based on Charles Dickens'
*A Christmas Carol,* can be found in "A Suggested Lesson Planning Sequence,"
p. 22, Day One. Many of these activities I use in order to prepare my students
for their first expository paragraph/argument on the literature we are currently
studying. Parts of four of the five exercises thereafter also refer to the selection
from *A Christmas Carol,* those exercises involving **TS** (topic sentence errors),
**E** (elaboration), **B** (blending textual support), **L** (listing plot details),
**P** (paragraph errors), **O** (off-topic), and **A** (adding transitions).

### A *selection from* A Christmas Carol

The door of Scrooge's counting-house was open that he might keep
his eye upon his clerk, who in a dismal little cell beyond, a sort of
tank, was copying letters. Scrooge had a very small fire, but the clerk's
fire was so very much smaller that it looked like one coal. But he
couldn't replenish it, for Scrooge kept the coal-box in his own room;
and so surely as the clerk came in with the shovel, the master pre-
dicted that it would be necessary for them to part.

"A merry Christmas, Uncle! God save you!" cried a cheerful
voice. It was the voice of Scrooge's nephew.

"Bah!" said Scrooge, "Humbug!"

This nephew of Scrooge's was all in a glow; his face was ruddy
and handsome; his eyes sparkled, and his breath smoked again.

"Christmas a humbug, Uncle! You don't mean that, I am sure?"

"I do," said Scrooge. "Merry Christmas! What right have you to be
merry? What reason have you to be merry? You're poor enough,"
grumbled Scrooge.

"What right have you to be dismal? What reason have you to be
morose? You're rich enough."

"Humbug."

"Don't be cross, Uncle!" said the nephew.

"What else can I be," returned the uncle, "when I live in such a
world of fools as this? Merry Christmas! What's Christmas time to you
but a time for paying bills without money; a time for finding yourself
a year older, but not an hour richer. If I could work my will," said
Scrooge indignantly, "every idiot who goes about with 'Merry
Christmas' on his lips, should be boiled with his own pudding, and
buried with a stake of holly through his heart. He should!"

"Uncle!" pleaded the nephew.

"Let me leave it alone, then," said Scrooge. "Much good may it do
you! Much good it has ever done you!"

"There are many things from which I might have derived good,
by which I have not profited. I have always thought of Christmas time,
when it has come round—apart from the veneration due to its sacred
name and origin—as a good time; a kind, forgiving, charitable, pleasant time: the only time I know of, in the long calendar of the year,
when men and women seem by one consent to open their shut-up

hearts freely, and to think of people below them as if they really were fellow-passengers to the grave, and not another race of creatures bound on other journeys. And therefore, uncle, though it has never put a scrap of gold or silver in my pocket, I believe that it has done me good, and will do me good; and I say, God bless it!"

"Good afternoon," said Scrooge.

"Don't be angry, Uncle. Come! Dine with us tomorrow. I want nothing from you; I ask nothing of you; why cannot we be friends?"

"Good afternoon," said Scrooge.

"I am sorry, with all my heart, to find you so resolute. We have never had any quarrel, to which I have been a party. But I have made the trial in homage to Christmas, and I'll keep my Christmas humour to the last. So A Merry Christmas, Uncle!"

"Good afternoon," said Scrooge.

"And a Happy New Year!"

"Good afternoon," said Scrooge.

His nephew left the room without an angry word. He stopped to bestow the greetings of the season on the clerk, who, cold as he was, was warmer than Scrooge; for he returned them cordially.

"There's another fellow," muttered Scrooge, "my clerk, with fifteen shillings a week, and a wife and family, talking about a Merry Christmas. I'll retire to Bedlam."

This lunatic, in letting Scrooge's nephew out, had let two other people in.

"Scrooge and Marley's, I believe," said one of the gentlemen, referring to his list. "Have I the pleasure of addressing Mr. Scrooge, or Mr. Marley?"

"Mr. Marley has been dead these seven years," Scrooge replied.

"We have no doubt his liberality is well represented by his surviving partner," said the gentleman. At the ominous word "liberality," Scrooge frowned, and shook his head.

"At this festive season of the year, Mr. Scrooge," said the gentleman, taking up a pen, "it is more than usually desirable that we should make some slight provision for the Poor and Destitute, who suffer greatly at the present time."

"Are there no prisons?" asked Scrooge.

"Plenty of prisons," said the gentleman, laying down the pen again.

"And the Union workhouses? Are they still in operation?"

"They are. Still," returned the gentleman, "I wish I could say they were not."

"Oh! I was afraid, from what you said at first, that something had occurred to stop them in their useful course," said Scrooge.

"Under the impression that they scarcely furnish Christian cheer of mind or body to the multitude, a few of us are endeavoring to raise a fund to buy the Poor some meat. What shall I put you down for?"

"Nothing!" Scrooge replied.

"You wish to be anonymous?"

"I wish to be left alone," said Scrooge. "Since you ask me what I wish, gentlemen, that is my answer. I don't make merry myself at

Christmas and I can't afford to make idle people merry. I help to support the establishments I have mentioned—they cost enough; and those who are badly off must go there."

"Many can't go there; and many would rather die."

"It's not my business," Scrooge returned. "It's enough for a man to understand his own business, and not to interfere with other people's. Mine occupies me constantly. Good afternoon, gentlemen!"

## ASSIGNMENT #2 REVISING FOR B (BLENDING TEXTUAL SUPPORT)

**Directions** Review section on blending text, p. 67; correct passages below.
1. It says in the text that the nephew, "a kind, forgiving, charitable, pleasant time…when men and women seem by one consent to open their shut-up hearts freely."
2. Scrooge doesn't want to make a donation. It says, "Nothing!" after the men say, "What shall I put you down for?"
3. Scrooge threatened his clerk after Bob cheered Scrooge's nephew. "Let me hear another sound from you and you'll keep your Christmas by losing your situation."

## ASSIGNMENT #3 EXTENDING THE ELABORATION OF AN IDEA E3, E4

**Directions** Review the explanation and examples for revising **E3** or **E4**, p. 71, and then extend the elaboration of the following sentences.
1. Bob Cratchit is an ideal father. An ideal father values relationships more than material wealth. For example, when Mrs. Cratchit tells Bob that Martha is "not coming," he reacts "with a sudden declension in his high spirits. . . Not coming upon Christmas Day!'"
2. Even when Scrooge's own nephew visits him at work to wish him a merry Christmas, the old man deprecates the nephew's cheerful spirit, insisting that "Christmas is a time for paying bills without money, and a time for finding yourself a year older, but not an hour richer."
3. Scrooge is unable to be generous under any circumstance. For example, the narrator describes the "clerk's fire [as] so very much smaller that it looked like one coal." Here the reader sees that the clerk doesn't have a large fire.

## ASSIGNMENT #4 ADDING TRANSITIONS A1, A2

**Directions** After the topic sentence, either attach a transitional clause or phrase, or insert a separate transitional sentence.
1. The opening scene of *A Christmas Carol* presents the conflict between selfishness and selflessness. The narrator explains that Scrooge's "clerk's fire was so very much smaller that it looked like one coal."
2. Dickens depicts Scrooge as the archetypal curmudgeon. Scrooge's only response to his nephew's invitation to dinner is "Good afternoon," a statement repeated four times.
3. Scrooge's nephew represents the spirit of youthful optimism. He questions his uncle, "What reason have you to be morose? You're rich enough."

## ASSIGNMENT #5 REVISING FOR <u>O</u>/<u>O2</u> (OFF-TOPIC) ETC.

**Directions** Review the explanation and examples for revising **O/O2,** p. 78, and then revise the following examples of beginnings of paragraphs. Note that the writer may need to address other symbols such as **B3/B4** or **E3** or **T.**

1. Dickens shows Scrooge's loathing of Christmas through his lack of compassion for others. His clerk's fire was "so very much smaller that it looked like one coal." In addition, the clerk couldn't "replenish it [the fire], for Scrooge kept the coal box in his own room."

2. Dickens portrays Scrooge as a greedy selfish man. One reads of how "the door of Scrooge's counting house was open that he might keep his eye upon his clerk," demonstrating his feeling of superiority and seniority over everyone, especially his dedicated worker. Finally, it reads, "Scrooge had a very small fire" but the clerk's fire was "much smaller."

3. Scrooge has no sense of generosity or care for others even though it is the holidays. Although Scrooge shows no holiday cheer, his clerk, Bob Cratchit, returns Scrooge's nephew's greetings of the season cordially. Scrooge ridicules Mr. Cratchit, "My clerk, with fifteen shillings a week, and a wife and family, talking about a Merry Christmas."

## ASSIGNMENT #6 DESTROYING A PARAGRAPH

**Directions** Choose a paragraph from the preceding section of *Complete Expository Paragraphs.* Cross out concrete details; replace with vague diction, weak verbs. Remove places where elaboration has been extended; remove word, logic glue.

# CONSTRUCTING THE PAPER

## DEFINITIONS

### • Subject

A subject may be a broad concept, field of study, a play, a character, a novel, a poem, or pattern either assigned to the student by the teacher or chosen by the student.

### • Topic

A more specific, more narrow aspect of the subject. Here the writer may focus on, among other things, a reoccurring image in a literary work, a setting, the language used by the author, or a specific event.

### • Thesis Statement

A thesis statement is a statement that presents the writer's approach, or insight, toward the topic; a statement that presents an opinion about its topic; a statement that identifies a new way of examining the topic; a statement that provides an answer to an implied question. More specifically, *a literary thesis* invites the reader to resee a text through a different lens, to recognize a pattern, or to understand a character more deeply.

**Thesis Statement Formula = Topic + Debatable Opinion**

# HOW DOES THE WRITER GENERATE A TOPIC FOR A THESIS?

### Option One: Ask and answer questions about the literature

A writer may generate ideas by asking and answering a series of questions about the work of literature he or she is studying. The answer to a question may then be written as a thesis statement.

#### • Theme

Does the story depict an abstract idea, a moral or psychological struggle, an aspect of human life? Does the plot suggest an analogy?

#### • Character

Does a character change, and why or how? What are a character's prominent qualities? What is the function of a character—is he or she the hero, the servant, the sage, the antagonist, a Christ figure, a tempter, a trickster? Is a character similar to another, perhaps a double? Is a character an exact contrast of another, perhaps a foil? Does the character react in the same manner when confronted by another character or setting?

#### • Plot

What is the conflict? Is the work a comedy, a tragedy, an epic? Is it a picaresque, a bildungsroman, a fable, an allegory?

#### • Setting

What is important about the setting? Are there multiple settings? How are they different? What does the landscape or dwelling suggest about theme or character?

#### • Style

How does the writer use imagery, diction, language, syntax to express tone or mood? What is the tone? Is there a motif; what is significant about it?

#### • Symbol

What does a symbol mean? What is its role in the story? Does its function change?

#### • Allusions

Does the plot of the story or a character remind the reader of someone historical, biblical, mythological?

#### • Point of view

What is the function of the narration? How does first person, third person omniscient, objective, or third person limited affect the story?

### Option Two: Use Aristotle's topics

Aristotle's topics provide a way for a writer to generate an idea for a thesis statement, to create an actual thesis statement or, at least, to narrow the subject. Aristotle suggests these topics represent the way we think and argue a subject.

## • Definition

When a writer considers definition, he or she says what something is. For instance, a character is___, a symbol is___, or a series of actions is___. With this approach, the writer explores the essential qualities of the definition as applied to the literary text. Possible definitions include

The conch in *Lord of the Flies* represents democracy.

In Dickens' *A Christmas Carol*, Bob Cratchit represents the ideal father.

Scout in *To Kill a Mockingbird* is a lady.

## • Comparison

When a writer argues by comparison, he explains how two or more items are either similar (analogous), identifying the qualities or aspects of similarity, or how these items are different (disparate), identifying the qualities or aspects that exhibit contrast.

Biddy and Estella in Dickens' *Great Expectations* are contrasting influences on Pip's maturation.

In *A Tale of Two Cities*, the battle between the human and the inhuman is resolved, with Stryver fleeing as a hypocrite and the unlikely Carton rising as a phoenix from the ashes of desperation to save humanity.

## • Consequence

When a writer uses consequence, he or she says something causes or is caused by something else. Possible created consequences include

Dickens' *A Christmas Carol* demonstrates that exploring one's memory can bring about self-improvement.

In Dickens' *A Christmas Carol*, Scrooge is isolated because of his obsession with money.

Thomas Hardy argues in his poem "Convergence of the Twain" that human pride caused the ship to sink.

# ONCE THE WRITER HAS CHOSEN A TOPIC, HOW DOES THE WRITER DISCOVER A THESIS STATEMENT?

## • Freewrite

Take the topic—perhaps it is a character, or a setting, or a symbol, or a motif—and *begin writing in complete sentences whatever comes to mind*. Write *without stopping for five, ten, or fifteen minutes*. Writers should not be concerned with organization or making logical sense. The goal is to discover possible ideas. The act of writing helps one penetrate the topic more deeply, assisting in the writer's discovery of an opinion about the topic. Writers should force themselves to write words or phrases, even if the only thing being written for awhile is, "I'm not sure what to say."

- Consider writing questions about the topic, aspects that are confusing, evoke strong emotion, or are particularly complicated.
- Consider unusual comparisons within the literary text, observations that don't at first seem logical.
- Consider journalistic questions: who? what? when? where? why? how?
- Concentrate on one plot detail that would serve as evidence; begin recalling as many concrete details as possible about this scene.
- Consider whether there exists any cause-effect relationships.

### • Brainstorm

Unlike freewriting, brainstorming may simply be *making a list of short phrases or incomplete ideas*. Writers may list as many concrete details as they can remember regarding the topic. Writers may employ the journalist's questions: who? what? when? where? why? how? What is important is to list whatever comes to mind. The process of making a list will cause writers to make associations, recognize possible comparisons, remember illustrations, etc.

### • Search for evidence

Search and list possible evidence (concrete showing details in the literary text) related to the topic.

> ...Where does the evidence occur in the plot?
> ...Whose actions support the topic? When do these occur?
> ...What do characters say?
> ...What does the narrator say? How does she or he say it?
> ...Go through the literary text and write down *key passages* that might relate to the topic.

Writers should carefully reread the collection of evidence gathered.

### • Reflect

While reflecting on this evidence, writers may, and should strive to, *discover a pattern*. Writers should recognize that in order to write a thesis statement that goes beyond plot and beyond an obvious pattern, they must take time to reflect on the text. A sophisticated thesis statement rarely is written spontaneously; an intelligent thesis statement is rarely written without first reflecting on the potential textual evidence. To attempt to write a thesis statement without reflecting and rereading sections of the literary text is to invite frustration and writer's block. Only after careful reflection on possible textual evidence can an intelligent thesis emerge.

## HOW DOES THE WRITER FORMULATE A THESIS STATEMENT?

> Broad Subject:...................... *A Christmas Carol*
> Specific Topic:...................... Bob Cratchit
> Question about the topic:... Why is he important to the story?
> Thesis:................................. Bob Cratchit represents the ideal father.

### *Check the thesis statement: topic + debatable opinion*

1. Can the writer identify the topic of the thesis statement? The subject might be a symbol, a character, a motif, an archetype, or an aspect of DIDLS (diction, imagery, details, language, sentence structure).
2. Can the writer identify the opinion? Or does the statement merely identify something in the text?
3. Does the thesis merely summarize or only point out an obvious detail or pattern?
4. Does the diction in the thesis include vague or abstract words that contain too many meanings, thus preventing a clear focus?

***Examples of thesis statements without an opinion***
- Ebenezer Scrooge is forced to remember events of the past.
- Huck and Jim experience several conflicts during their travel down the river.
- There are many symbols in the book.
- Dickens repeats images of "hands" throughout the novel.
- Matthew Arnold's sea metaphor plays a significant role in the poem.

***Examples of thesis statements with an opinion***
- Scrooge's encounters with the ghosts illustrate the transformative power of memory.
- Huck and Jim's friendship moves through three stages: the meeting, the challenge and survival, and developing love.
- The archetype of clothing reflects Huck's desire for individuality.
- In *Great Expectations* the hands motif indicates Pip's location in the journey toward maturity.
- The sea metaphor allows Matthew Arnold to develop a political commentary on the Victorian Age, a time in which man is isolated and void of religious conviction, a situation that can only be rectified by human love.
- The diction and imagery Twain uses in relaying Huck's story reveals his personal struggle with freedom and civilization.

## AFTER WRITING THE THESIS STATEMENT, WHAT NEXT?

### • Organize the evidence
After looking at the list of textual passages, consider the best way to organize the evidence. Look for patterns. Perhaps the evidence can be grouped chronologically, according to sections of the text. Perhaps the evidence can be grouped by aspects of the definition in the thesis statement or the parts of the analogy. Review the organization choices below that were previously discussed with paragraphing: time, place, idea. *Beware:* Some young writers attempt to organize their papers and write topic sentences without first examining the evidence. *Allow the evidence to determine the organization of the essay.*

## AFTER ORGANIZING EVIDENCE, WHAT DOES THE WRITER DO?

### • Create topic sentences
Write topic sentences that will support the thesis statement. Topic sentences show the reader how the writer is organizing the evidence. **Bold-faced phrases** *in the sample topic sentences that follow demonstrate the writer's organization choice; the* <u>underlined words</u> *act as glue tying the topic sentence to the thesis statement.*

***Topic Sentence (TS) = Organizing Element + Aspect of Thesis***

**Organization Choices**

1. Time: Organize chronologically, moving through the events in the novel or poem. (Note that I have only given examples of two topic sentences; these thesis statements often will require more.)

> Thesis  The conch in *Lord of the Flies* represents the decay of order and civilization.
>
> TS1  In **chapter one,** the <u>conch</u> is discovered and revered for its power to call the children to an ordered meeting.
>
> TS2  In **chapter three,** the conch shows signs of losing its <u>civilizing</u> power.

2. Place: Organize according to locations in the text.

> Thesis  The marriages in *Great Expectations* depict the variety of virtues and vices present in this British community.
>
> TS1  Near the story's beginning , the reader encounters the **home of Joe and Mrs. Joe,** a home where <u>truth</u> and <u>innocence</u> are <u>preyed upon.</u>
>
> TS2  Later, the reader visits **the Pockets' home,** a place of <u>idleness</u> and <u>self-centeredness.</u>

> Thesis  In *The Scarlet Letter,* Hester models the emotional strength uncharacteristic of a stereotypical seventeenth century woman.
>
> TS1  Exiting the **prison door,** Hester's demeanor shows the reader her <u>assertiveness.</u>
>
> TS2  At **the governor's house,** Hester forcefully displays her <u>confidence.</u>

---

**TS ≠ plot detail only**

A topic sentence that contains only a plot detail does not communicate an organization choice or an aspect of the thesis. For example, *Piggy discovers the conch near the lagoon in chapter one* is a plot detail and not a topic sentence.

---

3. Idea: This approach includes papers organized by a definition, a classification, an analogy/comparison, a comparison-contrast, or a cause-effect. The topic sentences, then, articulate separate parts of the thesis statement. For example, topic sentences might define the aspects of a definition, classify the evidence into categories, identify one cause, etc.

> Thesis  In *The Tempest* Prospero possesses the qualities of leadership all communities hope to produce.
>
> TS1  Prospero <u>demonstrates an ability **to restrain his emotions.**</u>
>
> TS2  Prospero <u>recognizes that **those who commit crimes must receive consequences.**</u>

> Thesis  In *The Canterbury Tales,* Chaucer uses his characters to explore three moral categories.
>
> TS1  The **lowest level** Chaucer describes is one of complete <u>depravity.</u>
>
> TS2  Chaucer's **second moral plane is defined** by the <u>perpetration of evil acts: sloth, selfishness, and hypocrisy.</u>

| Thesis | In *Great Expectations* Pip finds himself in a situation paralleling the parable of the prodigal son. |
|---|---|
| TS1 | The **Bible's <u>parable</u> begins** with the <u>prodigal son</u> who, dissatisfied with his present <u>situation</u> in life, asks his father for his inheritance. |
| TS2 | After he leaves his home and father, Pip, the <u>prodigal,</u> **squanders** his inheritance on a life of dissipation. |

| Thesis | In *A Tale of Two Cities,* the battle between the human and the inhuman is resolved, with Stryver fleeing as a hypocrite and the unlikely Carton rising as a phoenix to save humanity. |
|---|---|
| TS1 | The reader first meets <u>Stryver,</u> the **self-important opportunist,** contrasted to <u>Carton,</u> **a self-deprecating servant,** at the trial of Charles Darnay in the Old Bailey. |
| TS2 | Next, in <u>Stryver's</u> office, the reader glimpses the nightly business interactions between **an underestimated jackal** and **a roaring lion.** |

## CHECK THE DICTION OF THE TOPIC SENTENCES

### • Word glue

Does the writer use word glue to connect the topic sentences with the thesis statement? The writer may use synonyms or exact words from the thesis statement. The writer or reader should be able to draw circles around common words in the thesis and topic sentences. If the writer can't, the reader might not understand how the writer plans to prove the argument. *As in the previous examples that demonstrate organization choices, pp. 114–115, the <u>underlined words</u> here are the glue tying the topic sentence to the thesis.*

| Thesis | In *Great Expectations* the use of the hands motif indicates Pip's location in the **journey toward maturity.** |
|---|---|

### • Original First topic sentence

Pip lives in a household of violence and poor relationships. *(This is merely a plot detail.)*

### Revised

Pip first encounters the <u>impressionable stage of childhood,</u> wherein Pip is not yet able to evaluate situations critically; consequently, Pip surmises an association between <u>hands</u> and acrimonious relationships.

### • Original Second topic sentence

Pip begins to hate his life at the forge after he visits Miss Havisham and Estella. *(This is merely a fact from the chapter.)*

### Revised

Shortly after early childhood, Pip begins to grow into the more contemplative stage of preadolescence, a stage in which he begins to question his surroundings as well as draw conclusions about them.

Thesis   Coleridge's "Rime of the Ancient Mariner" illustrates man's proclivity since the Fall to **sin without cause,** to possess the **opportunity of reconciliation,** and to have the option to **do penance,** all in hopes of receiving forgiveness.

### • Original First topic sentence

The Mariner's misfortunes begin by abruptly and without cause killing the albatross. *(A plot detail.)*

#### Revised

Since the Fall, man often discovers himself <u>sinning without cause</u> and sometimes without explanation.

### • Original Third topic sentence

The narrator learns that the Mariner must now tell his tale. *(A plot detail.)*

#### Revised

With <u>reconciliation</u> comes <u>penance,</u> another stage on a path to forgiveness.

## MORE EXAMPLE THESIS STATEMENTS + TOPIC SENTENCES

Topic   Scout in *To Kill a Mockingbird*

Thesis   *To Kill a Mockingbird* by Harper Lee focuses the attention of the perspicacious reader on Scout's growth as she transforms from a carefree child into a true lady, one who is a lady at heart, not just a lady in appearance.

TS1   As Scout's father, Atticus plays an important role in teaching her important <u>values that a true lady</u> must possess.

TS2   In addition to Atticus' lessons, Miss Maudie Atkinson, Scout's benign neighbor, helps her <u>grow up to be a true lady.</u>

TS3   Contradictory values of character and <u>appearance</u> confront Scout as she becomes <u>a lady of character.</u>

Topic   Nature imagery in *Romeo & Juliet*

Thesis   In *Romeo and Juliet,* William Shakespeare's skillful use of imagery borrowed from the world of nature paints a vivid portrait of the emotional and physical make-up of man.

TS1   Various <u>light images taken from nature</u> reveal Juliet's brilliant <u>beauty</u> and suggest her <u>growing fears.</u>

TS2   Shakespeare's ingenious utilization of <u>bird imagery</u> creates a lucid picture of man's <u>physical qualities.</u>

TS3   Shakespeare also uses <u>bird imagery</u> to create man's <u>emotional characteristics.</u>

TS4   The use of other <u>animal imagery</u> produces a clear model of the <u>complex emotional nature</u> of man.

Topic    Dictatorial power in Homer's *Odyssey*

Thesis   The grip of power of Antinoos and Eurymachos is analogous to the authority of twentieth century dictators.

TS1     The leaders of the suitors and twentieth century dictators are demagogues who appeal to people's fears and emotions to get them to carry out their commands.

TS2     Both the leaders of the suitors and contemporary dictators rule by force rather than by law or respect for their position.

TS3     Despite the facade of power that Antinoos and twentieth century dictators possess, their positions as leaders are not very stable.

TS4     Both groups also blame the problems of their leadership on others.

Topic    New Testament revisited in *A Tale of Two Cities*

Thesis   Through images synonymous with Christ and imagery depicting the events before the Crucifixion, Dickens identifies the death of Sydney Carton with the death of Christ.

TS1     Before Dickens enters Carton into his Passion story, he first gives the reader *images of Carton's similarities to Christ.*

TS2     Having formed a connection between Carton and Christ, Dickens now begins his version of the Passion story.

TS3     Dickens imitates several aspects of the Last Supper of Jesus.

TS4     Dickens also alludes to Pontius Pilate and the trial of Jesus that determines his sentence.

## A FINAL WORD ABOUT ORGANIZATION/CONTENT

### • How many paragraphs?

A writer must decide how many paragraphs are necessary to prove or illustrate his or her argument. Each aspect of a student's thesis statement may be equivalent to one or more paragraphs. For example, in longer papers over 1,500 words, a writer will likely use a combination of *one-idea* paragraphs, *subordinate paragraphs,* and *glue paragraphs* (see p. 49). In shorter papers, however, those under 1,500 words, a student may be able to use single-idea paragraphs, explaining each aspect of his thesis statement with one paragraph per aspect.

## THE SHOWING-TELLING INTRODUCTION

An introduction should both grab the reader's attention (through elaborative "**show**ing") and clearly state (**tell**) the thesis. There are several methods of grabbing the reader's attention:

1. Quote another literary text that helps introduce the subject;
2. Paraphrase another literary text;
3. Quote the literary text that serves as the foundation for the writer's paper;
4. Paraphrase a scene from the literary text the writer will discuss;
5. Create a very brief, but showing, story that is relevant to the overall thesis of your essay.

### Transition between showing introduction and thesis statement

After the showing part of the introduction, the writer *must write one or two transitional* sentences that smoothly connect that aspect of the introduction to the thesis, or telling, statement.

## SAMPLE SHOWING-TELLING INTRODUCTIONS

- The **bold-faced sentence** makes the *transition* from the showing introduction to the thesis statement
- The underlined sentence is the *thesis,* or telling, statement.

### Method 1–2
*by Aaron Vilfordi*

Gazing upon a shimmering blue sea with the cool wind blowing over a pearly white vessel, Mary Shelley's Frankenstein tells his apprentice, Robert Walton, to "Learn from my miseries, and do not seek to increase your own" (156). The dying Frankenstein admonishes Walton to refrain from the mistake Frankenstein has made, the mistake of usurping the heavenly task of creating life. With Victor's admonishment, he receives some absolution and regains his humanity by compassionately influencing another to think of the consequences before acting on such dreams, although his arrival at this stage is too late. **Charles Dickens' Pip, although a comic hero, emulates Frankenstein in the way he, too, makes bad choices, finally rediscovering his true humanity through his concern and love for his old friend, Joe.** Pip starts out as an innocent boy but is soon corrupted by the dream of becoming a gentleman. Pip struggles with this dream, his life changing for the worse. Finally, Pip realizes what he has done and what he has lost. Unlike Frankenstein, Pip is able to learn from his mistakes and change before his life becomes a tragedy. He receives absolution by restoring his love for Joe. <u>Pip, the main character in Charles Dickens' *Great Expectations,* escapes Victor Frankenstein's tragic life because he completes a journey through four stages that allow him more completely to rediscover his true humanity: innocence, corruption, arrogance, and reconciliation.</u>

**Method 5**                                                           *by Michael Stysly*

Mark wipes the blood from his nose on his torn white shirt, grabs his L.L. Bean backpack, and jogs toward home. Behind him he can hear his classmates' derision—"Run, run, look at him run home to Mama"—but he doesn't look back; rather, he begins to imagine his destination, his tree house, built over a year ago with the help of his father. Rounding the corner, most of his tears now dried, he can see the large red oak in his back yard, the rope ladder dangling from the small opening above the ground about 15 feet. From the street he can't see the entire house because dense foliage covers its sides, protected both from the storms and hateful stares of his peers. He reaches the rope, pauses to gaze down Ridge Avenue and across the Smith's front yard, and reaches for the wooden planks, rising, swaying back and forth in the air, but moving deliberately upward out of reach, closer to safety. His small hands push the square covering and slide it open, pulling himself up on to the floor. He reaches down and pulls up the rope ladder, his breathing still staggered, as if there were a limited amount of oxygen. The rope piled beside him, he closes the door opening and feels safe. **Now he has time; now he can temporarily escape the cruelty of his world. Like Mark's tree house,** <u>the river for Huckleberry, in Mark Twain's *Adventures of Huckleberry Finn,* serves as a symbol of refuge, a world that provides an escape from the cruelties of everyday life, a place where hope and love prosper.</u>

**Method 4**                                                           *by Daniel Lawson*

A man in black slithers through the shadows along the wall. He caresses the velvet bag filled with gold coins, just to assure himself of its continued existence. The poor soul he swindled it from this time is a widow with little money. After he had his way with her in bed, he sold her "passage into the Kingdom of Heaven," as he likes to put it. It didn't matter what he called it, as long as he got his money and a little fun on the side, too. He finally reaches the monastery, sneaks through his bedroom window, and falls asleep. **This is not a holy priest. He is a lying criminal who backstabs the helpless for money and, sometimes, sex.** He is <u>the kind of clergyman Chaucer often depicts in *The Canterbury Tales,* one who desires wealth, breaks vows, and exploits the common man.</u>

**Method 1**                                                           *by Ben Bireley*

As they were going out, they met a man from Cyrene named Simon, and they forced him to carry the cross to a place called Golgotha. There they offered Jesus wine to drink, mixed with gall, but after tasting it, he refused to drink it. When they had crucified him, they divided up his clothes by casting lots. And sitting down, they kept watch over him there. Above his head, they placed the written charge against him: This is Jesus, King of the Jews. Two robbers were crucified on his left. Those who passed by hurled insults at him, shaking their heads and saying, "You who are going to destroy the temple and build it in three days, save yourself! Come down from the cross if you are the Son of God!" (Matthew 27:32–40)

This excerpt from the Bible is part of the Passion story of Christ, one of the most popular stories in Western Civilization. The popularity of the story makes the symbols associated with it easily discernible to any perspicacious reader; therefore, **writers often use imagery and symbolism relating to Jesus' story to convey their thematic ideas. *A Tale of Two Cities,* by Charles Dickens, is one such example.** Through images synonymous with Christ and imagery depicting the events before the Crucifixion, Dickens identifies the death of Sydney Carton with the death of Jesus.

### Method 5                                                    *by Joseph McGill*

"Be healed, my brother! Rise up and walk by the healing power of the Holy Spirit!" the minister screams passionately into the microphone. He lays his hands on the young cripple's shoulders, and the boy, on cue, throws down his crutches and embraces the minister. No one in the entire congregation suspects it is a hoax; they sit dumbfounded, amazed by the evangelist's miraculous "healing powers." The minister plays for the rolling cameras, hugging the boy even tighter and squeezing tears out of the corners of his eyes. He can almost hear the telephones ringing non-stop in the back of the "church" with people willing to donate thousands of dollars to "aid his parish." Finally, after the crowd's "Amens!" and "Praise the Lords!" subside, the minister rises again to the microphone and begins his collection speech. "Be generous and give all you can to the good Lord! He looks favorably on those who contribute to his Kingdom and those who spread his message!" He barely contains a greedy grin as the baskets make their way around the church, stuffed with checks and bills. **This sly minister's exploitation of his parishioners resembles the corruption that Chaucer highlights in *The Canterbury Tales.*** Chaucer reveals three main areas of corruption in the Medieval church: a focus on worldly pleasures, a violation of basic Christian theology, and an exploitation of parishioners. These criticisms alert the reader to the human qualities of the clergy; like their parishioners, they, too, are people who sin and make mistakes.

### Method 2                                                    *by Russell Lemmer*

Colonel Sherburn cocks his neck to the left again, proceeds until he feels the second pop, and then returns his eyes to the vast ocean of angry faces that amalgamate to form the bloodthirsty mob. He gingerly spits upon the rooftop, and his eyes once again return to the ocean. "Lynch him! Hang him good!" yells a face, although it cannot be determined exactly which countenance made the entreaty. The ferment is allayed by the silence that succeeds the cry, and the faces begin to turn, left, right, left, right, as if each one were looking for back-up. A clap of thunder, a lightening bolt, the rain pelts harder than before as if aiming to injure. The Colonel still surveying, his lips begin to move and a speech follows. The speech that he delivers is short, yet memorable. It is about how a man will follow a crowd blindly, without purpose and without reason. Though briefly mentioned, the character of Colonel Sherburn plays a significant role in the novel *Huckleberry Finn.* Twain uses this character to get his point across about slavery: People do not even know why they continue it anymore, but they do it because the next man does. **In many novels, minor characters such as the Colonel play a tremendous role in the story. Such is the case with the character of Mr. Pumblechook in Charles Dickens' novel *Great Expectations*.** <u>Pumblechook serves as the stereotypical, middle-class Englishman whose shallow treatment towards others, with respect to their social class, reflects the way society as a whole treats them.</u>

*Method 3* *by Jeff Erfe*

It was the best of times, it was the worst of times, it was the age of wisdom, it was the age of foolishness, it was the epoch of belief, it was the epoch of incredulity, it was the season of Light, it was the season of Darkness, it was the spring of hope, it was the winter of despair, we had everything before us, we had nothing before us, we were all going direct to Heaven, we were all going direct the other way—in short, the period was so far like the present period that some of its noisiest authorities insisted on its being received, for good or for evil, in the superlative degree of comparison only. (1; bk. 1, ch. 1)

As early as the opening sentences of *A Tale of Two Cities*, Charles Dickens sets up a recurring theme the reader will encounter throughout the novel: **the restive, combative duality between various opposing forces in the plot. The relationship between Mr. Stryver and Sydney Carton is one such example.** Stryver, although a minor character, plays a significant role as Carton's foil: he epitomizes greedy, inhuman, business-like formality against Carton's selfless and emotional tenderness. <u>In the end, as with all other dualities in the novel, the battle between the human and the inhuman is resolved, with Stryver fleeing as a hypocrite and the unlikely Carton rising as a phoenix from the ashes of desperation to save humanity.</u>

## ASK THESE QUESTIONS ABOUT THE INTRODUCTION

- From the first few words, has the writer *grabbed the reader's attention?*
- Are the *verbs* active and in the present tense?
- Has the writer re-created *a brief but significant scene* that demonstrates a point in his or her essay—a scene or situation from a literary text (the one being discussed or an analogous tale from a different text) or from contemporary life that effectively leads into the thesis?
- Has the writer written a *transition sentence or sentences* that connect the attention-grabber to the thesis statement?
- Is the writer's *thesis statement* clearly stating *a topic + a debatable opinion?*
- Has the writer used a variety of *sentence structures* in the introduction?

## THE NON-SUMMARY CONCLUSION

1. The writer <u>does not summarize</u> the essay or merely restate the thesis; a well-written essay needs no summary in its concluding paragraph because the clarity of its organization throughout would make a summary conclusion merely redundant.
2. Instead, the writer connects the thesis to a larger issue—to the community, to the writer himself or herself, to other works of literature.
3. Blend thesis, or primary idea, into this larger issue.
4. Where appropriate, the writer might consider finishing the conclusion by "bookending" the attention-grabber from the introduction, or the writer might even subtly allude to a major detail from the body.

## SAMPLE CONCLUDING PARAGRAPHS

### Subject: Scout in To Kill a Mockingbird                    by John Tapee

Scout eventually transforms into a true lady of character. This examination of Scout's growth as she matures into a lady reminds the reader of Pip in *Great Expectations*. In that novel, Magwitch believes that money and looks will make Pip a gentleman, but Joe, the true gentleman, teaches Pip to be such a man by teaching him qualities that will help him mature. Through his education and maturity, Pip, like Scout, eventually becomes a true gentleman, comforting Magwitch his deathbed and, truly penitent, returning to expiate his abandonment of Joe. In today's society as well, the term "lady" can be misunderstood to mean a lady in appearance. While Mother Teresa, one of the most beneficent people of our time, is the true lady, she would not be considered one by someone who believes that the title of "lady" is merited based on appearance. Through this scrutinization of Scout's growth, the reader can clearly see that she matures into a real lady—not a lady like many of the "ladies" of Maycomb, but one who cares about who she is, not what she looks like.

### Subject: Leadership                    by Dustin Reyes

Leadership is a quality that has the potential to overleap any obstacle placed in the path of man's upwardly marching accomplishments. Throughout history, times of trial for mankind have been survived due to the efforts of leaders. However, just as true leadership can be utilized for positive ends, leadership can be perverted to serve the needs of those who, through guile and deceit, purport to honor it. An example that springs to mind is the rise to power of Adolf Hitler in post-war Germany. However, just as the leadership of Churchill eventually vanquished Hitler's malice, there is always the hope that positive leadership provides salvation and justice.

### Subject: Odysseus                    by Andre Valdivia

After taking note of all of Odysseus's shortcomings, people can look to him as an even greater hero than before because we can better relate to him. Usually, people tend to make a hero seem like the epitome of everything desirable and appealing in a person, and in doing so, we make that hero seem superhuman. Then, when we try living up to these superior standards we have created, we hold ourselves in disdain when we fall short because we are not perfect, or we become severely disappointed when we discover our hero is not as great as once thought, which was the case with John F. Kennedy. Odysseus is not perfect; however, despite all the instances where he lacks virtue, he is still extremely revered by Greek society and is considered a hero because he is abundantly more beneficent than malevolent. Odysseus, therefore, can serve as the true paragon of a hero, one to whom mankind can relate. Unlike some superhuman creation, Odysseus is human because he falls into temptation and he makes mistakes, just like everyone else. So rather than comparing oneself to an image of perfection we conjure up only to find ourselves constantly wanting, we can look to Odysseus and see a true human hero.

**Subject: Great Expectations** *and the prodigal son*      *by Patricio Delgado*

Because a parallel between *Great Expectations* and the parable of the prodigal son exists, two pieces separated by more than 1,800 years, we may deduce that their basic theme of sinning, repenting, and forgiving is timeless. In other words, every human of every age in some way or another asks for his inheritance, or sins by pursuing his own selfish desires, becomes unhappy and unfulfilled in this pursuit, and re-evaluates his situation, returning to God or remaining in a state of misery. Because this theme includes the option to repent, we discover a permeating feeling of hope surrounding humanity. No matter in what era or place, we shall not be denied forgiveness and salvation if we repent for our sins, if we do as the prodigal son and Pip did and give up our selfish and self-centered pursuits in favor of God and His love. For this reason, *Great Expectations* as a whole is a novel about hope for humanity rather than despair.

**Subject: Tragic theory and** *Frankenstein*      *by Joe McGill*

By examining *Frankenstein* as a tragic story, the true richness of the story is revealed, and all characters have a place in the plot. Robert Walton, who appears in the "frame story," does not seem to have much importance in the novel unless looked at from the tragic perspective. From the tragic perspective, however, Walton's place in the novel is not only obvious but crucial. At the end of the story, Walton's decision to return home serves as the pointing towards reconciliation. After listening to Victor's advice, Walton and his crew head home, which symbolizes that the violation of nature has ceased. Also, by examining the story as a tragedy, the reader can understand why Shelley spends so much time describing Victor's family. She gives many detailed descriptions of the family so the reader will know the characters and realize the abject suffering that Victor endures because of their deaths. Shelley's masterpiece of writing can only be fully appreciated if the reader views the story as part of the tragic realm.

**Subject: The Canterbury Tales**      *by Mauricio Delgado*

In criticizing the Church, Chaucer beckons us to be more like the parson who transcends his own poverty, preferring to give "to poor parishioners both from Church offerings and his property." What Chaucer describes and denounces in the timeless and universal *The Canterbury Tales* not only occurs in the Church but in our own community, our own classroom. We should avoid falling into the greed, hypocrisy, and abuses that plague these members of the clergy, and follow the true teachings of Jesus Christ. Even in the sacred Jesuit community, I see students who degrade others because of their financial situation; I see students who learn about justice in theology class one period, yet ridicule a student the next period. Most importantly, though, I see myself in many of these situations, going against my inherited beliefs and hurting another person. What is clear, though, is that we are human beings who sin and make mistakes. Members of the clergy, though seemingly holy, are also people who can fall into evil.

### Subject: The Odyssey
*by Michael O'Hanlon*

The voluminous number of similarities between the leadership of the suitors and twentieth century dictators reveals a pattern of rule that tyrants follow. Intimidation and threats have always been used by despots to control dissension and to subjugate the population at large. Many leaders who rely on these methods consistently blame others, especially dissenters, for problems that they themselves have caused or are unable to solve; in addition, they coerce people to go along with and carry out this persecution. These types of regimes, whether on a small or large scale, usually end with the violent death of the rancorous rulers at the hands of heroic forces fighting for justice, thus offering hope to those suffering from unjust leaders. For these reasons, the Odyssey serves as a paradigm of rule by malevolent rulers, a paradigm that traverses time.

## ASK THESE QUESTIONS ABOUT THE CONCLUSION

- What's significant about this thesis—is it worth discussing?
- Does the conclusion avoid merely summarizing the main points of the paper?
- Does the writer attempt to discuss what is significant about the paper's thesis?
- Does the writer attempt to relate the thesis to our contemporary culture in an elaborately extensive fashion?
- Does the writer attempt to relate the thesis to other works of literature?
- Does the writer attempt to "bookend" with the situation in the attention-grabber of the introduction?
- Should the writer extend the elaboration of an idea by providing a more concrete example?
- Are there any wordy structures? Are there any vague or confusing statements that could be more precise?
- Do some sentences need combining? Are a variety of sentence structures used?

Steve Kovatis                                                                Kovatis 1
Dr. Degen
English 3
23 April 1997

### Simon and the Tao

A bird sings its sweet song from the trees. The warm sun penetrates the foliage and illuminates intermittently the soft, tender earth below. Walking through this forest, the simplicity of the truth of the earth begins to appear; the Tao begins to reveal itself. "When the Tao is taught, / people know where to go and what to learn / Because they know that they will not be harmed / But will receive great peace" (Lao 44). This promise of achieving peace and harmony by discovering the Tao, the mysterious, omnipresent, and multifariously defined "way" of the truth, has echoed throughout Chinese civilization through the teachings of Lao Tzu. In *Lord of the Flies,* Simon presents us with a modern day example of the proper search, according to Taoist tradition.

Taoism first stresses the union with nature, becoming one with the Tao, or path, which our surroundings reveal to us. Nature provides us with a wholeness, for "One who does not separate his being from the nature of universal wholeness lives with the universal virtue of wholeness" (Lao 8). Literally, and figuratively through the novel, "Simon turned away...and went where the just perceptible path led him" (56; ch. 3), demonstrating Simon's union with nature in three ways. First, the image of Simon turning away from the group shows a sense of individuality, a rejection of following the ideas of the community. Second, the passage glorifies nature, indicating that it indeed is a "just" and correct path to follow; additionally, it implies a "perceptible" path, discernable to Simon. Third, though diffident, Simon follows that path he sees in nature, and he surrenders himself to the direction that nature indicates, **a point central to the Taoist message of following nature.** Similarly, in another instance, Simon "knelt down and the arrow of the sun fell on him" (57; ch. 3), giving the image of the sun, **representative of greater nature,** pointing him in the direction of harmony. In response to this call of the wild, Simon "cocked a critical ear at the sounds of the island," willing and able to listen to the directions he has been given. Simon even reunites with nature in death. According to Taoism, "In the natural flow of energy transformation / Mankind conforms itself to Earth" (Lao 31). When Simon dies, "Somewhere over the darkened curve of the world, the sun and moon were pulling" (154; ch. 9) at Simon's body, encouraging him to join the sea. Then, "softly, surrounded by a fringe of inquisitive bright creatures, itself a silver shape beneath the steadfast constellations, Simon's dead body moved out toward the open sea," joining that which had guided him since his arrival on the island.

> Steve extends his elaboration of the quotation from Lao by weaving its ideas into Simon's situation at various points in the tale.

> Both the analysis modifier and, in the sentence thereafter, the appositive phrase, serve to maintain the reader's focus on this paragraph's topic, Simon's union with nature.

Simon also demonstrates the mystical, the "Esoteric," aspect of Taoism. Here, Taoism essentially argues that by "cultivating 'stillness' a few key individuals in each community could become perfect receptacles for Tao" (Smith 201), which then in turn would "cultivate perfect cleanliness of thought and body" (Smith 201). As previously indicated, Simon "turns away" from the group to cultivate his **stillness,** to become receptive to the Tao. In solitude, Simon consistently retreats to his small clearing in the forest. As he sits there, "**nothing moved** but a pair of gaudy butterflies that danced round each other in the hot air" (57; ch. 3), indicating Simon's willingness **to be still** and let nature move while he observed, always learning. According to Taoism, **a still person** would also **"radiate a kind of healing"** for the larger group. For example, Piggy waits for his serving of meat from Jack's first hunt, but Jack "meant to leave him in doubt" (73; ch. 4) and withholds Piggy's portion, as Piggy drools with hunger. Here Simon "shoved a piece of meat over the rocks" (74; ch. 4) to a starving and drooling Piggy, **a clear act,** at least on a small scale, **of healing** or alleviating a small form of suffering.

In this second body paragraph, Steve develops the topic of Simon as mystic by keeping the reader focused on the idea of stillness as a generator of healing in the story.

Lastly, grasping a part of the Tao brings with it a knowledge greater than that of the community, greater than traditional knowledge. "To return to the true self / End[s] the endless search / for segmented, intellectual knowledge" (Lao 23). As the tension mounts during an early assembly concerning what to do about the beast, Simon proposes that "maybe there is a beast…maybe it's only us" (89; ch. 5), taking a clear leap beyond the group as well as beyond the realm of logic. Simon does not see a beast in the traditional sense that the others see it, namely a large, gross monster, but as a disease in the human character. He is the only one in the group to discover the reification of the beast that has poisoned, and will continue to poison, the unity and purity of the tribe. How ironic, then, that this reification by the tribe eventually causes his own demise, as the tribe mistakes him for the imaginary beast and kills him. In this same demonstration of an almost omniscient knowledge, Simon later affirms to Ralph that he "will get back all right" (111; ch. 7) to England, a statement originated from no logical source. Simon then does not elaborate on his statement, for when challenged as to how he knows this, Simon only reiterates his original thesis, which later turns out to be true, **a knowledge from an inexplicable origin, a knowledge above the comprehension of the rest of the tribe.**

Note the style of the final sentence of this paragraph—it ends in parallel analysis modifiers.

Simon's example depicts the acme of proper Taoist existence. Such an example becomes especially helpful because one of Lao Tzu's teachings is that the "Tao, the path of subtle truth / cannot be conveyed with words / the subtle truth is indescribable" (Lao 1). In absence of words, we must turn to human examples to lead us to the proper search for the Tao; specifically, we must at least evaluate Simon's example. Taoism must be understood and lived by the whole person, beyond the realm where words fall short, and Simon provides us with that silent leadership. Only by truly understanding, beyond the realm of language, can we reap the benefits, and only then can we be in harmony with heaven; in this way, we must follow Simon's footsteps.

**Works Cited**

Golding, William. *Lord of the Flies.* New York: Putnam, 1954.

Lao Tzu. *Tao The Ching.* Rpt. in *The Complete Works of Lao Tzu.* Trans. Ni Hua Chung. Los Angeles: Shrine of the Eternal Breath of Tao, 1989.

Smith, Huston. *The Religions of Man.* New York: Harper & Row, 1958.

*Note. Generally, a student should place the "Works Cited" entries on a separate page. For some teachers, adding the entries after the concluding paragraph is acceptable. Always consult your teacher if you are unsure.*

Brian Campbell

Dr. Degen

AP English

22 May 2002

### Macbeth, Banquo, and the Initial Revelation of Character

'Bah! Humbug!' Scrooge responds to his nephew, who is "all in a glow" about the Christmas season. In this famous opening scene of *A Christmas Carol,* Charles Dickens uses dialogue between Scrooge and his nephew to reveal their opposed personalities. In fact, these two contrasting personalities provide the conflict for the entire novel—generosity battles greed. Perhaps Dickens borrowed this technique from William Shakespeare, who uses short scenes in the openings of his plays to establish the conflict eventually to be resolved. In Shakespeare's *Macbeth,* the dialogue early in the play among Macbeth, Banquo, and the three witches reveals important aspects of the two thanes' characters. Macbeth, the commanding war hero, follows ambition over reason, a choice that actually leads him toward demise rather than power; Banquo, however, depends more on reason and is portrayed as a noble, but cautious, skeptic.

First, Macbeth asserts his power over others. After he hears the witches' "prophetic greeting" (1.3.78), for example, Macbeth, **dissatisfied with their incomplete predictions,** demands of the three, "Stay, you imperfect speakers, tell me more" (1.3.70) and "Speak, I charge you" (1.3.78), **commands that degrade the sisters by implying their servitude toward Macbeth.** Macbeth's use of "imperfect" (1.3.70), for instance, takes on a double meaning, **implying both "incomplete" and "defective,"** which insults the witches as being flawed, possibly in contrast to Macbeth's opinion of his perfect self.

> Among the sentence structures Brian uses in the first body paragraph are both a present and a past participial phrase, as well as an analysis modifier.

Macbeth's military might, ironically, is powerless to withstand the witches' guile. Earlier in the play, Macbeth "like valor's minion / carved out his passage" and "unseamed [the merciless Macdonwald] from the nave to the chops" (1.2.16–22). Now this strength becomes futile because Macbeth allows the sisters to control him through his desires, particularly his ambition to become king, a desire that has manifested itself in the thane's "horrible imaginings" (1.3.139) of the king's murder, a murder that would allow Macbeth to seize the throne. As the witches tamper with his ambition to become king, Macbeth's "bold commands" seem to wither and, instead,

> Brian focuses on the ease with which Macbeth changes once he learns of the witches' prophecies concerning him. The dominating military figure shrinks to a beggar.

more closely resemble entreaties to the witches: "Stay. . . tell me more" (1.3.70). The image of Macbeth, chasing after the witches, suggests his supplication to them and actually becomes humorous as the noble warrior, who "fixed Macdonwald's head upon [the] battlements" and fought near Forres like a "[cannon] overcharged with double cracks" (1.2.23,37), now follows after the three weird sisters, practically begging them for information.

Banquo, unlike Macbeth, depends upon reason, which he displays through his repeated skepticism. As he addresses the witches, Banquo first wonders: "Live you? Or are you aught / that man may question? (1.3.42–43) . . . Are ye fantastical, or that indeed / which outwardly ye show?" (1.3.53–54). Refusing to immediately believe the witches' prophecies as credible, Banquo maintains an objective distance to prevent being misled by a false prophecy, this distance securing himself from harm; in fact, he makes certain not to submit himself to the witches, but instead emphasizes his own power: "Speak then to me, who neither beg nor fear / your favors nor your hate" (1.3.60–61). Banquo understands that if he does not take the initiative to dominate the witches, then they may successfully manipulate his ambition for their own gain. In addition, in questioning the existence of the witches—"Were such things here as we do speak about, / or have we eaten on the insane root / that takes the reason prisoner?" (1.3.83–85)—he describes reason as a tool that allows one to perceive reality, his questions demonstrating the reasoning process, considering all logical possibilities to explain the mysterious disappearance of the three weird sisters.

> Here the writer immediately contrasts what the opening scene has revealed of Macbeth's pliable character with Banquo's determination not to be so easily manipulated by that which conflicts with his reason.

Furthermore, Banquo still remains cautious even after Macbeth becomes the thane of Cawdor. **The prophecy having been fulfilled,** Banquo does not heighten his trust in the witches and believe them now to be honest in their predictions; instead, he warns Macbeth, "Oftentimes, to win us to our harm, / the instruments of darkness tell us truths, / win us with honest trifles, to betray's / in deepest consequence" (1.3.123–126). With the mention of "honest trifles," Banquo acknowledges that, although the witches' predictions have come true, the sisters may be using that anticipated newfound trust to plot evil deeds. Banquo's adamant skepticism illustrates his refusal to yield reason even after the witches are proven to be credible. This skepticism, though it seems unnecessary and rather cold, aids Banquo in preventing outside forces—the witches, for example—from dominating him; otherwise, without his disbelief, Banquo, no matter how powerful he may be, would fall under the control of others, just as Macbeth does.

> In this sentence beginning with an absolute phrase concerning the truth of one of the prophecies, Brian emphasizes Banquo's skepticism about these "honest trifles"and, in the sentences that follow, explicates his judicious advice to Macbeth.

Shakespeare and, later, Dickens demonstrate to the reader the importance of beginning scenes, how they serve to establish some of the major themes of the play or novel. One recognizes, too, that paying attention to what characters say and how they say it will implicitly reveal a character's strengths and weaknesses. Even in our lives today, we may practice observing seemingly insignificant scenes more carefully, listening to language people use in dialogue with one another, uncovering unarticulated conflict or character strengths and weaknesses. Perhaps, as in the case of Scrooge, recognizing conflict can lead to self improvement.

### Works Cited

Dickens, Charles. *A Christmas Carol.* New York: Penguin, 1984.
Shakespeare, William. *Macbeth.* New York: Bantam, 1988.

## CONSTRUCTING THE PAPER ASSIGNMENTS AND ACTIVITIES

### Assignment #1: Writing Thesis Statements (TH)

Directions: Revise the following thesis statements, ensuring that each has a clear topic + opinion. Review p. 112.

1. Scrooge views two important feasts—the feast of the Cratchit family and the feast of his nephew.
2. The ghost of Christmas past forces Scrooge to observe painful scenes of his childhood.
3. Three ghosts influence Scrooge—the ghost of Christmas past, the ghost of Christmas present, and the ghost of Christmas future.

### Assignment #2: Writing Progress Chart

Note: This assignment is given to students after they have received written feedback from the teacher on several compositions, compositions the teacher has previously marked using the editing symbols listed on the **Editing Symbols** chart, pp. 196–197. Students gather their compositions and essay tests and concentrate on the symbols marked on those papers.

Directions: Students examine all their compositions and tests they have written up to this point in the year. Select an example of each type of writing problem that the teacher has marked on each composition and essay test. Write down the original version of the sentence or sentences, including the error marked. Below it, write your revised, corrected version.

#### Requirements

1. List at least one example of each editing symbol (e.g. **W, O, TS, P, C, G**) that has been used by the teacher. Not every student will have an example of every editing symbol. See pp. 196–197 for the complete list.
2. Please type.
3. If the student is listing an example of editing symbol **G**, identify the specific grammatical problem. For example, did the writer incorrectly label an absolute phrase?
4. Highlight the revised material.

### Partial Example of a Writing Progress Chart

Since this is only a partial example of such an assignment, it contains only three categories. Student writers, however, will need to show an example of *each symbol* found in their papers. Use the format found in chapter two to list original sentence and revised sentence.

### Problem/Editing Key    Example & Revision

W .................................... Original: Throughout our lives, we are exposed to a lot of different teachings and one of them, in our society, is the value placed upon a life in which we are successful.
Revised: Our society teaches the value of success.

C .................................... Original: There is physical decay in Victor Frankenstein. The cleric is like Victor. Both seek to "explore unknown powers, and unfold to the world the deepest mysteries of creation."
Revised: This physical decay occurs in Victor Frankenstein, who, like the cleric, seeks to "explore unknown powers, and unfold to the world the deepest mysteries of creation."

G .................................... Original: **After I opened the door,** I walked into the room. (not a noun clause)
Revised: After I opened the door, I walked into the room, and I realized **that my feet had collided into a box of bowling trophies.** (noun clause)

# 4

## GRAMMAR FOR STRUCTURE AND SYNTAX

### PHILOSOPHY OF GRAMMAR INSTRUCTION

- Specific aspects of grammar should and can be taught in conjunction with—rather than in isolation from—the writing process in order to facilitate the development of a gradually maturing writing style.
- The core belief here is that most students should, by the time they are in eighth or ninth grade—and on through the end of high school—be able to focus on the building blocks of sentence structure: clauses and phrases. As students understand more about the functions of clauses and phrases and how to use them as communication tools of written language, the better, more interesting writers they will become.
- Throughout the school year, students are gradually introduced to (and revisit) specific structures. They are given opportunities for practice in recognizing and understanding the usage of each structure, in correct punctuation involving the structure, and in sentence combining activities. Finally, they are expected to use each structure in their compositions once they have been taught it. By knowingly using each structure, the gradual ability to manipulate each one increases. As more structures are taught and practiced during the year, students are expected to include all of them in their writings.

### What is the difference between a phrase and a clause?

A phrase is a group of words.

A clause is a group of words with a subject and a verb.

A phrase itself will *not* have a subject and a verb; within a phrase, as we shall see, there may be a subordinate clause, which, of course, contains a subject and a verb, but that clause will be functioning as a noun, adjective, or adverb in that phrase.

## CLAUSES

# Two Categories of Clauses

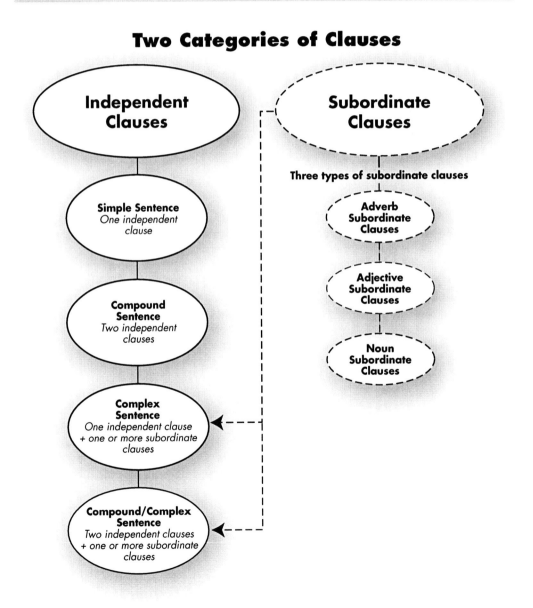

### What is the difference between independent and subordinate clauses?

Both categories of clauses contain, by definition, subject-verb combinations; independent clauses, however, can stand on their own as sentences, while subordinate clauses are always subordinate to (or dependent upon) an independent clause in order to exist in a sentence. Subordinate clauses begin with words that join them to independent clauses; these words are subordinating conjunctions and relative pronouns.

## SUBORDINATE CLAUSES

### What words begin subordinate clauses?

**Subordinating conjunctions** usually begin the adverb subordinate clause.

| | | | |
|---|---|---|---|
| after | as though | once | unless |
| although | because | provided that | until |
| as | before | since | when* |
| as if | even though | so that | whenever |
| as long as | if | than | where* |
| as soon as | in order that | though | while |

\* *when* and *where* may also begin adjective or noun subordinate clauses

**Relative pronouns** often begin adjective and noun subordinate clauses.

| | | | |
|---|---|---|---|
| that | who | whichever | whose |
| how | whom | whoever | whether |
| what | which | whomever | why |

## ADVERB SUBORDINATE CLAUSES (ADVSC)  (Exercises, pp. 162, 164–165)

- **Function:** Modify verbs, adjectives, or adverbs.
- **Provide this information:** The **ADVSC** tells *how? when? where? why? to what extent?* or *under what condition?* about the word being modified.
- **Begin** with subordinating conjunctions (see the list above).
- **Location in a sentence:** Anywhere, usually before or after the independent clause.
- **Punctuation rules:**
  1. If the **ADVSC** begins the sentence (or, in other words, is located before the independent clause), always place a comma after it.
  2. If the **ADVSC** is located after the independent clause, a comma is usually not needed.

  *Because I did not study for the test sufficiently,* I barely passed.

  *Whenever Miranda looks at me,* I just want to hide my face *until she goes away.*

  My sister will need to do the dishes *as soon as she can so that she will be ready when her friends arrive.*

  *Although we have already purchased our tickets to the concert,* I want us to arrive there *before the doors to the arena open since all seats are general admission.*

## ADJECTIVE SUBORDINATE CLAUSES (ADJSC)   (Exercises, pp. 163–166)

- **Function:** Modify nouns or pronouns.
- **Provide this information:** The **ADJSC** tells *what kind?* or *which one?* about the word being modified.
- **Begin** with relative pronouns, plus at times *where* and *when* (see list, p. 133).
- **Location in a sentence:** The **ADJSC** always follows the noun or pronoun being modified.
- **Punctuation rules:**

  1. If the **ADJSC** is *essential* to the meaning of the sentence, *do not separate it* from the independent clause with commas.
  2. If the **ADJSC** is *not essential* to the meaning of the sentence, *separate it* from the rest of the sentence *with commas.*

> **Teaching and learning punctuation**
> The punctuation rules for a specific structure are best taught and learned at the time the structure itself is taught and learned.

The musicians *whom we enjoyed more than any others* were the members from North Texas University's One O'clock Lab Band.

Jairo Salazar, *who has attended this school for only six months,* has already achieved the highest grade point average in his class.

Shakespeare's sonnets, *which I've read more than once,* are among my favorite poems.

Have you seen the new car *that Kenny is driving*?

The reason *why Margot dislikes her biology class* has nothing to do with her teacher, Mrs. Heredia, *whom she likes,* and everything to do with snakes and fetal pigs, *which the students are dissecting.*

## USING WHO, WHOM, THAT, AND WHICH

Use *who* and *whom* to refer to **people**; use *that* and *which* to refer to **things**.

### Who and Whom

Use *who* under two circumstances: when the subordinate clause requires a subject or when it requires a predicate nominative (that is, when the subordinate clause's main verb is a linking verb).

Use *whom* when the subordinate clause requires a direct object (because the clause has an action main verb and already has a subject).

- The student *who won the award* is Tanisha.
- Does anyone know *who he is*?
- Joseph Montgomery, *whom I have known for a year,* is my best friend.

### That and Which

Use *that* to begin essential adjective subordinate clauses; use *which* to begin nonessential adjective clauses.

- The novel *that I am reading* is terrific.
- Wuthering Heights, *which I began last night,* is a terrific read.

## NOUN SUBORDINATE CLAUSES (NSC)   (Exercises, pp. 164–166)

- **Function:** The **NSC** can function as any noun can function: as a subject, a predicate nominative, a direct object, an indirect object, an object of the preposition, or an appositive.
- **Provide this information:**
    1. If the **NSC** is a subject (**S**), it tells *who* or *what* the sentence is about.
    2. If it is a predicate nominative (**PN**), it identifies the subject.
    3. If it is a direct object (**DO**), it tells *whom?* or *what?* receives the verb's action.
    4. If it is the indirect object (**IO**), it tells *to whom? to what? for whom?* or *for what?* an action is done.
    5. If it is an object of the preposition (**OP**), it is being connected to another word in the sentence by that preposition.
    6. If it is an appositive (**AP**), it is identifying a noun that comes before it.
- **Begin** with relative pronouns, plus at times *where* and *when* (see list, p. 133).
- **Location in a sentence:**
    1. If the subject (**S**) , the **NSC** is usually at the beginning of the sentence.
    2. If it is a predicate nominative (**PN**), the **NSC** follows a linking verb.
    3. If it is the direct object (**DO**), the **NSC** follows an action verb.
    4. If it is the indirect object (**IO**), the **NSC** comes between an action verb and a direct object.
    5. If it is an object of the preposition (**OP**), the **NSC** follows a preposition.
    6. If it is an appositive (**AP**), the **NSC** comes right after the noun it identifies.
- **Punctuation rule:** The **NSC** is *not separated* from the rest of the sentence *by commas* unless it is functioning as a nonessential appositive.

> *How* Louis survived four days in a blizzard on Mt. McKinley is the subject of his new book. **NSC = S**

> A solution to the problem is *what I am seeking.* **NSC = PN**

> Achilles believes *that Agamemnon has dishonored him.* **NSC = DO**

> Ms. Jamison will give *whoever needs one* a ticket to the fair. **NSC = IO**

> The meaning of *whatever you just said* is apparently beyond my understanding. **NSC = OP**

> Yesterday's Supreme Court ruling, *that anyone accused of a crime must first be read their Miranda rights,* has been established practice for some time. **NSC = AP**

> ***Sometimes the word that begins a noun subordinate clause may be omitted.***

> Alfonso's mother said *he must leave at this instant.* The relative pronoun *that* has been omitted before the **NSC**, which is functioning as a **DO** in this sentence.

## COMPLEX, COMPOUND, AND
## COMPOUND-COMPLEX SENTENCES (Exercises, pp. 163–166)

**Complex Sentence (CX)**
*One independent clause + one or more subordinate clauses*

- *When Macbeth remembers meeting the witches,* his lust for power increases.
- King Lear, *whose old age did not produce excessive wisdom,* makes a fatal decision *that destroys his family.*
- The autographed baseball, *which John Henry has had on his bookshelf for years,* will bring him thousands of dollars *as soon as the next auction is held.*

**Compound Sentence (CP)**
*Two independent clauses*

- Two witnesses noticed the man in question beforehand, but neither of them saw the crime being committed.
- Johnny rode his bicycle to the grocery store; his front tire had a flat along the way.
- Marcella decided to study the Chinese language in college; in fact, she made this decision her junior year of high school.

**Compound-Complex Sentence (CPCX)**
*Two independent clauses + one or more subordinate clauses*

- The playwright *whom Roberto enjoyed more than any other* was Shakespeare, and his interest in becoming an actor grew from the moment *when he acted the part of Mercutio in the school play.*
- Mercutio's unpredictable temperament sometimes startled people; however, Romeo, *who was his closest friend,* ignored most of his explosive outbursts.
- *After Tybalt killed Mercutio,* Romeo entered the fray; this decision would change the entire direction of his life.

---

### WHAT ARE THE THREE WAYS TO JOIN TWO INDEPENDENT CLAUSES TOGETHER TO FORM A COMPOUND OR COMPOUND-COMPLEX SENTENCE?

If you closely examine the three sentence examples above for both the compound sentence and the compound-complex sentence, you will observe that all three ways are demonstrated. They are

- with a *comma followed by* a coordinating conjunction ——→ **, yet**
- with a solo semicolon ——→ **;**
- with a conjunctive adverb *preceded by a semicolon* and *followed by a comma* ——→ **; consequently,**

*See p. 152 for the list of seven coordinating conjunctions and the list of conjunctive adverbs.*

## PARTICIPIAL PHRASES AS ADJECTIVES

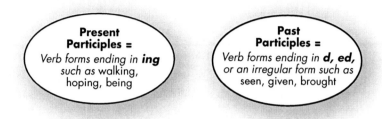

**Present Participles =**
Verb forms ending in **ing** such as walking, hoping, being

**Past Participles =**
Verb forms ending in **d, ed,** or an irregular form such as seen, given, brought

*Present participial phrases PrPP*   (Exercises, pp. 167–170)

*Past participial phrases PaPP*   (Exercises, pp. 169–170)

- **Function:** Modify nouns or pronouns.
- **Contain** the present or past participle and any complements (such as direct objects or predicate nominatives) or modifiers (adjectives and adverbs, whether they be single words, phrases, or subordinate clauses).
- **Provide this information:** The **PrPP** and **PaPP** tell *what kind?* or *which one?* about the word being modified.
- **Location in a sentence:** The **PrPP** and **PaPP** will appear directly before or after the noun or pronoun it modifies.
- **Punctuation rules:**
    1. When the **PrPP** or **PaPP** begins the sentence (that is, it comes directly before the noun or pronoun it modifies), always separate the phrase from the rest of the sentence with a comma.
    2. When the **PrPP** or **PaPP** follows the noun or pronoun it modifies, separate the phrase from the rest of the sentence with commas if it is a *nonessential* phrase; if the **PrPP** or **PaPP** is *essential,* no commas are used.

### Essential or nonessential participial phrase?
- The student *running down the hall* slipped on the banana peel. (The **PrPP** is essential, for it identifies which student is being referred to. No commas needed.)
- Carlton, *running down the hall,* slipped on the banana peel. (The **PrPP** is not essential to the meaning of the sentence: The reader knows who slipped on the peel. Use commas.)
- The kite *blown away by the fierce wind* is the only one of ours that remains lost. (The **PaPP** is essential, for it identifies which kite is being referred to. No commas needed.)
- Janelle's kite, *blown away by the fierce wind,* is the only one of ours that remains lost. (The **PaPP** is not essential for identifying the kite. Use commas.)

### Verb or adjective?

When is a present or past participle functioning as a **verb**? When it has a helping verb before it: (present) *is* running, *has been* galloping, *might be* recording, *would have been* consuming; (past) *had* given, *will be* finished, *are* written, *were* cooked.

When is a present or past participle acting as an **adjective**? When it has no helping verb in front of it and is, at that time, modifying a noun or pronoun.

- Forrest Gump became a *running* machine at one point in his life.
- Parents of the children brought *baked* goods to the school festival.

### Present participial phrases

- *Running for his life,* Forrest eventually escaped from the young men out for a joyride in their pickup.
- Forrest, *running for his life,* eventually escaped from the young men out for a joyride in their pickup.

- *Crouching down on the red asphalt track,* Royce stretches his hamstrings as a final precaution and positions himself on the starting blocks.
- Royce, *crouching down on the red asphalt track,* stretches his hamstrings as a final precaution and positions himself on the starting blocks.

- *Throwing tomatoes at passing cars yesterday,* the boys were severely disciplined by their parents today.
- The boys *throwing tomatoes at passing cars yesterday* were severely disciplined by their parents today.

### Past participial phrases

- *Envied by the flat-footed Achilles,* Hector inspects his worn Nikes and quickly brushes off some dirt.
- Hector, *envied by the flat-footed Achilles,* inspects his worn Nikes and quickly brushes off some dirt.

- *Destroyed in the heat of recent battle,* the forlorn village stood silently in the frosty night.
- The forlorn village, *destroyed in the heat of recent battle,* stood silently in the frosty night.

- *Ripped apart in an encounter with a crazed mongrel,* the teddy bear has been mailed to the teddy bear repair factory.
- The teddy bear *ripped apart in an encounter with a crazed mongrel* has been mailed to the teddy bear repair factory.

## ABSOLUTE PHRASES

**Absolute phrases (AbP)**   (Exercises, p. 173)
- **Function:** Modify all or part of the sentence to which it is connected.
- **Contain** a noun that is immediately followed by an adjective, often—but not always—a participle or participial phrase.
- **Location in a sentence:** The **AbP** is frequently found either at the beginning or at the end of a sentence.
- **Punctuation rule:** The **AbP** is separated from the rest of the sentence by a comma.

> The boy stares into space, *his face being white with fear.*

> *His strength invincible,* Beowulf undertakes the formidable challenge.

> *The act of violence having been committed,* Macbeth shakes with terror.

> "Ronald Reagan appears out of the darkness, *his head bowed in conversation with a vaguely familiar man in business."*
> —*U.S. News,* Jan.'96

## GERUND PHRASES AS NOUNS

**Gerund phrases (GP)**   (Exercises, p. 170)
- **Function:** Act as the subject, predicate nominative, direct object, indirect object, object of a preposition, or appositive of a clause or sentence.

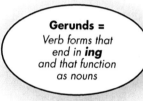

**Gerunds =**
*Verb forms that end in **ing** and that function as nouns*

- **Contain** the gerund and any complements (such as direct objects or predicate nominatives) or modifiers (adjectives and adverbs, whether they be single words, phrases, or subordinate clauses).
- **Provide this information:**
    1. If the **GP** is a subject (**S**), it tells *who* or *what* the sentence is about.
    2. If it is a predicate nominative (**PN**), it identifies the subject.
    3. If it is a direct object (**DO**), it tells *whom?* or *what?* receives the verb's action.
    4. If it is the indirect object (**IO**), it tells *to whom? to what? for whom?* or *for what?* an action is done.
    5. If it is an object of the preposition (**OP**), it is being connected to another word in the sentence by that preposition.
    6. If it is an appositive (**AP**), it is identifying a noun that comes before it.
- **Location in a sentence:**
    1. If the subject (**S**) , the **GP** is usually at the beginning of the sentence.
    2. If it is a predicate nominative (**PN**), the **GP** follows a linking verb.
    3. If it is the direct object (**DO**), the **GP** follows an action verb.
    4. If it is the indirect object (**IO**), the **GP** comes between an action verb and a direct object.
    5. If it is an object of the preposition (**OP**), the **GP** follows a preposition.
    6. If it is an appositive (**AP**), the **GP** comes right after the noun it identifies.

- **Punctuation rule:** The **GP** is *not separated* from the rest of the sentence *by commas* unless it is functioning as a nonessential appositive.

> *Keeping one eye on her watch and another at the door* was very difficult for Estellita. **GP = S**

> Latrell's favorite activity is *playing chess.* **GP = PN**

> The great challenge, *keeping the peace,* now presents itself. **GP = AP**

> "A compromise proposed *trimming spending for welfare, food stamps, and other projects.*" —*Life,* December 1995 **GP = DO**

> The thought of *reading over five chapters in my physics text tonight* makes me a bit sleepy. **GP = OP**

## VERB FORMS ENDING IN *ING:* PARTICPLES OR GERUNDS?

Remember that function is what determines whether *knocking,* for example, is a participle or a gerund. When its function is as an **adjective,** *knocking* is a **participle**.

> The girl *knocking on the door* pleaded for someone to answer.

Here *knocking* is a **participle** because the phrase *knocking on the door* modifies girl.

When the function is that of a **noun,** *knocking* is a **gerund.**

> *Knocking on the door* caused temporary pain.

Here *knocking* is a **gerund** because it acts as the subject of the sentence, which is a noun function.

## INFINITIVE PHRASES AS ADVERBS, ADJECTIVES, NOUNS

### Adverb infinitive phrases (ADV-IP)   (Exercises, pp. 171–172)
- **Function:** Modify verbs, adjectives, or adverbs.
- **Contain** the infinitive and any complements (such as direct objects or predicate nominatives) or modifiers (adjectives and adverbs, whether they be single words, phrases, or subordinate clauses).

> **Infinitives =**
> *Verb forms preceded by **to,** such as* to talk, to destroy, to warn, to love

- **Provide this information:** The **ADV-IP** tells *how? when? where? why? to what extent?* or *under what condition?* about the word being modified.
- **Location in a sentence:** You might find an **ADV-IP** anywhere in the sentence, usually at the beginning of it or somewhere after the verb.
- **Punctuation rule:** If the **ADV-IP** *begins* the sentence, place a comma after it; otherwise, no comma is usually needed.

> The students rose *to cheer the performance.*

> *To annoy his baby sister,* Esteban began calling her "a little cockroach."

> Nikita worked harder than anyone else at track practice *to ensure that she would win a full athletic/academic scholarship to Duke.*

### Adjective infinitive phrases (ADJ-IP)
- **Function:** Modify nouns or pronouns.
- **Contain** the infinitive and any complements (such as direct objects or predicate nominatives) or modifiers (adjectives and adverbs, whether they be single words, phrases, or subordinate clauses).
- **Provide this information:** The **ADJ-IP** tells *what kind?* or *which one?* about the word being modified.
- **Location in a sentence:** The **ADJ-IP** always follows the word it modifies.
- **Punctuation rule:** The **ADJ-IP** will usually never be separated from the rest of the sentence by commas.

> Many writers have a tendency *to use too many commas.*

> The challenge *to bench press three hundred pounds* was successfully met by three of our school's athletes.

> The one *to ask about life in Thailand* is Tiffany.

### Noun infinitive phrases (N-IP)
- **Function:** The **N-IP** can function as any noun can function: as a subject, a predicate nominative, a direct object, an indirect object, an object of the preposition, or an appositive.
- **Contain** the infinitive and any complements (such as direct objects or predicate nominatives) or modifiers (adjectives and adverbs, whether they be single words, phrases, or subordinate clauses).
- **Provide this information:**
    1. If the **N-IP** is a subject (**S**), it tells *who* or *what* the sentence is about.
    2. If it is a predicate nominative (**PN**), it identifies the subject.
    3. If it is a direct object (**DO**), it tells *whom?* or *what?* receives the verb's action.
    4. If it is the indirect object (**IO**), it tells *to whom? to what? for whom?* or *for what?* an action is done.
    5. If it is an object of the preposition (**OP**), it is being connected to another word in the sentence by that preposition.
    6. If it is an appositive (**AP**), it is identifying a noun that comes before it.
- **Location in a sentence:**
    1. If the subject (**S**), the **N-IP** is usually at the beginning of the sentence.
    2. If it is a predicate nominative (**PN**), the **N-IP** follows a linking verb.
    3. If it is the direct object (**DO**), the **N-IP** follows an action verb.
    4. If it is the indirect object (**IO**), the **N-IP** comes between an action verb and a direct object.
    5. If it is an object of the preposition (**OP**), the **N-IP** follows a preposition.
    6. If it is an appositive (**AP**), the **N-IP** comes right after the noun it identifies.
- **Punctuation rule:** The **N-IP** is *not separated* from the rest of the sentence *by commas* unless it is functioning as a nonessential appositive.

> *To invest with success in stocks* may require a knowledge of economics that you do not possess at this time. **N-IP = S**

Jermaine's goal, *to bicycle across South America from Venezuela to the southernmost tip of Chile,* has been something he has trained for during the past two years. **N-IP = AP**

Consuela plans *to graduate a year early from Harvard Theological Seminary.* **N-IP = DO**

King George's decision was *to deploy British troops to the colonies across the Atlantic.* **N-IP = PN**

## APPOSITIVE PHRASES

### *Appositive phrases (AP)* (Exercises, p. 174)

**Appositive =**
*A noun or pronoun used to **identify** another noun or pronoun*

- **Function:** Identify or provide additional information about another noun or pronoun.
- **Contain** the appositive and any words that modify it, be they single words, phrases, or subordinate clauses.
- **Location in a sentence:** An **AP** is usually located directly after the noun or pronoun it is identifying; occasionally, the **AP** will begin the sentence directly before the noun or pronoun it is identifying.
- **Punctuation rule:** If the **AP** *is nonessential,* separate it from the rest of the sentence with commas; if it is an *essential* **AP**, do not use commas.

The startling announcement, *an edict from the king,* trumpets over the loudspeaker.

*A strikingly inventive person,* Najeera has the admiration of all of her peers.

My friend *Katie McAllister* departs for Cambridge University tomorrow.

Clarence Darrow, *the most famous American defense lawyer at the turn of the previous century,* is the great-grandfather of our algebra teacher.

The Hannah-McCloskey kidnapping and murder, *this city's crime of the century,* was never solved.

## NOUN: A WORD, PHRASE, OR CLAUSE THAT NAMES A PERSON, PLACE, THING, OR IDEA

### e.g. words as nouns
*car, London, toy, hate.*

### gerund phrases as nouns
*Recording a Top Ten hit* is this musician's primary ambition.
David received a ticket for *running a red light.*

### infinitive phrases as nouns
Shaniqua wants *to defeat her opponent decisively.*
*To serve in the Peace Corps* remains Donyelle's intention.

### noun subordinate clauses
*Whoever finishes the test first* will probably fail it.
Clay did not hear *that tomorrow's concert has been cancelled.*

## THE FUNCTIONS OF THE NOUN IN A CLAUSE OR SENTENCE

### Nouns can be the subject (S) of a clause or sentence.

The *town* of Weatherford celebrates its Peach Festival every July.
> [The single-word *town* is the **S** of this sentence.]

*Listening to her favorite singer* puts Alicia in a splendid mood.
> [The gerund phrase *listening to her favorite singer* is the **S** of this sentence.]

*To speak slowly and distinctly* is something that Jackie rarely does.
> [The infinitive phrase *to speak slowly and distinctly* is the **S** of the sentence. This sentence contains an adjective subordinate clause, *that Jackie rarely does*, and *Jackie* is the **S** of that clause.]

*Which of the hockey teams will win the Stanley Cup* is anybody's guess at this point in the series.
> [The noun subordinate clause *which of the hockey teams will win the Stanley Cup* is the **S** of the sentence; since *which of the hockey teams will win the Stanley Cup* is a clause, it, too, contains a subject, and that **S** is which.]

*That he risks injury and even death* makes Alberto's job as a stunt man especially uninviting for most people.
> [The noun subordinate clause *that he risks injury and even death* is the **S** of this sentence; the pronoun *he* is the **S** of the noun subordinate clause itself.]

> **What is a subject?**
> A subject is *who* or *what* the clause or sentence is about. Any noun can be a subject, which means a single-word noun, a gerund phrase, a noun infinitive phrase, or a noun subordinate clause may be functioning as the subject.

***Nouns can be the predicate nominative (PN) of a clause or sentence.***

> William Faulkner was a *winner* of the Nobel Prize for Literature.
>> [The single-word *winner* is the **PN** of this sentence.]

> Karen's future goal is *singing for a living.*
>> [The gerund phrase *singing for a living* is the **PN** of this sentence.]

> Tabitha's favorite line from Shakespeare has always been "*to be or not to be.*"
>> [The compound infinitive phrase *to be or not to be* is the **PN** of this sentence.]

> Johnny is *who will receive my vote for class president.*
>> [The noun subordinate clause *who will receive my vote for class president* is the **PN** of this sentence.]

**What is a predicate nominative?**
A predicate nominative is a noun that follows a linking verb and identifies the subject. Any single-word noun, gerund phrase, noun infinitive phrase, or noun subordinate clause can be a predicate nominative.

## IS THAT NOUN REALLY FUNCTIONING AS A PREDICATE NOMINATIVE?

First, make sure it follows a linking verb (see p. 148). Keep in mind that, since the predicate nominative identifies the subject, you can interchange the two. Therefore, to test whether a noun that follows a linking verb is actually the predicate nominative, rearrange the parts of the sentence: Make the predicate nominative the subject and the subject the predicate nominative. If you can do that so that the sentence retains its original meaning, you know that you have a predicate nominative. e.g. Singing for a living is Karen's future goal. *Goal* is now the predicate nominative here; *singing for a living* is now the subject.

***Nouns can be the direct object (DO) of a clause or sentence.***

> Randolph tossed his *cap* into the air at graduation.
>> [The single-word noun *cap* is the **DO**.]

> Carla Sue's dad enjoys *dancing to the music of the Rolling Stones.*
>> [The gerund phrase *dancing to the music of the Rolling Stones* is the **DO**.]

**What is a direct object?**
A direct object, when a sentence or clause has one, is a noun that follows action verbs and receives the action of that verb. Direct objects answer the questions *what?* or *whom?* after an action verb. Any single-word noun, gerund phrase, noun infinitive phrase, or noun subordinate clause can function as a direct object.

> Judge Holland decided *to dismiss the case for lack of evidence.*
>> [The infinitive phrase *to dismiss the case for lack of evidence* is the **DO**.]

> Although my sister likes *eating pineapple pizza,* I knew *that she would not even taste any of the pepperoni.*
>> [The adverb clause *although my sister likes eating pineapple pizza* begins the sentence; the gerund phrase *eating pineapple pizza* is the **DO** of that clause. The noun clause *that she would not even taste any of the pepperoni* is the **DO** in the independent clause.]

### Nouns can be the indirect object (IO) of a clause or sentence

Henry handed his best *friend* the secret diary.
[The single-word noun *friend* is the **IO**.]

If Juanita brings the *class* donuts Friday, Andre may bring soft drinks.
[*Class* is the **IO** in the adverb subordinate clause that begins this sentence.]

Kimberly gives *repairing automobiles* her undivided attention.
[The gerund phrase *repairing automobiles* is the **IO**.]

This particular class has shown *whoever teaches them* a masterful approach toward studying.
[The noun subordinate clause *whoever teaches them* is the **IO**.]

> **How can an indirect object be distinguished from a direct object?**
> An indirect object, if there is one, always comes between the action verb (never a linking verb) and the direct object; in addition, the indirect object answers one of these questions after an action verb: *to whom? for whom? to what? for what?* Any single-word noun, gerund phrase, and noun subordinate clause can be an indirect object. It is doubtful that you will discover many infinitive phrases functioning as indirect objects because of the word "to" in the infinitive; however, if one were to write *The literary committee gave **To Kill a Mockingbird** an award*, then ***To Kill a Mockingbird*** would be an infinitive phrase as indirect object.

### Nouns can be the object of a preposition (OP) in a clause or sentence

Paula listens to *music* around the *clock*.
[In this sentence the single-word noun *music* is the object of the preposition "to" and the single-word noun *clock* is the object of the preposition "around."]

Jaye believes that she lost her hearing from *playing in a heavy metal band.*
[This sentence contains a subordinate clause, *that she lost her hearing from playing in a heavy metal band.* Within the subordinate clause, the gerund phrase *playing in a heavy metal band* is the object of the preposition "from." Within the gerund phrase, there is also a prepositional phrase, *in a heavy metal band,* and *band* is the object of the preposition "in."]

I addressed the letter to *whom it may concern.*
[The noun subordinate clause *whom it may concern* is the object of the preposition "to."]

### Nouns can be the appositive (AP) in a clause or sentence

My friend *Erica* sends all of her favorite singers fan mail.
[The single-word noun *Erica* is the **AP** identifying the friend in this sentence.]

Jeffrey's hobby, *building model airplanes*, keeps him busy most every weekend.
[The gerund phrase *building model airplanes* is the **AP** identifying the hobby.]

Only a few of us were amazed by Geraldo's somewhat complicated wish, *to become both a professional football player and a professional ballet star before the age of 25.*

> **What is an appositive?**
> An appositive is a noun that is located next to another noun and identifies it in some way. Any single-word noun (with or without modifiers), gerund phrase, noun infinitive phrase, and noun subordinate clause can be an appositive.

[The noun infinitive phrase *to become both a professional football player and a professional ballet star before the age of 25* is the **AP** identifying the wish.]

Dat's belief, *that the sale of handguns should be prohibited,* caused a major debate between him and his friend Stephen, who thought he couldn't be more unwise.

[The noun subordinate clause *that the sale of handguns should be prohibited* is an **AP** identifying the belief; the single-word noun *Stephen* is an **AP** identifying the friend.]

## PRONOUN: A WORD USED IN PLACE OF A NOUN

e.g. *I, me, you, he, him, her, it, myself, herself, yourself, each, neither, who, which, somebody, few, most.*

## THE FUNCTIONS OF THE PRONOUN IN A CLAUSE OR SENTENCE

***Anything a noun can be, a pronoun can be.***

**A pronoun's antecedent:** a word or group of words to which a pronoun refers. e.g. The engineer of the train blew *its* whistle repeatedly. (*Train* is the antecedent of *its.*)

A pronoun *must agree with its antecedent in number;* in other words, when the antecedent is singular, the pronoun should be singular. This is especially tricky regarding indefinite pronouns.

### Indefinite Pronouns

| Singular | | | Plural | Singular or plural |
|---|---|---|---|---|
| anybody | everyone | nothing | both | all |
| anyone | everybody | neither | few | any |
| anything | everything | somebody | many | most |
| each | one | someone | others | none |
| either | no one | something | several | some |
| | nobody | | | |

**Subject-verb agreement**
When the subject is a <u>singular</u> indefinite pronoun, ignore any prepositional phrase that may immediately follow that pronoun. *Each of the boys is ready to play* is grammatically correct. *Each,* not *boys,* is the subject.

### Quick Review

Nouns—and pronouns—can function as **subjects, predicate nominatives, direct objects, indirect objects, objects of prepositions,** and **appositives** in a sentence or clause. Since nouns function in this way, that means that **gerund phrases, noun infinitive phrases,** and **noun subordinate clauses** have these same functions.

One other function of any noun—or pronoun— is in **direct address,** as in *Gloria, did you bring your homework?* In this interrogative sentence, *Gloria* is a noun of direct address.

### The his or her dilemma

To write *Everyone must sit down quietly at his or her desk before receiving his or her test materials* is a grammatically correct sentence construction. After all, *everyone* is always a singular indefinite pronoun (one of those peculiarities of the language that we might as well accept without undue stress) and, if the group in question has both males and females, then it is appropriate that the personal pronouns *his or her* be used in this situation. Admittedly, this is very awkward and when continually using *his or her* in sentences, the writing becomes inelegant, indeed.

### What's a solution?

- Go to the plural. *Students must sit down quietly at their desks before receiving their test materials.*
- Eliminate the need for personal pronouns. *Students must be seated in order to receive test materials.*

In other words, if you don't want to go overboard with *his or her,* which easily happens, take a different approach.

## VERBS

# Two Categories of Verbs

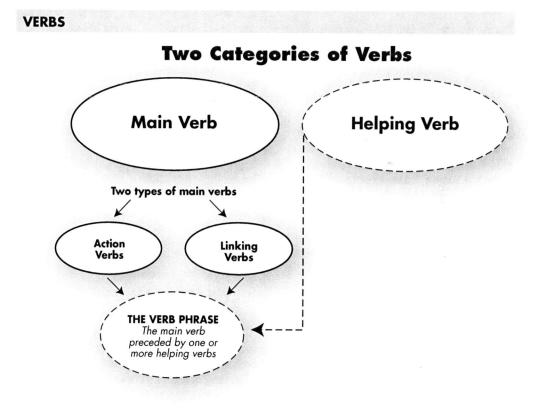

### How is a helping verb distinct from a main verb?

Helping, or auxiliary, verbs are only used when a sentence or clause contains a *verb phrase;* in other words, there is no helping verb unless the verb consists of more than one word. Moreover, the helping verb always precedes the main verb, whether that main verb is an action verb or a linking verb. Therefore, the main verb is always the last word in a verb phrase. If the clause or sentence contains only one word as the verb, then that verb is always the main verb.

# THE _BE_ VERB CAN BE EITHER A HELPING VERB OR A LINKING MAIN VERB

**BE**
_as a linking main verb_

**am is are was were be been being**

**BE**
_as a helping verb_

When the **BE** verb is either the _only verb_ in the clause or sentence, or it is the _last word in a verb phrase,_ then the **be** verb is the **main verb.**

Shelly _is_ the secretary of the homecoming committee.

The twins, Darius and Shawanna, have _been_ ill for a week now.

Everyone believes that Joshua will _be_ shy like his father.

### More about linking verbs

Linking verbs, almost always followed by either predicate nominatives or predicate adjectives, include the **be** verb plus sensory verbs like **sound, taste, appear, feel, look, smell,** and verbs that express condition like **become, remain, seem, stay, grow.**

The sensory and condition verbs can be either action or linking verbs. How do you tell if one of these is action or linking?

• If you can substitute a **be** verb and the sentence makes sense, it's linking.

• See if what follows the verb is a predicate nominative or predicate adjective.

• What are these verbs—action? linking?

Tybalt _looked_ surly.

Juliet _looked_ at the stars in the night sky.

The Friar _grows_ a variety of herbs.

Mercutio _grows_ more and more belligerent.

When the **BE** verb appears before a main verb, it is always a helping verb in that clause or sentence.

The lady in the lavender blouse <u>has _been_ waiting</u> for you since eight o'clock.

The bass player _was_ <u>jumping</u> backwards at the time that the lead singer fell off the stage.

Both letters _were_ <u>composed</u> on a word processor by Gwendolyn.

### How many helping verbs are there? 23

| | | |
|---|---|---|
| am | is | are |
| was | were | be |
| been | being | |
| have | has | had |
| do | does | did |
| may | might | must |
| shall | should | will |
| would | can | could |

### Can a helping verb only function as a helping verb?

If it precedes a main verb, it is always functioning as a helping verb. However, _if_ any of these verbs are used as either the _only verb_ in the clause or sentence or the _last word in a verb phrase,_ then what is often one of the 23 helping verbs is now functioning as a main verb.

• Tommy _has_ five fingers on his right hand.

• Mikey will _do_ it.

**Forms of the verb**

| Present tense | Past tense | Past participle | Present participle |
|---|---|---|---|
| go / goes | went | (has) gone | (is) going |
| bring / brings | brought | (has) brought | (is) bringing |
| talk / talks | talked | (has) talked | (is) talking |

*Other tenses*

| Present perfect | Past perfect | Future | Future perfect |
|---|---|---|---|
| He has run. | He had run. | He will run. | He will have run. |
| He has seen. | He had seen. | He will see. | He will have seen. |

**Voice**

| **Active Voice** | vs. | **Passive Voice** |
|---|---|---|
| Quentin *eats* the pizza. | | The pizza *is eaten* by Quentin. |

| | |
|---|---|
| An action verb is in active voice when the subject performs the action of the verb. Unless a specific reason determines a need for passive voice, most writers will want to concentrate on the judicious use of active voice verbs. | An action verb is in passive voice when the action of the verb is done to or performed on the subject. Passive voice is formed by using a **be** verb (such as *is, are, was,* or *were*) with the past participle form of the verb. |

## MODIFIERS: ADJECTIVES, ADVERBS, AND PREPOSITIONAL PHRASES

## ADJECTIVE

a word, phrase, or clause that describes, specifies, limits, or modifies nouns or pronouns. They tell *what kind, which one, how many,* or *whose* about the word modified:

**Adjectives**
*answer the questions*
*what kind?*
*which one?*
*whose?*
*how many?*

> **e.g. words as adjectives**
> a *rotten* apple, the *green* ink
> *several* assignments, *my* computer
>
> **prepositional phrases as adjectives**
> the house *on the corner*, a teacher *with a strict demeanor*
>
> **present participial phrases as adjectives**
> The student *hurdling down the hallway* fell into the trash can.
> *Polishing the antique table,* Carol suddenly noticed a distinct smell *drifting in from the kitchen.*

### past participial phrases as adjectives

*Knocked down by an inside fast ball,* the batter slowly dusted himself off and prepared for the next pitch.

Sonja Martinez, *disturbed by the raucous behavior of her classmates,* asked the counselor for a transfer.

### infinitive phrases as adjectives

The most important team *to beat this time* is the Yankees.

The counselor *to see about college entrance exams* is Mrs. Juarez.

### adjective subordinate clauses

Anthony, *who missed two weeks of school because of pneumonia,* asked for tutorial assistance from some of his teachers.

The twenty-two answers *that I missed on the algebra exam* certainly didn't help my grade.

## ADVERB

a word, phrase, or clause that modifies a verb, adjective, or another adverb. They tell *how, when, where, why, to what extent,* or *under what condition* about the word modified: e.g. he *carefully* reads; she ran *immediately; here* sat the monster; a *very* red apple.

**Adverbs**

*answer the questions how? when? where? why? to what extent? under what condition?*

### e.g. words as adverbs

I *cautiously* approached the grey fox.

We attended the play *yesterday.*

Jason's laughter sounded *extremely* ridiculous to my ears.

The children ran *outside* to play after the thunderstorm.

### prepositional phrases as adverbs

The children ran outside to play *after the thunderstorm.*

*Underneath my sister's bed,* our tri-color collie slept.

### infinitive phrases as adverbs

*To irritate his older brother,* Tony repeated his every word.

Felicia's mother wrapped the rolls with a towel *to keep them warm.*

The children ran outside *to play after the thunderstorm.*

### adverb subordinate clauses

*Because I could not locate my tennis shoes,* I wore high heels to school.

No one will pass Mr. Hollister's exam *unless you study well.*

*As the graduation ceremony ended,* everyone stood to sing the school song.

## PREPOSITION

a word that connects the noun or pronoun that follows it to some other word in the clause or sentence. A **prepositional phrase** begins with a preposition and ends with a noun or pronoun, the **object of the preposition.**

### A list of some prepositions

| | | | | |
|---|---|---|---|---|
| aboard | at | down | off | to |
| about | before | during | on | toward |
| above | behind | for | onto | under |
| across | below | from | out | underneath |
| after | beneath | in | outside | until |
| against | beside | inside | over | up |
| along | between | into | past | upon |
| among | but (except) | like | since | with |
| around | by | near | through | within |
| as | concerning | of | throughout | without |

### A list of some compound prepositions

| | | | |
|---|---|---|---|
| according to | because of | in front of | next to |
| ahead of | by means of | in spite of | on top of |
| along with | in addition to | instead of | out of |

### *Functions of prepositional phrases in a clause or sentence*

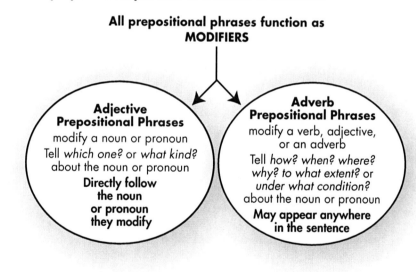

**All prepositional phrases function as MODIFIERS**

**Adjective Prepositional Phrases**
modify a noun or pronoun
Tell *which one?* or *what kind?* about the noun or pronoun
**Directly follow the noun or pronoun they modify**

**Adverb Prepositional Phrases**
modify a verb, adjective, or an adverb
Tell *how? when? where? why? to what extent?* or *under what condition?* about the noun or pronoun
**May appear anywhere in the sentence**

The bench *beneath the elm trees* needs a serious repair.

The debate *concerning school vouchers* is scheduled for Friday.

I did not notice any girl *in pedal pushers.*

Kaneisha walked *around the track* sixteen times.

*Underneath the open prairie sky,* the imposing farm house stood alone.

Mr. Donnegan exercises seriously *because of health problems.*

## CONJUNCTION: A WORD THAT JOINS WORDS, PHRASES, OR CLAUSES TOGETHER

### Coordinating Conjunctions

Connecting words that join words, phrases, or clauses that are grammatically alike—frequently, though not exclusively, used to join independent clauses

*and   but   for   or   nor   yet   so*

### Correlative Conjunctions

Connecting words that join groups of words that are grammatically alike—sometimes used to join independent clauses

*both...and   either...or   neither...nor   not only...but also*

### Conjunctive Adverbs   (Exercise, p. 19, day eight, #2)

Connecting words that are used to join independent clauses

**to show contrast:** however, nevertheless, instead, on the other hand, still

**to add more information on the same subject:** furthermore, moreover, in addition

**to show the effect or result of a cause:** therefore, consequently, as a result

**to show similarities:** likewise, similarly

**to show the opposite of what is intended:** otherwise

**to emphasize a fact in a stronger or more specific way:** in fact, indeed

**Punctuation rule:** When joining two independent clauses together with a conjunctive adverb, put a semicolon before it and a comma after it.

Tanya wanted to travel to Florida; *therefore,* she worked all summer to pay for her trip.

### Subordinating Conjunctions

Subordinating conjunctions are used to form a subordinate clause; they appear at the beginning of the clause.

| | | | | |
|---|---|---|---|---|
| after | because | that | when* | Subordinating conjunctions begin *adverb subordinate clauses;* those marked with asterisks may sometimes begin *adjective* or *noun subordinate clauses.* |
| although | before | since | whenever | |
| as | even though | so that | where* | |
| as if | if | than | while | |
| as long as | in order that | though | till | |
| as soon as | once | unless | wherever | |
| as though | provided | until | | |

# PARTS OF SPEECH FOR STRUCTURE AND SYNTAX

**Nouns**

| What parts of the sentence can nouns be? | subject, predicate nominative, direct object, indirect object, object of the preposition, appositive, and noun of direct address |
| --- | --- |
| What phrases and clauses function as nouns? | gerund and infinitive phrases + noun subordinate clauses |

**Pronouns** — can be whatever nouns can be

**Verbs**

| What are the two categories of main verbs? | action verbs and linking verbs |
| --- | --- |
| What are the complements that follow action verbs? | direct objects and indirect objects |
| | *What questions do direct objects answer after the action verb?* whom? or what? |
| | *What questions do indirect objects answer after the action verb?* to whom? or to what? for whom? or for what? |
| What are the complements that follow linking verbs? | predicate nominatives and predicate adjectives |
| What are the four forms of the verb? | present tense, past tense, present participle, and past participle |
| What are the two verb forms that require a helping verb in front of them in order to function as a verb in the sentence? | present participles and past participles |
| What are the 23 helping verbs? | am/is/are/was/were/be/been/have/has/had/do/does/did/can/could/shall/should/may/might/must/will/would/being |

**Prepositions**

| Is a subject or a complement in a prepositional phrase? | no; do not confuse the object of the preposition with either a subject or a complement |
| --- | --- |

**Adjectives**

| What do adjectives modify? | nouns or pronouns |
| --- | --- |
| What are the questions that adjectives answers? | what kind? which one? whose? how many? |
| What phrases and clauses function as adjectives? | prepositional, participial, and infinitive phrases + adjective subordinate clauses |

**Adverbs**

| What do adverbs modify? | verbs, adjectives, other adverbs |
| --- | --- |
| What are the questions that adverbs answer? | how? when? where? why? to what extent? under what condition? |
| What phrases and clauses function as adverbs? | prepositional and infinitive phrases + adverb subordinate clauses |

# RHETORICAL PATTERNS AND VARIATIONS FOR SENTENCES

**Anadiplosis** Repetition of the ending segment at the beginning of another segment:
- When *I give, I give* myself. —Walt Whitman
- All that *Tracy has stated, she has stated* with her usual zeal.

**Anaphora** Repetition of the beginnings of sentences or clauses:
- *Let us march* to the realization of the American dream. *Let us march* on segregated housing. *Let us march* on segregated schools. *Let us march* on poverty. —Martin Luther King, Jr.
- *Down fell the* tender saplings, *down fell the* aging sycamore, *down fell the* graceful willow, *down fell the* mighty oak under the battering ram of the storm.

**Antithesis** Repetition by contrasting of parallel elements:
- That's *one small step for* a man, *one giant leap for* mankind. —Neil Armstrong
- Shelby's elastic voice *dug deeply into the well of* the lyric's pain before it *climbed forcefully into the open air of* the song's ultimate joy.

**Asyndeton** Omitting conjunctions between words, phrases, or clauses:
- He has been beaten, tortured, interrogated, manipulated.

**Epanalepsis** Repetition of the beginning at the end of a clause or sentence:
- *Blood* hath bought *blood*, and *blows* have answer'd *blows*. —Shakespeare's *King John*
- The *object* of our quest is not our journey's sole *object*.

**Epistrophe** Repetition of endings in consecutive clauses or sentences:
- I'll have *my bond!* Speak not against *my bond!* I have sworn an oath that I will have *my bond!* —Shylock in Shakespeare's *Merchant of Venice*.

**Parallelism** Repetition of like structures:
- I thought that *had I not planned* to have a party while my parents were gone for the weekend, or *had I not gone* to pick up the fourth passenger in a car my parents told me was designed for three teenagers, or *had I not run* the red light ten minutes before the wreck, or *had we not stopped* to buy cigarettes for my friend, I would surely have avoided the entire incident. —Nick Crivello

**Parataxis** A series of phrases or clauses without conjunctions:
- I eat, I dance, I read.

**Polysyndeton** Using conjunctions between words, phrases, or clauses:
- A man with no hat, *and* with broken shoes, *and* with an old rag tied round his head. A man who had been soaked in water, *and* smothered in mud, *and* lamed by stones, *and* cut by flints, *and* stung by nettles, *and* torn by briars; who limped, *and* shivered, *and* glared, *and* growled; *and* whose teeth chattered in his head as he seized me by the chin. —Charles Dickens' *Great Expectations*

## ADDITIONAL PUNCTUATION FOR CLARITY

The primary comma and semicolon rules have been discussed with the punctuation rules that accompany each explanation for clauses and phrases. While there is no attempt in this text to create a complete list of all punctuation rules, some additional ones helpful to the writer include the following:

**Comma**   (Exercises, pp. 174–176, 178)

Do not use a comma when the coordinating conjunction *and* joins two verbs or predicates that share a common subject.

- Macbeth stabbed the guards *and* wiped the blood on his arms.

**Semicolon**   (Exercises, pp. 176–178)

Usually a comma is placed before a coordinating conjunction that joins two independent clauses; however, use a semicolon with that coordinating conjunction if there are already several commas in one or more of the independent clauses.

- The hijackers, having repeatedly asked for the jet to be fueled with three times the amount needed to reach Paris, set a 5 p.m. deadline for being allowed to leave the Marseilles airport; but the authorities remained determined to keep the airliner on the ground in Marseilles.

Use a semicolon to separate items in a series when the items themselves already contain commas.

- Byzantine trade included furs such as sable, mink, and fox; precious stones such as rubies, gold, and ivory; and fabrics such as silk, muslin, and damask.

**Colon**   (Exercises, pp. 177–178)

Use a colon to introduce a part of a sentence that exemplifies, restates, or explains the preceding part. (*If what follows the colon is a sentence, rather than a fragment, capitalize the first word.*)

- All essays contain portions that need improvement: The paragraphs, sentences, and words may be victims of the red pen.

Use a colon to introduce a series or list. What comes before the colon, however, must be an independent clause, a complete sentence.

- **Incorrect** Advance Placement English students will study: *Beowulf, Macbeth, The Tempest, Paradise Lost, Return of the Native,* and *Great Expectations.*
- **Correct** Advance Placement English students will study powerful works of literature: *Beowulf, Macbeth, The Tempest, Paradise Lost, Return of the Native,* and *Great Expectations.*

## COMMON PROBLEMS WITH STRUCTURE AND SYNTAX

Comma splices, run-ons, faulty parallelism, fragments, subject-verb agreement, pronoun-antecedent agreement

### Comma Splice (CS)

A comma splice occurs when two sentences—that is, two independent clauses—are joined together with a comma only. A coordinating conjunction should follow the comma in such a case.

#### Original

John walked down to the candy store, he decided to buy Jolly Ranchers.

#### Possible Revisions

John walked down to the candy store, and he decided to buy Jolly Ranchers. (Writer places a coordinating conjunction after the comma.)

John walked down to the candy store; he decided to buy Jolly Ranchers. (*Writer joins the two independent clauses with a semicolon.*)

John walked down to the candy store where he decided to buy Jolly Ranchers. (*Writer turns the second independent clause into an* **ADVSC** *with the subordinating conjunction* where.)

John, deciding to buy Jolly Ranchers, walked down to the candy store. (*The writer turns the second independent clause into a* **PrPP**.)

#### Original

Michael loves violent action films, however, his girlfriend enjoys romantic ones.

#### Possible Revisions

Michael loves violent action films; however, his girlfriend enjoys romantic ones. (*Since* however *is a conjunctive adverb, the writer changes the comma after* films *to a semicolon.*)

Michael loves violent action films, but his girlfriend enjoys romantic ones. (*The writer replaces the conjunctive adverb* however *with the coordinating conjunction* but; *the only comma required is the one after* films.)

Although Michael loves violent action films, his girlfriend enjoys romantic ones. (*The writer removes the conjunctive adverb* however *and turns the first independent clause into an* **ADVSC** *with the subordinating conjunction* although; *the comma after* films *remains because of punctuation requirements for the* **ADVSC** *at the beginning of sentences.*)

### Run-On (RO)

A run-on sentence is similar to a comma splice since it contains more than one sentence—more than one independent clause—but, in this case, the writer doesn't add any punctuation whatsoever to join these two structures.

#### Original

My uncle retrieves my aunt from her search we start toward the lobby.

#### Possible Revisions

My uncle retrieves my aunt from her search, and we start toward the lobby. (*The writer adds the coordinating conjunction* and *preceded by a comma.*)

My uncle retrieves my aunt from her search; we start toward the lobby. (*The writer uses a semicolon to join the two independent clauses.*)

After my uncle retrieves my aunt from her search, we start toward the lobby. (*The writer turns the first independent clause into an* **ADVSC** *with the subordinating conjunction* after; *a comma after the* **ADVSC** *is required.*)

### Faulty Parallelism (//)

Sentences often contain two or more words, phrases, or clauses in a series or as pairs. These units must be parallel; that is, they must be of the same type.

#### Original

John argued angrily with his teacher and was boisterous.

#### Revision

John argued angrily and boisterously with his teacher.

#### Original

Dorothy asked the teacher what she had to do to improve her grade and about the exam.

#### Revision

Dorothy asked the teacher what she had to do to improve her grade and what questions he would place on the exam.

#### Original

Michael asked that he receive an "A" in English, more help on his essay, and being allowed to turn it in late.

#### Revision

Michael asked that he receive an "A" in English, that he have more help on his essay, and that he be allowed to turn it in late.

### Sentence Fragments (SF)

Because sentences must have a subject and a verb, sometimes writers confuse a subordinate clause for a complete sentence because subordinate clauses have a subject and verb. Subordinate clauses must be attached to independent clauses.

#### Original

Pip accepted an offer to travel to London. Because he wanted to become a gentleman.

#### Revision

Pip accepted an offer to travel to London because he wanted to become a gentleman.

Sometimes writers think phrases, which do not have a subject and a verb, can stand as an independent clause.

#### Original

Sending Joe and Biddy a gift instead of visiting them.

#### Revision

Pip sends Joe and Biddy a gift instead of visiting them.

### Subject-Verb Agreement (SV)

Subjects that are singular require singular verbs, and subjects that are plural require plural verbs. This general practice becomes tricky **when the subject is an indefinite pronoun**. Such indefinite pronouns as *either, neither, each, everyone*, and *everybody* are always singular and take a singular verb.

#### Original

Either of those girls *are* certain to perform well in the competition.

#### Revision

Either of those girls *is* certain to perform well in the competition.

Another situation that can cause difficulty in subject-verb agreement occurs **when the subject is followed by a prepositional phrase**. The noun following a preposition is the object of the preposition; the subject of the sentence or clause is never in a prepositional phrase.

#### Original

The singer, along with the other members of the band, *are* always acting silly.

#### Revision

The singer, along with the other members of the band, *is* always acting silly.

### Pronoun-Antecedent Agreement (PA)

When we write sentences, our pronouns and antecedents must agree in number, gender, and person. Remember that a pronoun is a word used in place of a noun; some examples include *I, me, you, he, few, most, their*. A pronoun's antecedent is a word or group of words to which a pronoun refers. See pp. 146–147 for specific examples, a list of indefinite pronouns, and commentary regarding the *his / her* dilemma. Among the problems that arise when using pronouns, and their potential solutions, are these that follow.

### Avoid vague, confusing, or ambiguous pronoun reference.

#### Original

When Michelle purchased some groceries, they asked her for her Kroger's discount card.

#### Revision

When Michelle purchased some groceries, the cashier asked her for her Kroger's discount card.

#### Original

The teacher discussed the student's failing grades with her mother after she finished drinking the cup of coffee.

#### Revision

After the teacher finished drinking the cup of coffee, she discussed the student's failing grades with her mother.

### Singular indefinite pronouns (see p. 146) act as singular antecedents.

#### Original

Each of the students at Englewood Girls' Academy will purchase their books Tuesday.

#### Revision

Each of the students at Englewood Girls' Academy will purchase her books Tuesday.

#### Revision

The students at Englewood Girls' Academy will purchase their books Tuesday.

### A collective noun takes a singular pronoun when considered a unit; considered in terms of individual parts, the collective noun takes a plural pronoun.

#### Original

The faculty unanimously voted to increase their salaries by four percent.

#### Revision

The faculty unanimously voted to increase its salaries by four percent.

# EXTENDING ELABORATION WITH MODIFICATION[1]

(Exercises, p. 161)

### Analysis Modifiers

**Method** End the original sentence with a comma, *choose a noun* (with or without modifiers) *that emphasizes details you have just cited*, and then continue your analysis. Study these examples.

• The Pardoner tries to sell a "holy relic" even to the "widow who mightn't have a shoe," a *defilement* of Christian theology that provides further evidence of the Church's corruption.

• Joe extends his "restoring touch" unto Pip, "aiding and comforting [him]…by giving [Pip] gravy," a *benevolent deed* that demonstrates not just his concern for Pip, but his willingness to help and care for him.

### Repeat Word Modifiers

**Method** End the original sentence with a comma, *repeat a key word*, and then continue extending your elaboration. Study these examples.

• By omission, the narrator implies that she possesses something beyond the physical realm that warrants his love, *something* intangible to the five senses.

• Hester chooses to live in the town in which she has sinned, *live* despite the daily ridicule not only from townspeople but also from clergymen.

• The Pardoner is both deceptive and greedy, *deceptive* in his selling of false relics to naïve believers, *greedy* in his desire to make a profit using his position in the church.

## Sample Modifications

• **Duke Theseus represents a leader who attempts to balance the feminine and the masculine.**

### Elaboration with repeat word modifier

Duke Theseus represents a leader who attempts to balance the feminine and the masculine, the *masculine* that restores the order King Creon disrupted, the *feminine* that grants clemency to Arcite and Palamon.

### Elaboration with analysis modifier

Duke Theseus represents a leader who attempts to balance the feminine and the masculine, a *combination* that allows him to maintain an image of strength along with compassion, a *combination* that places love before violence.

• **While living with Pap, Huck is in a dangerous situation.**

### Elaboration with repeat word modifier

While living with Pap, Huck is in a dangerous situation, a **situation** that requires quick thinking and imagination if he is to survive.

### Elaboration with analysis modifier

While living with Pap, Huck is in a dangerous situation, an **environment** that often involves physical and mental abuse.

---

[1] Adapted from Williams, Joseph M. Style: Ten Lessons in Clarity & Grace. Boston: Scott, Foresman, 1989. 131–132.

# SENTENCE STRUCTURE AND STYLE EXERCISES

## Sentence Combining: Repeat Word Modifiers/Analysis Modifiers

**Directions:** Combine each group of sentences using one or more *repeat word* or *analysis* modifiers. Underline or highlight the modifiers created. You may delete extra words if necessary.

1. They sit in front of a large bay window, where these souls pensively sit. They hope if they look over their shoulders their family, bearing gifts, will burst through the door. These are not material gifts, but gifts one cannot find at Macy's. These are gifts of affection, love, and compassion.

2. Adding to this self-inflicted torture, Dimmesdale battles Chillingworth. He is a physician who does not abate Dimmesdale's pain but is a "chief actor in the poor minister's interior world." He is able to "arouse him with a throb of agony."

3. Scrooge disdainfully comments about his nephew's monetary status: "You're poor enough." This shows how Scrooge evaluates individuals by their monetary value.

4. Near this prison rests "a portion of the virgin soil…a cemetery." Cemeteries often remind one that death might affect this community, too.

5. In addition, Wealhtheow also presents to Beowulf "two arm-wreaths, with robes and rings also, and the richest collar." These gifts represent Hrothgar and Wealhtheow's gratitude towards Beowulf for killing the notorious Grendel. Beowulf cleanses the hall.

6. Chaucer depicts the knight as a virtuous pilgrim. He is a person who fights for the Church. He rejects extravagance in exchange for humility.

7. Bob Cratchitt's office fire is smaller than Scrooge's. This detail is ironic considering Bob's heart is much warmer than his boss'.

8. Cratchitt's office is described as a "dismal little cell." The word *cell* suggests that he is imprisoned by Scrooge's cruelty.

9. Frankenstein realizes that his experiment, if successful, will transcend all previous scientific discoveries. This accomplishment would exalt the doctor to a position of great fame.

10. Scrooge sees the Christmas season as devoid of tangible value. This is a view of the world that is base and political. His cynicism thwarts a relationship with his nephew.

## Sentence Combining with Adverb Subordinate Clauses

The following six words are subordinating conjunctions that may begin adverb subordinate clauses. Three of the subordinating conjunctions suggest a contrasting relationship between the two clauses of the sentence; three are used to indicate a cause and effect relationship.

| for contrast | **although** | **even though** | **while** |
| for cause and effect | **because** | **since** | **as** |

**Directions:** In the following pairs of sentences, combine one sentence with the other by turning one of the sentences into a subordinate clause and attaching it to the other. Attach six subordinate clauses *before the independent clause*. Place six subordinate clauses *after the independent clause*. Be sure your combination makes logical sense; not just any combination will do. Also, be sure to follow the comma rules with regard to adverb subordinate clauses, p. 133. Make one combination per pair. Use all six subordinating conjunctions by the end.

1. A 1948 law says that women cannot be assigned combat duty. It is possible women will be involved in combat in the next war.

2. The thief will get away with the crime. Someone will report him to the police.

3. The play's director stated that rehearsals begin an hour earlier today. She feels that the actors need much more practice.

4. Michelangelo's sculpture *Pieta* is now displayed only behind a protective glass shield. It was damaged by a lunatic.

5. Over fifteen inches of snow fell during the night. The school district decided to have school anyway.

6. I do not have any money. I'll have to borrow twenty dollars from someone else.

7. Other composers may have been more inventive. None have captured the American spirit like Duke Ellington.

8. Sheryl has practiced vigorously for months. She is ready to win all three track and field events that she's entered.

9. Over ten inches of ice glazed the streets. The school district decided to call off school.

10. People always become ill at one time or another. There is a great demand for students, both female and male, to enter the nursing profession.

11. An innocent man was executed for the crime. The real murderer was eventually caught and signed a confession.

12. The linebacker suffered a hamstring injury in last week's game. The coaches expected him to play Sunday.

### Sentence Combining with Adjective Subordinate Clauses

**Directions:** Combine each pair of sentences below to form one sentence containing an adjective clause that modifies the boldfaced word. Underline the adjective subordinate clause. Punctuate the new sentence correctly.

1. **Guillermo** is normally very shy in class. He surprised all his peers by delivering an impassioned speech on capital punishment.

2. The award-winning **film** created additional revenue for Steven Speilberg. The film combined actual war footage with fabricated scenes.

3. **Charles Dickens** spent part of his youth working in a shoe factory. Later in life he became a successful writer.

4. The three boys planned a **joke**. The joke involved hiding water balloons in the bottom of the girls' book bags.

5. The **girls** did not realize the balloons were in their bags when they threw them on the ground. The girls became very angry once the water seeped out from the bottom of the bags.

6. The girls decided to plot their **revenge**. The revenge will be much more creative and clandestine than the boys' so-called joke.

7. The governor decided to veto the latest welfare reform **bill**. This piece of legislation would obligate working mothers to work only 20 hours per week, rather than the current requirement of 30.

8. Yvette has a **belief** regarding wealth. Acquiring wealth is extremely necessary for success in life.

9. **Ariel** is an ethereal spirit in Shakespeare's *The Tempest*. Ariel serves the magician Prospero.

10. Disguised as a beggar in his own palace, Odysseus manages to demonstrate **restraint.** This prevents him from prematurely revealing his identity.

### Writing Complex Sentences with Adjective Subordinate Clauses

**Directions:**
- Create five original complex sentences, each one containing a correctly punctuated adjective subordinate clause.
- Each adjective clause must begin with a different relative pronoun. The five relative pronouns to be used are *whose, who, that, whom,* and *which.*
- Highlight the adjective subordinate clause.
- Identify the subject and verb in your adjective subordinate clause.

## Writing Compound-Complex Sentences with Adjective and Adverb Subordinate Clauses

**Directions:**
- Create five original compound-complex sentences, each one containing a correctly punctuated adjective and adverb subordinate clause.
- Highlight the adjective and adverb subordinate clauses.
- Identify the subject and verb in your adjective and adverb clauses.
- To join together the two independent clauses in each sentence, use either solo semicolons or correctly punctuated conjunctive adverbs.

## Noun Subordinate Clauses and Adjective Subordinate Clauses

**Directions:**
- Identify the subject and verb in every clause, subordinate and independent.
- Underline each subordinate clause.
- If the subordinate clause is an adjective, identify it as **ADJSC** and draw an arrow to the word it modifies.
- If the subordinate clause is a noun, identify it as **NSC** and write its function in the sentence next to the identification (e.g. **NSC-S** or **NSC-OP**).

1. Sparta was the ancient Greek city-state where physical strength and skill were most highly admired.

2. In Athens, which was Sparta's greatest rival, intellectual achievement was greatly valued.

3. The Athenian belief in democratic values was what the Spartans could never understand.

4. The Athenian whose leadership brought his city-state to pre-eminence was Pericles.

5. That Athens grew economically, culturally, and militarily under Pericles became a threat to Spartan interests.

6. The news that Athens had invaded the Spartan peninsula of Peloponnesus caused the Spartans to prepare for war.

7. The Spartans knew why the Greeks had invaded their territory.

8. They sent a declaration of war to those leaders who were prepared to receive it.

9. From what became known as the Peloponnesian War arose the Greek world's first renowned historian, Thucydides.

10. Reading Thucydides will benefit anyone who believes knowledge of the past may prevent problems in the future.

### Writing Complex Sentences with Noun Subordinate Clauses

**Directions:**
- Create five original complex sentences, each one containing a noun subordinate clause.
- Each noun clause must begin with a different relative pronoun. The five relative pronouns to be used are *who, that, what, how,* and *why*.
- Underline the noun subordinate clause.
- Identify the subject and verb in your noun subordinate clause.

### Three Types of Subordinate Clauses: adverb, adjective, and noun

**Directions:**
- Identify the subject and verb in every clause, subordinate and independent.
- Underline each subordinate clause.
- If the subordinate clause is an adjective, identify it as **ADJSC** and draw an arrow to the word it modifies.
- If the subordinate clause is an adverb, identify it as **ADVSC** and write the question it answers next to the identification. (e.g. **ADVSC-WHY?**)
- If the subordinate clause is a noun, identify it as **NSC** and write its function in the sentence next to the identification (e.g. **NSC-PN** or **NSC-DO**).

1. After he looked at me for a moment, the man turned me upside down and emptied my pockets.

2. When he came to the low church wall, he got over it like a man whose legs were numb and stiff.

3. She was not a good-looking woman, and I had the general impression that she must have forced Joe Gargery to marry her by hand.

4. That I was going to rob Mrs. Joe almost drove me crazy with guilt.

5. As soon as the great black velvet pall outside my window was shot with gray, I got up and went downstairs.

6. He crammed what little food was left into the breast of his gray jacket.

7. Joe, who had ventured into the kitchen after me, drew the back of his hand across his nose with a conciliatory air.

8. Joe threw his eyes over the handcuffs and pronounced that the job would necessitate the lighting of his forge fire.

9. The cattle turned their heads from the wind and sleet and stared angrily as if they held us responsible for what annoyed them.

10. That the shouting was made by more than one voice soon became apparent.

11. Because one of the soldiers, who carried a basket in lieu of a gun, dropped to his knees to open it, my convict took the opportunity to look round him for the first time and saw me.

12. The "something" I had noticed before clicked in the man's throat.

## Simple, Compound, Complex, and Compound-Complex Sentences

**Directions:**
- Identify the subject and verb in each clause.
- Underline each subordinate clause
- Identify each clause as **ADVSC**, **ADJSC**, and **NSC** and explain why it is that type of clause. (Follow directions for such an explanation on the preceding page's directions for "Three Types of Subordinate Clauses.")
- Identify the entire sentence as
    **S** simple = one independent clause
    **CP** compound = two independent clauses
    **CX** complex = one independent clause + one or more subordinate
        clauses
    **CPCX** compound-complex = two independent clauses + one or more
        independent clauses

1. Edmond Dantes, whose marriage to Mercedes was prevented by various villains, spent fourteen years in prison for a crime that he never committed.

2. The unfortunate jeweler was lying on the floor in a pool of blood, which flowed from three large wounds in his chest; a kitchen knife with only its handle showing had been plunged into the fourth wound.

3. He discovered that a slope had been made; moreover, the rock had slid down to its present position, where it had been fixed in place by another rock about the size of a building stone, which had been used as a wedge.

4. Before inviting the two new cardinals to dinner, Cesar Borgia asked his father about a famous key opening a certain cupboard and a ring containing a lion's head.

5. He stopped in the hall and called for a servant to announce him to Noirtier, but nobody answered.

6. They poured some rum down his throat; complaining of a sharp pain, he soon opened his eyes and groaned.

7. As he stood knocking vainly on the door, Maximilien saw his father walking from the bedroom and pressing to his side an object that he tried to conceal beneath his coat.

8. That Dantes spent the years of his captivity planning an all-encompassing revenge against his enemies will not be a surprise to whoever has read about his travails.

9. Villefort buried the evidence of his affair under a full moon and before the curious eyes of a man he did not notice.

10. A novel of deception and desire, *The Count of Monte Cristo* provides the serious reader with a hero, Edmond Dantes, whose adventures require both mental and physical dexterity; however, what may serve as the ultimate cause of his success is his patience.

### Sentence Combining with Present Participial Phrases

**Directions:**
- Combine the following sentences by turning one of them into a present participial phrase.
- Make two combinations per pair, one before the noun it modifies and one after it.
- Underline each present participial phrase.
- Use commas where necessary.

e.g. Miami's citizens *have* already *experienced* two hurricanes this year. They *are* very well *prepared* for any future catastrophe.

**The writer has four options for combining these sentences.**

Miami's citizens, *having already experienced two hurricanes this year*, are very well prepared for any future catastrophe.

*Having already experienced two hurricanes this year*, Miami's citizens are very well prepared for any future catastrophe.

Miami's citizens, *being very well prepared for any future catastrophe*, have already experienced two hurricanes this year.

*Being very well prepared for any future catastrophe*, Miami's citizens have already experienced two hurricanes this year.

1. Sergeant Simpson reprimands the private very severely. He forcefully removes one of his stripes.

2. Tamika traveled to the airport in a yellow van. She arrived twenty minutes early.

3. The coach has called two straight running plays with no success. He then decides to signal for a long pass.

4. The philosopher spoke to the English II classes at Garland High. She urged the students to study metaphysics before they graduate.

5. My cat refused to eat any food in his tray. He seemed to be on a hunger strike until we allowed him to lick off the dinner plates.

6. Hiroshima, Japan, had been destroyed by an atomic bomb in 1945. It was rebuilt over a period of fifteen years.

7. The robin eats at the bird feeder each morning. The bird is occasionally joined by a pair of sparrows.

8. The oak was struck by lightning. It split in half and fell to the ground.

9. The Secretary of State flies into Kashmir this weekend. She attempts to work out a peaceful settlement in the region.

10. Michael Stipe promotes the sale of his autobiography. Each weekend he visits bookstores and signs autographs.

### Sentence Combining with Past Participial Phrases

**Directions:**

- Combine the following sentences by turning one of them into a past participial phrase.
- Make two combinations per pair, one before the noun it modifies and one after it.
- Underline each past participial phrase.
- Use commas where necessary.

e.g. The coach of the basketball team *was concerned* about Randolph's inability to make free throws. He decided to bench him for the second half.

**The writer has two options for combining these sentences in this case.**

The coach of the basketball team, *concerned about Randolph's inability to make free throws*, decided to bench him for the second half.

*Concerned about Randolph's inability to make free throws*, the coach of the basketball team decided to bench him for the second half.

**Hint:** When looking at a pair of sentences, you must first *find a verb phrase containing a past participle*. The verb phrase with a past participle is the one that contains a helping verb. *To form the past participial phrase, jettison the helping verb and retain the past participle.* In the above case, of the two sentences involving the coach and Randolph, only the first sentence has a past participle in the verb—*was concerned*, with *was* being the helping verb and *concerned* the past participle form of the verb. If both sentences in the pair have past participles, then you will likely have four options for combining the sentences because you may select either past participle to begin the past participial phrase.

1. Columbus was exhausted by a series of storms on his fourth voyage. He stayed in his cabin for the duration of the journey.

2. Magellan was enraged by the actions of two mutinous captains on his journey. He executed them posthaste.

3. The caterpillar is denied an opportunity to live. It is swatted onto the floor a few feet in front of me.

4. The free safety for the football team was injured in the play. He writhes helplessly on the ground.

5. Shannon's softball team was defeated in the state championship game. It was awarded the Hollander Trophy for Highest Team Batting Average.

6. Primal Scream's "Exterminator" was played three times in one hour on 3WK Underground Radio on my computer's Real Player. It drove my little sister out of my bedroom.

7. He was surprised at the violence contained in the news report. He quickly turned the channel to MTV.

8. Odysseus was instructed by Athena to disguise himself in his own house. He dined with the suitors and restrained his outrage at their supercilious behavior.

9. Her finished poems had been placed in a secret drawer by Emily. They were found twenty years after she died.

10. Grendel was easily defeated by Beowulf. The monster fought and yelled but fled to the swamps to bleed to death.

### Identifying Present and Past Participial Phrases

**Directions:** Underline the participial phrase. Draw an arrow to the word it modifies. Identify it as **PrPP** or **PaPP**.

1. Admired by Johann Sebastian Bach, Vivaldi's compositions included instrumental works and operas.

2. The first European explorers arriving in South America had found that many Indian tribes farmed the land.

3. Located at this time in the Cairo museum, Tutankhamen's coffin is made of solid gold.

4. The encyclopedia, containing more than 40,000 entries, provides an enormous range of information.

5. Pip, turning from the Temple Gate as soon as he had read the warning, made his way to Fleet Street, where he obtained a carriage and drove to Covent Garden.

6. Pip, obligated by his sense of duty to his benefactor, puts his life in peril on Magwitch's behalf.

7. The child racing through Aunt Nikita's vegetable garden soon disappeared behind the stone wall encompassing the next-door neighbor's back yard.

8. The building we lived in was gray, as were the streets, filled with slush the first few months of my life there. [Sentence from Judith Ortiz Cofer's "Silent Dancing."]

9. Sometimes I'd come home to find her lounging in the bamboo chair on the back porch, eating melon, or lying on the couch with a bowl of half-melted ice cream balanced on her chest. [Sentence from Naomi Shihab Nye's "Maintenance."]

10. I left the suburb folded in light, the white beams already taking on a grayish glitter, a dog barking somewhere. [Sentence from Eavan Boland's "The Woman, The Place, The Poet."]

### Identifying Gerund Phrases and their function

**Directions:**
- Underline the gerund phrase.
- Tell if it is used as a subject (**GP-S**), direct object (**GP-DO**), object of the preposition (**GP-OP**), or the predicate nominative (**GP-PN**).

1. Fearing to have the news of Estella's marriage to Drummle confirmed by the newspaper caused Pip to stop his subscription to the local daily.

2. Joe's primary mission in London was restoring me to good health.

3. Composing ragtime piano pieces was Scott Joplin's special talent.

4. Because ragtime musicians did make a practice of writing down their music, some critics did not accept ragtime as a legitimate form of jazz.

5. Imagine telling that to Scott Joplin!

6. Making an errata page is sometimes part of the publishing business.

7. At the age of twelve, Billy the Kid began living a life of crime.

8. Portraying Billy as the Robin Hood of the frontier became common with dime-novel authors of the day.

9. By covering his exploits with glamour, writers turned the story of a vicious murderer into a Wild West legend.

10. A favorite occupation for writers of stories, novels, and films is retelling the legend of Billy the Kid.

### Distinguishing Between Gerund and Present Participial Phrases

**Directions:** Because present participles and gerunds are both verb forms that end in *ing*, it may be tricky to tell them apart unless you keep in mind their function in the sentence: A present participial phrase functions as an adjective; a gerund phrase, of course, functions as a noun. Each sentence below contains either a present participial phrase or a gerund phrase.
- If it is a participial phrase, underline it and draw an arrow to the word it modifies.
- If it is a gerund phrase, underline it and tell how it is being used in the sentence (e.g. **GP-DO**).

1. Dancing as a cultural activity probably started with ancient religious ceremonies.

2. Moving into other areas of life, it later became a form of recreation and entertainment.

3. Medieval performers, lacking a stage, danced in a great hall.

4. Members of the audience would enjoy dancing of every description.

5. The only drawback was charging the customer astronomical prices for each performance.

6. After establishing academies of dance, the country's minister for cultural affairs created multiple scholarship opportunities for talented children.

7. The most popular scholarship, paying full tuition for the entire six-year program, is granted to ten students each year.

8. One academy has a renowned year-long course in dance exercise that the country's soccer players, hoping to qualify for the World Cup team, must take and pass.

9. The dancers completing the six-year program in ballet compete for positions with various ballet troupes throughout the continent.

10. Those studying theatrical dance often audition for roles in musicals staged in New York City and London

## Identifying Infinitive Phrases and their function

**Directions:**
- Underline the entire infinitive phrase.
- Identify the phrase as **N-IP**, **ADJ-IP**, or **ADV-IP**.
- If the phrase is a noun, identify the reason (**N-IP=S**, **N-IP=OP**, etc.).
  If the phrase is an adjective, draw an arrow to the word it modifies.
  If the phrase is an adverb, identify the reason (**ADV-IP=WHY**, **ADV-IP=WHERE**, etc.) and draw an arrow to the word it modifies.

1. One of the passengers decided to attack the hijacker. *N-IP = DO*

2. To provide myself some necessary relaxation, I rented a cabin at Possum Kingdom Lake for the three-day weekend. *ADV-IP = why*

3. If you are interested in receiving a job application, Mrs. Cunningham is the secretary to ask at this time. *ADJ-IP which*

4. "To dream the impossible dream" is the first line of my favorite song. *N-IP = S*

5. The lieutenant's orders were to dismiss the troops forthwith. *N-IP = DO*

6. The best place to view the skyline is near White Rock Lake. *ADJ-IP*

7. Latreisha wanted to take swimming lessons so that she would feel more comfortable when she goes on the Alaskan cruise. *N-IP = DO*

8. Parker listened to *West Side Story* to calm his nerves before the interview with the theater director at the university. *ADV-IP = why*

9. Demetria proposed a theory that the Vikings were probably the first to circumnavigate the world. *ADJ-IP*

10. To stop the argument between Jacob and Minh, Julia told them to split in half the hundred-dollar bill they had found.

*ADV-IP = why*          *N-IP = DO*

## Infinitive, Gerund, and Participial Phrases

**Directions:** Each sentence contains an infinitive, gerund, present participial, and/or past participial phrase. Some of these sentences contain more than one such phrase.

First, determine whether a phrase is a participial phrase or a gerund phrase.
- If it is a participial phrase, underline it and draw an arrow to the word it modifies.
- If it is a gerund phrase, underline the phrase and tell how it is functioning (**GP-S**, **GP-OP**, etc.) in the sentence.
- If it is neither a participial phrase nor a gerund phrase, then it is an infinitive phrase. Underline it and tell its function (**N-IP=DO**, **ADJ-IP**, **ADV-IP=HOW**, etc.).

1. Working overtime is the only way Sara can earn enough money to support her family.

2. The motorcycle parked by the fire hydrant will receive a ticket from the police officer.

3. To part with her collie upset Enriqueta so much that her parents tried to assure her that getting a new dog would be a very high priority in the next few weeks.

4. Francine's primary interest is acting in a community theater.

5. The driver of the blue Chevy pickup was given a ticket for running a stop sign.

6. Concerned about the hurricane, the residents of the island community left their homes.

7. The vacationers, swimming leisurely, had no knowledge of the danger in the water.

8. The authorities wondered whether postponing the concert would be preferable to cancelling it altogether.

9. To activate the community's interest in banning boom boxes in the nearby park, a neighborhood group circulated a petition to bring the matter before the city council.

10. I suppose that finding a pickup painted metallic black was more important to Ricky than the price he would have to pay for it.

11. The loud crying in the next room caused the lady to make an inquiry; however, she soon discovered that to cry loudly does not always signify a serious problem.

### Sentence Combining with Absolute Phrases

**Directions:** Combine the following sentences by creating an absolute phrase out of one sentence in the pair and joining that phrase to the other. Underline or highlight the absolute phrase.

- Removing the "be" verb from the sentence creates an absolute phrase.

  **Original**

  > Julia listened in stunned silence. Her smile was vanishing from her face.

  **Revision**

  > Julia listened in stunned silence, *her smile vanishing from her face.*

  **Original**

  > The furnace was broken. We huddled under blankets and waited for dawn.

  **Revision**

  > *The furnace broken,* we huddled under blankets and waited for dawn.

- Turning a regular active verb into a participle creates an absolute phrase.

  **Original**

  > She looks up and smiles at her uncle. Long strands of silky hair fall limply on her face.

  **Revision**

  > She looks up, *long strands of silky hair falling limply on her face,* and smiles at her uncle.

1. She cheerfully punches the keys T-H-E E-N-D and looks up with a proud crescent stretching across her lips. Her eyes gleam brightly as she reads over the masterpiece.

2. My mother keeps bellowing names, and soon her friends and relatives converge on the house. Her voice draws life from the dream's dark corners. [from Bernard Cooper's *Maps to Anywhere*]

3. John waited in the classroom. His fingers tapped on the desk nervously.

4. The community was restored. Prospero decides to throw away his magic staff and leave his recent past behind him.

5. The bank robbers fled the scene within minutes. The security guard saw part of the license plate numbers.

6. Mrs. Jones stared at the class. She had two research papers in her hand. She gritted her teeth.

7. John knelt on the fifty-yard line. He looked up at the tied score. He realized the team only had ten seconds.

8. Her heart races as she rushes away from the foreboding footsteps. The freezing wind chills her to the bone.

9. Mark's bedroom was a disaster. He had dirty underwear draped on the waste paper basket. He had soiled socks under the bed.

10. Three rugby players walked into the locker room together. One was soaked in sweat.

### Sentence combining with Appositive Phrases

**Directions:** Combine the following pairs of sentences by turning one of the sentences in each pair into an appositive phrase. Underline the appositive phrase.

1. Jerry Jones is the owner of the Dallas Cowboys. He is currently interviewing potential head coaches.

2. Edmond Dantes is a master of disguises. He meticulously plans a variety of strategies for achieving his ultimate goal.

3. The *Pharoan* is a ship owned by the Morrell family. It was decimated during a severe storm at sea.

4. Dr. Gregory wrote a new book on Elizabeth Bishop. She teaches at Harvard University.

5. That student has received scholarship offers from eight different universities. She is a recent immigrant from Tanzania.

6. He subscribes to the *The Georgia Review*. This literary magazine publishes some of the finest nonfiction in the Unites States.

7. Dinah plans to move to New York City and play in the house band at The Blue Note. She has been a jazz pianist since high school.

8. Rod Steiger was an Academy Award-winning actor. He was best known for his roles in *On the Waterfront, The Pawnbroker,* and *In the Heat of the Night.*

9. Chuck Palahniuk is the author of *Fight Club*. He has become Darrell's favorite novelist.

10. Patrice boasts a .355 batting average. She is the starting shortstop on her high school baseball team.

### Commas with Introductory Elements

**Directions:** Place commas after the introductory elements in each sentence. Introductory elements that require commas include the following: introductory adverb subordinate clauses, introductory present and past participial phrases, introductory adverb infinitive phrases, an introductory group (two or more) of prepositional phrases, and any introductory words.

1. After the principal entered the classroom everyone became uncomfortably quiet.

2. With the fall of Rome in A.D. 476 the empire crumbled.

3. Continuing to plan out his strategies Odysseus rests against the doorway as he listens to the heaving noises coming from Polyphemus' throat.

4. Provided that his ship is able to pass by Charybdis safely Odysseus and his mariners will take a chance on a moderately more successful encounter with Scylla.

5. If you had seen Polyphemus milking his ewes you might have carried away a somewhat different impression from that of Odysseus.

6. Yes it is difficult to excuse the eating of six of Odysseus' men.

7. Closed for a week of overdue repairs to its facilities my favorite pizza parlor was unavailable for a visit by my English class.

8. Although I have not seen the movie *The Client* I heard the book was much better.

9. To defend his client effectively the lawyer hired a private investigator.

10. Because Vivian was always making people laugh she decided to use her natural clumsiness as a stepladder to a career in comedy.

### Using Commas with Coordinating Conjunctions: Compound Sentences vs. Compound Predicates

**Directions:**
- If the coordinating conjunction is used in order to join independent clauses to form a compound sentence or a compound-complex sentence, *place a comma before* it.
- If the coordinating conjunction is used in order to join compound parts of a predicate, *do not place a comma before* it.
- To be sure whether you have a compound sentence or a compound predicate, identify the subject and verb in each clause, both independent and subordinate clauses. (Remember that all verbs in the compound predicate will have the same word as the subject; all verbs in the compound sentence will have different words as the subject.)
- Underline any subordinate clauses.
- Identify each sentence as simple (**S**), compound (**CP**), complex, (**CX**), and compound-complex (**CPCX**).

1. Theseus held out his hand to Hercules and hoped that his cousin would rethink his plan to kill himself.

2. Walking in the parade before the sacrifice, Ariadne noticed the Athenian hero and immediately fell in love with him.

3. Theseus leapt toward the hideous animal and grasped its bulging throat.

4. It took not only his strength to accomplish this arduous task but also his intelligence.

5. Hercules could not seem to control his emotions effectively and he often felt penitent about the resulting actions.

6. Theseus was sometimes a little bit supercilious and, therefore, convinced that he could do whatever he wanted to do whenever he pleased.

7. Atlas came back with the apples but did not give them to Hercules.

8. Psyche betrays her husband's wishes and proceeds to take a quick glance at him.

9. This shouldn't come as much of a surprise because the Athenians admired knowledge over brawn and believed that wit vanquished any enemy.

10. Hercules destroyed every member of his family with implacable fury but he would not have contemplated such a gruesome action if he were in his right mind.

11. Heroes might be those people who rescue passengers from a grisly plane crash or simply rescue a pet cat from a tree.

12. Although Psyche never wandered without purpose, she traveled great lengths on many of her journeys and she would have been hopelessly lost without succor.

### Using Semicolons

**Directions:** Apply the rules for usage of semicolons, pp. 136 and 155, to the following sentences. Be prepared to explain why using the semicolon in each sentence is necessary. Whatever punctuation already appears in the sentence is appropriately used.

1. The pastel drawings are lovely nevertheless, they should be sprayed with a fixative.

2. The weather is very strange we should have had a hard frost at least three weeks ago.

3. Cooking in front of television cameras can be embarrassing for example, I have seen cooks spill batter all over the stove and drop food on the floor.

4. The story of the woman with multiple personalities shows the disease's brutal cause, bizarre symptoms, and strange development but the woman's tale is not ever sensationalized.

5. The most significant dates of the Civil War were April 12, 1861 July 3, 1863 and April 9, 1865.

6. The participants in the exhibit are Judi Parker, who paints in water color Simon Rogers, who is a potter and Peter Mondavian, who sculpts in transparent plastic.

7. Paper airplanes are not airplanes at all they should be called paper gliders.

8. I want to get a roommate who makes up the bed and understands the proper use of hangars consequently, I filled out a questionnaire to help determine roommate compatibility.

9. Blenders, food processors, and instant food have eliminated most slicing, dicing, and pureeing yet the time required for putting together a meal seems the same.

10. California, Texas, and New York are the three most populous states and Florida and Arizona are the fastest growing.

Why are the uses of the semicolon in these three sentences that follow incorrect? Revise and explain.

11. Even though Sophocles wrote 124 plays; only seven plays by him still exist.

12. I have checked the following sources; encyclopedias, almanacs, indexes, and periodicals.

13. Stacey has to leave basketball practice for his ballet rehearsal at five o'clock, otherwise; the director will have to assign his role to another dancer.

### Using Colons and Semicolons

**Directions:** Place colons and semicolons where they belong in the following sentences. All commas currently in these sentences are correct and should be left alone.

1. The following items appeared in error on our credit card bill twelve folding chairs, which we did not order one automatic juice squeezer, which we returned and three Christmas tree ornaments, for which we paid cash.

2. Tuition for the music school is not high moreover, many scholarships are available.

3. Paris, Venice, and Amsterdam are all beautiful cities but my favorite city anywhere in the world is Cairo.

4. Perhaps inspired by Diego Rivera's work, artist Judith Baca helped create the world's longest mural the one-mile-long piece, entitled *The Great Wall of Los Angeles*, shows the contributions made by ethnic groups to the city.

5. In the Olympics the first-place winner gets a gold medal second-place, a silver medal and third-place, a bronze medal.

6. It's obvious why you're tired you've been staying up too late.

7. Jim enjoys history, literature, and psychology yet his ambition is to become a math professor.

8. Before you paint, gather the necessary supplies paint, a palette, and brushes.

9. Remove the cable clamps in the reverse order from the way you connected them first, disconnect one of the black cable's clamps from the engine block then, disconnect the other from the assisting battery finally, disconnect the red cable's clamps from the positive terminals.

10. He admits he doesn't know yet what he will do with his life or how he will do it but he is sure it will have nothing to do with football.

## Using Commas, Colons, and Semicolons

**Directions:**
- Identify all subjects and verbs in each clause, subordinate and independent.
- Highlight all subordinate clauses.
- Place punctuation where it belongs.

1. In the prologue to his epic Homer asks a muse to sing through him.

2. The mariners who ate the lotus were eventually plucked from the ship by a ravenous twelve-necked hyenamaid an odious creature that even the brave Odysseus feared.

3. Telemachus the only son of Ithaca's king searched for his father for a year being unable to find any information about him he returned to his mother's palace so that he could help her with keeping the suitors under control.

4. In order that everyone have an opportunity to listen to the sirens Odysseus decided that his mariners disturbed by the idea that only he might listen to their song should remove the beeswax from their ears for a maximum of ten seconds.

5. Circe who was enchanted by this man who did not fear her granted Odysseus' request for help that would put him on the road home.

6. To discern the values of Greek culture from a study of Homer's epics all Greek school children were required to read both the *Odyssey* and the *Iliad* from an early age therefore the primary curriculum of the nation was centered on these two texts.

7. Odysseus' largest ship destroyed by one of Zeus' lightning bolts was unable to survive the voyage home.

8. The reunion of Odysseus with his son which was assisted by the goddess Athena produced a flood of tears and a plan for reclaiming their kingdom.

9. The slaughter of the suitors reminds the careful reader of an earlier Homeric simile like the monster Scylla from which six of his mariners could not escape Odysseus is compared to a fisherman pulling his prey in by a net.

10. Penelope the woman who resisted the pressure of the suitors to abandon Odysseus for dead and choose one of them as her new husband refuses to disarm herself until the conqueror of these men has passed a final test.

### Imitating Syntax and Style of Authors

**Directions:** Write your own sentence, purposely imitating the syntax and style of each of the following sentences composed by other authors.

e.g. **author** Ito Romo *El Puente*

Lola tripped, and when she did, she leapt forward, falling flat on her face, her nose against the pavement.

Imitation of syntax and style

Macbeth reflected, and after he decided to kill the king, he proceeded with his plan, condemning his soul to hell, the earth about to tremor.

1. **Author** Kyla Dunn "Cloning Trevor"

   A human egg, retrieved just hours earlier from a young donor, was positioned under a microscope, its image glowing on a nearby video monitor.

2. **Author** Philip Roth "My Baseball Years"

   It was different, however, on Sundays out at Ruppert Stadium, a green wedge of pasture miraculously walled in among the factories, warehouses, and truck depots of industrial Newark.

3. **Author** Annie Dillard *An American Childhood*

   He chased us silently over picket fences, through thorny hedges, between houses, around garbage cans, and across streets.

4. **Author** Charles Bowden "Teachings of Don Fernando"

   His voice courtly, his face calm, his body singing of ease, I will trust him completely.

5. **Author** Robert Fagles *Iliad*

   Lord marshal Agamemnon rose up in their midst, streaming tears like a dark spring running down some desolate rock face, its shaded currents flowing.

### Potpourri: Putting Clauses and Phrases Together

**Directions:**
- Examine each sentence and identify all the subject-verb combinations—in other words, identify all the clauses, independent and subordinate.
- Identify each sentence as **S**, **CP**, **CX**, or **CPCX**—and explain why.
- Identify each subordinate clause as **ADVSC**, **ADJSC**, or **NSC**—and explain why your response is correct.
- Identify each **PrPP**, **PaPP**, **GP**, **IP**, and **AbP**—and identify its function.

1. That Bob Ewell acted pusillanimously in this story is further evidence that cowardice and bigotry go hand in hand.

2. To give Tom Robinson an opportunity to have his side of the story fairly presented to the jury, Judge Taylor decides that Atticus Finch should defend him.

3. Because Miss Havisham had been jilted, she began teaching Estella to treat men with contempt; to give her adopted daughter the chance to sharpen her skills is the reason why the wealthy lady issued Pip an invitation to play.

4. Whoever is Pip's benefactor has hired Mr. Jaggers to act as Pip's guardian when the former apprentice arrives in London.

5. Seeing the neighborhood from Arthur Radley's point-of-view becomes a major learning experience for Scout.

6. Boo Radley, disturbed by what he observes from behind his window, runs into the kitchen and grabs a knife; the only idea on his mind is defending his children from Bob Ewell.

7. Biddy, tears tumbling down her cheeks, watched Pip turn away.

8. Although the jury decides that Tom Robinson is guilty, a few of Maycomb's judicious people understand what has really happened; taking hours to deliberate Tom's fate is a small step forward in a town that has seen no progress since the Civil War ended.

9. His destruction imminent, the protagonist has remained a selfish, haughty, and ultimately ill-fated individual who long ago stopped growing as a human being.

10. The passion with which the lawyer for the defense presented her client's case to the jury distracted her listeners from the subtle thread of irrationality tying her case together.

## CREATING THE GRAMMATICAL STRUCTURE GUIDE

### Objectives
- To help students understand and identify grammatical structures correctly;
- To prepare students for learning how to manipulate these structures in their writing so that they may develop an increasingly sophisticated style.

**Directions:** Create your own grammar guide, defining grammatical structures and punctuation choices. Assignment should be typed.

### Required structure categories

| | |
|---|---|
| Present participial phrase | Absolute phrase |
| Past participial phrase | Appositive phrase |
| Gerund phrase | Noun subordinate clause |
| Adjective infinitive phrase | Adjective subordinate clause |
| Adverb infinitive phrase | Adverb subordinate clause |
| Noun infinitive phrase | Complex sentence |

Compound sentence w/ coordinating conjunction
Compound-complex sentence w/semicolon
Compound-complex sentence w/conjunctive adverb

1. Each structure category must be clearly identified and defined.

2. For each sample sentence, box or label the structure and, where necessary, identify its function in parentheses.

3. For each of the aforementioned structures, include two examples:
   - An original sentence of the student's own creation.
   - A sample sentence from a magazine or newspaper. Cite the source.

### Sample entry for a grammatical structure guide

### Noun subordinate clause

**Definition:** A clause (a subject and verb combination) that functions like a noun (subject, direct object, indirect object, predicate nominative, object of preposition, appositive, and noun of direct address). The clause begins with relative pronouns: *that, what, where, whether, how, who, whom, whoever, whomever, whose, why.*

### Sentences

1. Beowulf reaffirmed *that he would fight on, disregarding the long odds.* (direct object)
2. "*That gambling is All-American entertainment* was clear even at six one recent Sunday morning." —*U.S. News,* January 1996 (subject)

# APPENDIX

## GENERAL COMPOSITION ASSIGNMENT AND REVISION DIRECTIONS

These directions should be followed for paragraphs, essay test revisions, and major compositions, unless otherwise modified by the teacher.

### *Major Composition Requirements*

1. Composition must be **typed double-spaced.**
2. Composition should use the correct **MLA heading,** pp. 125, 127.
3. Composition should be written in **present tense** when discussing literary topics.
4. A student must **turn in all drafts with the final copy.**
5. All **new additions to final** copy—revised words, sentences, phrases—that did not appear in drafts must be highlighted with a highlighter marker.
6. A student must write a **showing-telling introduction,** p. 118.

7. **When a student quotes the literary text,** he or she must follow with a page number and chapter number in parenthesis for novels (450; ch.5); book or part and line numbers for long poems (3.45–48); line numbers for shorter poems (45–46); and act, scene, and line numbers for a play (2.3.45–49).
e.g. *Pip lowers his head and asks Joe "to forgive me for the wrongs I've done you" (56; ch.4).*

8. **A Works Cited** page should be placed at the end of the composition. If a student's only entry is the original text, he or she may place the entry, with "Works Cited" preceding it, after the conclusion. (See sample papers at the end of chapter three.)

9. Each body paragraph should contain **extensively elaborated** details.

10. A student should highlight and label one example of the following **sentence structures** that the teacher requires for the particular composition. (The teacher will modify this list per assignment, depending on the structures covered in class heretofore, but if he or she does not, the student is expected to include all required structures.)
    a. compound sentence w/conjunctive adverb (p. 136)
    b. compound-complex sentence (p. 136)
    c. present participial phrase (p. 137)
    d. past participial phrase (p. 137)
    e. absolute phrase (p. 139)
    f. repeat word modifier (p. 160)
    g. analysis modifier (p. 160)
    h. noun subordinate clause (p. 135)
    i. adjective subordinate clause (p. 134)
    j. adverbial subordinate clause (p. 133)
    k. infinitive phrase (p. 140)
    l. gerund phrase (p. 139)
    m. appositive phrase (p. 142)
    n. a sentence with consecutive parallel structures: two or more noun clauses, adverb clauses, present participial phrases, etc.
    e.g. *Miss Kate and Miss Julia were there, gossiping and laughing and fussing, walking after each other to the head of the stair, peering down over the banisters, and calling down to Lily to ask her who had come.*
    (Consecutive parallel present participial phrases in a sentence by James Joyce)

11. A student must highlight and use appropriately ___ SAT **words** from the vocabulary list. (Insert number of SAT words required on blank space.)

12. A student's **conclusion** should avoid summary or mere restatement of the thesis statement; instead, the conclusion ought to connect the thesis to one larger issue: a) to the community; b) to the writer of the composition; c) to other works of literature.

### Suggested Penalties

This depends, of course, on a teacher's point grading system.)

| | |
|---|---|
| no rough draft | –5pts. |
| no highlighting | –5pts. |
| no required structures | –5pts. |
| no Showing-Telling introduction | –5pts. |
| no Works Cited, MLA format | –2pts. |

### Requirements for Smaller Compositions

The numbers mentioned under each category are references to the preceding Major Composition Requirements.

#### Showing revision requirements

A student should apply the preceding Major Composition Requirements numbered 2, 3, 4, 5, and 10.

#### Paragraph requirements

A student should apply the preceding Major Composition Requirements numbered 2, 3, 4, 5, 7, 9, 10, and 11.

#### Essay test revisions

A student should apply the preceding Major Composition Requirements numbered 1, 2, 3, 4, 5, 7, 9, 10, and 11.

## MLA Documentation

### Parenthetical Citations are placed within the paper itself rather than as foot- or endnotes.*

For lines of **short poetry**: line numbers (45–46).

For lines of **longer poetry or epic**: first, refer to the canto, part, or book; next, if there are individual stanzas, refer to the stanza number; finally, refer to the line numbers; (1.2.5–7) refers to canto or book 1, stanza 2, lines 5–7.

For lines of a **play**: act.scene.line numbers (1.2.5–6).

For a **novel**: include the chapter with the page number (34; ch. 4); if the novel has book / section divisions, include that number as well (34; bk. 1, ch. 4).

For a **source without mention of the author's name** in the writer's essay: include the author's last name and the page number (Gower 41).

For a **source with mention of the author's name** in the writer's essay: include the page number only (4).

For a **source with more than one author, neither of whom are mentioned** in the writer's essay: include both authors' last names and the page number (Connors and Roberts 45).

For an **author with more than one entry in the works cited page**: include the last name of the author, and the title of the source followed by the page number (Stevenson, *The Poetry of Elizabeth Bishop* 67).

For a **quotation cited indirectly in another source**: include *qtd. in* and the last name of the author of the other source (the indirect source) and the page number (qtd. in Miller 304).

For a **quotation containing a question mark or an exclamation point**: retain this punctuation within the closing quotation mark and place a period after the parenthetical citation. *Mr. Lorry hopes to "see such a night again!"* (94; bk. 2, ch. 6).

For a **book or article with no author**: use the title and a page number ("Poetry of Donne" 65).

For **two authors with the same last name**: include the first initial of each author (or the entire first names if the initials are the same) and the page number (J. Jones and H. Jones 76).

For **a sacred text**: (Gen. 3.15), (2 Cor. 2.16), (John 2.1–4)

### General Composition Assignment and Revision Directions

These directions should be followed for paragraphs, essay test revisions, and major compositions, unless otherwise modified by the teacher.

### Example paragraph with parenthetical documentation

Telemachos is similarly pushed forward by his father's spirit. He tells Athene, after she questions him about his father, that "I for my part do not know. Nobody really knows his own father" (1.215–216). Telemachos must strive, however, to know his father, his past, in order to function in the present. In fact, "to know one's own father is to be part of the continuum of the human race and to see one's place in its future" (Gower 41). Telemachos must then seek to know his father. Athene recognizes this spiritual need: "Oh, for shame. How great your need is now of the absent / Odysseus" (1.253–4). Moreover, as Mary Lou Hoyle states, the entire "first five books of *The Odyssey* reveal the desperate conditions in Ithaka and thus the need for Odysseus the husband and father to return" (66). As a result of this deficit, Telemachos must "fit out a ship with twenty oars, the best you can come by, / and go out to ask about your father who is so long absent" (1.280–281).

### Works Cited

Gower, Dona. "Athena and the Paradigm of the Teacher." *Classic Texts and the Nature of Authority*. Ed. Donald and Louise Cowan. Dallas: Dallas Institute of Humanities and Culture, 1993. 36–49.

Hoyle, Mary Lou. "The Sword, the Plow, and the Song: Odysseus' Great Wanderings." *The Epic Cosmos*. Ed. Larry Allums. Dallas: Dallas Institute of Humanities and Culture, 1992. 59–88.

### MLA Works Cited Format

#### General rules for documenting text-based sources

1. Order of information and the punctuation that follows each item: Author's last name, author's first name. Title. City of publication: publisher, date published.
2. Place titles of books, epics, and plays in italics; place titles of articles, chapters, and short poems in quotation marks.
3. Use only first city of publication listed and the latest copyright date.

#### Book w/one author

Orwell, George. *Animal Farm*. New York: Signet, 1946.

#### A translation

Homer. *The Odyssey*. Trans. Robert Fagles. New York: Penguin, 1996.

### A book whose author is unknown

*Encyclopedia of Virginia.* New York: Somerset, 1993.

### Book w/two or more authors

Pressley, Michael, and Vera Woloshy. *Cognitive Strategy Instruction That Really Improves Children's Academic Performance.* Cambridge, MA: Brookline Books, 1995.

### An article in a reference book/multivolume work/encyclopedia

Cassidy, James. "The Great Dickens." *Nineteenth Century Literary Criticism.* 10 vols. Chicago: UP of Chicago, 1954.

Pettigrew, Thomas F. "Racism." *The World Book Encyclopedia.* 1998 ed.

### An introduction, a preface, a foreword, or an afterward to a text

Drabble, Margaret. Introduction. *Middlemarch.* By George Eliot. New York: Bantam, 1985. vii–xvii.

### Article in a scholarly journal

Fitzgerald, John. "The Misconceived Revolution: State and Society in China's Nationalist Revolution, 1923–26." *Journal of Asian Studies* 49 (1990): 323–43.

Baum, Rosalie Murphy. "Alcoholism and Family Abuse in *Maggie* and *The Bluest Eye.*" *Mosaic* 19.3 (1986): 91–105.

### An essay reprinted in an anthology or book

① ② ③ ④
Frye, Northrop. "The Mysticism of Macbeth." *Shakespearean Journal* 99

⑤ ⑫ ⑥ ⑦ ⑧
(1984): 990–95. Rpt. in *Shakespeare.* Ed. Robert D. Denham.

⑨ ⑩ ⑪ ⑫
Charlottesville: UP of Virginia, 1990. 18–27.

| | |
|---|---|
| ① | Author |
| ② | Title of Article |
| ③ | The article originally appeared in this journal. You'll find this source at the end of the article or on the bottom of the first page. |
| ④ | Volume number |
| ⑤ | Date of article |
| ⑥ | Rpt. = Reprinted |
| ⑦ | This is the book where you found the article, the place where it has been reprinted. |
| ⑧ | Edited by Denham |
| ⑨ | City of publication |
| ⑩ | Publisher |
| ⑪ | Year |
| ⑫ | Page numbers. |

Roberts, Sheila. "A Confined World: A Rereading of Pauline Smith." *World Literature Written in English* 24 (1984): 232–38. Rpt. in *Twentieth Century Literary Criticism.* Ed. Dennis Poupard. Vol. 25. Detroit: Gale, 1988. 399–402.

### Article in a newspaper

> Feder, Barnaby J. "For Job Seekers, a Toll-Free Gift of Expert Advice."
> *New York Times* 30 Dec. 1993: A38.

### Article in a magazine

> Bazell, Robert. "Science and Society: Growth Industry." *The New Republic* 15 Mar. 1993: 13–14.

### General rules for documenting online sources

1. Order of available information and the punctuation that follows each item: Author's last name, author's first name. Title of article, short story, poem, discussion forum posting [place *Online posting* afterwards]. *Title of book.* Abbreviation (if applicable) for editor, compiler, or translator, followed by the person's name. Any publication information for print version of source (publisher, city, date). *Title of project, database, periodical, professional site, or personal site* [place Home page afterwards]. Name of editor for project or database. Version number of the source; for a journal, include volume and/or issue number. Date of the electronic source, or latest update. Name of subscription service [use library name if it is the subscriber, along with its city and state]. The number range or total number of pages, paragraphs, or other sections, if they are numbered. Sponsoring institution. Date when researcher accessed the source [no period used after this date]. The URL of the source <in angle brackets>.
2. All entries contain as many items from #1 above as are available.
3. Apply text-based rules for use of quotation marks and italics for titles.
4. See <www.mla.org> for additional information about *online* documentation.

### Article in online newspaper or magazine

> Lodge, David. "Dickens Our Contemporary." *The Atlantic Online* May 2002. 14 June 2002 <http://www.theatlantic.com/issues/2002/05/lodge.htm>.

### Material from a scholarly project online

> Wollstonecraft, Mary. *A Vindication of the Rights of Woman.* London, 1892. *The Electronic Text Center.* Ed. David Seaman. 2002. Alderman Lib., U of Virginia. 29 July 2002 <http://etext.lib.virginia.edu/toc/modeng/public/WolVind.html>.

### Article in online reference database

> Doreski, C.K. "Proustian Closure in Wallace Stevens' 'The Rock' and Elizabeth Bishop's 'Geography III.'" *Find Articles.* 2002. 10 pp. Look Smart and The Gale Group. 19 April 2002. <http://www.findarticles.com/cf_0/m0403/n1_v44/ 20851473/p1/article.jhtml?term=Elizabeth+Bishop>.

### Basic Classical Rhetoric[1]

#### Persuasion

One of the four modes of discourse, **persuasion** seeks to convince the audience to adopt the writer's point of view, his argument. Today, persuasion occurs not only in print media, daily conversation, and public oratory, but also in visual media as well—billboards, TV ads, films, etc. What follows is a brief introduction to how persuasion works, according to Aristotle; it is designed to focus on persuasive strategies for effective writers. Knowledge of these strategies for convincing another can prove advantageous for any student. For one thing, understanding persuasion provides another method for analyzing both fiction and nonfiction; students may, for example, explore the persuasive appeals used by the speaker in the poem "To His Coy Mistress" or examine with greater insight a commentator's advocacy of a specific solution to a national issue. Moreover, as students become more adept at recognizing various methods of persuasion, they can incorporate these strategies into their own argumentation. Finally, recognizing persuasive techniques, along with the common fallacies associated with them, assists students in responding sensibly to the daily bombardment of solicitations and opinions.

#### Aristotle and Persuasion

The successful persuader, according to Aristotle, uses three types of appeals to convince others to change their opinions:

*logos*   the appeal to the audience's reason
*pathos*   the appeal to the audience's emotions
*ethos*   the appeal of the persuader's character

#### Logos

When we appeal to logic, to the audience's reason, we may argue using

- *induction* beginning with specific details and proceeding to draw a general conclusion

- *deduction* beginning with a general statement and proceeding to show specific examples as proof

- *authoritative sources* government research, statistics, expert opinion

- *definition* arguing that something meets the definition

- *analogy* arguing that one item is similar to another item

- *consequence* arguing cause and effect.

---

1 Most of the information in this section is adapted from Corbett, Edward P. J., and Robert J. Connors. *Classical Rhetoric for the Modern Student.* New York: Oxford University Press. 1999.

### Pathos

When we appeal to the emotions of the audience, we may argue using

- sensory images and metaphors that build rapport, create fear, evoke sympathy

- storytelling and narration

- diction that is emotionally connotative.

The emotional appeal can, of course, be misused by some writers for nefarious purposes, to make the audience act in a manner that contradicts what they would otherwise know to be logically sound; therefore, caution is needed by both writers and their audiences. However, the appeal to emotion ought not be discarded, for, when judiciously employed, it can provide motivation to change and act in a manner that supports reason.

### Ethos

When writers make an ethical appeal, they communicate to the audience their good character. Aristotle divides this appeal into three types: *phronesis,* that the writer is sensible; *arête,* that the writer has high moral character; *eunoia,* that the writer is benevolent. Ethos, therefore, involves the type of impression the writer creates in the mind of the audience. Any part of the discourse that causes the audience to question the judgment or integrity of the writer can have devastating effect on the persuasive success of the writer's argument.

***Successful writers who become skilled persuaders make choices,*** based on their audience and the occasion of their argument, as to how they arrange the three types of appeals. Reason alone, they know, does not often convince an audience to change. To spur change, or action, the writers must also appeal to emotion. Likewise, if the audience does not trust the judgment and good will of writers, the arguments these writers have made will not be convincing.

## Dispositio: Arrangement of the Classical Argument

- *exordium:* the introduction, where the writer/speaker introduces the topic, establishes its importance, and establishes the writer's ethos with the audience.

- *narratio:* outlines the current situation, or the basic facts

- *divisio:* explains the argument

- *confirmatio:* explains the evidence in support of the argument

- *confutatio:* refutes the opposing arguments

- *peroratio:* conclusion

### Common Logical Fallacies of Argumentation

A **non sequitur** is any conclusion that "does not follow" logically from the premises of an argument. Knowledge of such logical fallacies allows careful writers not only to counter arguments opposing their positions but also to avoid faulty reasoning on behalf of their own opinions.

- **Cause-effect** *[post hoc, ergo propter hoc;* "after it, therefore, because of it"]: arguing that because action A followed action B, B caused A. e.g. After Mark moved into the neighborhood, the crime rate increased.

- **Slippery slope:** arguing that one action will surely lead to a more serious consequence. e.g. Requiring trigger locks will result in the banning of all guns.

- **Either-or:** arguing that there exist only two options when, in fact, the issue is not a "black-or-white" one in which other options have been exhausted. e.g. You either support clean air standards, or you support the auto industry.

- **Faulty analogy:** arguing that because two things are alike in some ways, they are also alike in others, with no consideration given to their dissimilarities. e.g. Andy and John are from rural America. John doesn't like the city; Andy probably doesn't like the city either.

- **Begging the question** *[petitio principii]:* "circular reasoning," occurring when something is assumed as true that has yet to be proven. e.g. Michelle didn't steal the ice cream bar because she is an honest person. *To state that Michelle is honest begs the question about her involvement in the theft of the ice cream, neither proving her fundamental honesty nor demonstrating that she has been honest at every moment of her life, including at the time of the theft.*

- *Ad hominem* argument [to the man]: use of an appeal to emotion in a devious manner that, instead of addressing and refuting the argument made by the opponent, finds the writer attacking the character of the opponent.

- *Ad populum* argument [to the people]: another deceptive use of emotion by appealing to irrational fears and prejudices, rather than logic, in order to create support for a position or provoke hostility toward the position of an opponent. Sometimes public symbols and values are used in this deceitful way—*the flag, patriotism, motherhood*—as are terms intended as pejoratives—*radical, reactionary, left-wing, right-wing.* The emotions aroused by such words may create the illusion that the position being argued has actually been proven.

- **Hasty generalization:** arguing that, because a member of a group has a certain quality, all members of the group have that quality. e.g. All English teachers will correct your bad grammar.

- **Red herring** *[ignoratio elenchi;* "ignorance of the refutation"]: a term deriving from the practice of hunters "dragging a herring across the trace in order to lead the hounds away from their pursuit of the prey," a red herring is used by writers who argue by drawing attention to an irrelevant point. e.g. So what if I cheated on the exam? So did Fernando and Pauline.

# GRADING RUBRICS

### Essay Rubric

Students receive a copy of this rubric with their graded papers so that they can focus on areas of weakness. The teacher circles those items that pertain to the student's paper.

#### A-,A / 90,95 Clearly Outstanding

**Content** Introduction grabs attention; thesis articulates a persuasive, original opinion; topic sentences articulate precise aspect of argument; creative/original ideas and insights extensively elaborated, refreshing; goes beyond general commentary; excellent use of transitional sentences; conclusion effectively discusses the significance of the paper topic.

**Style** Appropriate use of sophisticated vocabulary, sentence variety, parallel structure, modification; language is concise and lucid, verbs active; effective punctuation.

#### B-,B,B+ / 80,85,88 Above Average

**Content** Thesis contains a legitimate opinion; clear/organizes paragraphs; introduction needs to grab the reader's attention more or needs additional work; topic sentences provide clear link to thesis; strong ideas developed; minor problems with textual examples, transitional sentences, elaboration; writer needs to improve the transition from the introductory story to thesis; conclusion adequate—may do some additional work.

**Style** Mechanically accurate; minor coherence problems; re-examine some word and logic glue; combine some sentences to eliminate wordiness and to provide variety and balance; minor problems with grammar, spelling, punctuation, redundancy; at times, blend quoted material more smoothly; for clarity, some sentences need revision; some topic sentences need tighter focus; a few verbs could be strengthened; strengthen link between paragraphs; some phrases too vague; begin to incorporate more sophisticated vocabulary and sentence structure.

#### C-,C,C+ / 70,75,78 Acceptable

**Content** Introduction needs development—analogy doesn't tie to thesis adequately; thesis needs revision of opinion; thesis contains little insight beyond comments made in class; one or more paragraphs have problems with elaboration, overall focus, support of thesis; more primary text needed; quoted material needs more explanation; transitional sentences between examples needed; summary rather than analysis of text; organization of ideas may need revision; more appropriate text needed; ideas need further explanation/analysis; illogical interpretation of text; text out of context; conclusion only summarizes main points or needs more elaboration.

**Style** Word glue transitions needed to improve paragraph coherence; some topic sentences need revision: summary, unclear, too broad, connection to thesis unclear; problems with sentence clarity, redundancy, punctuation, choppy sentences, weak verbs, wordiness, spelling, grammar; problems with transitions between paragraphs; some awkward incorporation of textual support; some vague sentences; little use of SAT vocabulary or sentence variety.

### D-,D,D+,F / 65,67,69,<60 Unacceptable/
### Does Not Meet Requirements

**Content** No showing introduction; body paragraphs not completely developed; thesis not evident, lacks a persuasive opinion; ideas lack development; little or no textual support; paper fails to adequately address thesis; topic sentences not supported, not linked to thesis; illogical analysis of text; research requirement not met; plagiarism; little change from first draft.

**Style** Serious problems with coherence, transitions within paragraphs; serious spelling, grammar errors; sentences need revision; vague/ confusing; wordy.

## Showing Writing Rubric

Students receive a copy of this rubric with their revised, graded paper. The teacher circles those items that pertain to the paper.

### A-,A / 90,95 Clearly Outstanding

Grammatical structures are accurately labeled; verbs are in the present tense and active; the paper contains few or no unnecessary "be" verbs; the student has extended the elaboration of each image beyond two sentences; almost no telling or little telling occurs throughout the piece; each sentence shows action or a specific, singular image; the student has extensively revised his or her composition; the first sentence grabs the reader's attention with specific showing detail; sophistication of writing style and vocabulary clearly indicated.

### B-,B,B+ / 80,85,88 Above Average

Most verbs are active; some "be" verbs could be revised; some places could be extended; the student may be listing new images with each new sentence, though this occurs infrequently; the first sentence attempts to grab the reader's attention, but it could use some additional concrete singular detail; some telling sentences exist, though not many; the paper contains creative ideas but some ideas need more elaboration and showing detail; some wordiness and redundancy need revision; the first draft shows evidence of revision, but additional revision would have added to the quality of this final draft; certain problems with sentence structure, grammar usage, punctuation, and/or capitalization are evident; some evidence of sophisticated writing style and vocabulary emerging.

### C-,C,C+ / 70,75,78 Acceptable

More than three grammatical errors exist; in general, the student has completed the assignment adequately; the student has revised parts of his or her paper, though not extensively; only relatively minor elaboration of details has been done; verbs need to be more active; avoid reliance on "be" verbs; sections of the paper contain listing—introducing a new image or detail with each sentence; there are places in which elaboration needs to be extended; too many plurals and vague words; the paper contains solid ideas, but the student's composition needs more development.

### D-,D,D+,F / 65,67,69,<60 Unacceptable/ Does Not Meet Requirements

The paper contains too many telling phrases or sentences; more substantial revision of the first draft is required; serious errors in grammar exist; the student must see the teacher for help; little revision has been done to the original; numerous "be" verbs and vague, plural words; student has not extended his elaboration of ideas; sentence structure, grammar usage, punctuation and/or capitalization procedures have not been followed.

## TRANSITIONAL WORDS

- **Time** after, afterward, at first, as, before, finally, immediately, later, next, now, previously, soon, then
- **Place** above, ahead, among, beyond, down, elsewhere, farther, here, in front of, in the background, near, nearby, next to, there
- **Idea** first, second, third, similarly, as, in the same way, for instance, likewise, however, one, two, three
- **Extending elaboration by**

| | |
|---|---|
| **comparing** | as, at the same time, by comparison, compared with, equally, in the same manner, like, likewise, similarly, the same as |
| **contrasting** | although, and yet, as, as if, as though, at the same time, but, by (in) contrast, conversely, different from, even so, unlike, even though, however, in spite of, instead of, neither, nevertheless, on the one hand, on the other hand, otherwise, provided that, though, unfortunately, whereas, yet |
| **emphasizing/ clarifying** | especially, for instance, in fact, indeed, that is, in other words |
| **adding another example** | moreover, most important, now, so, to repeat, additionally, again, also, especially, in addition, in fact, last, again, also, besides, equally important, furthermore, related to this, similarly, in contrast |

# QUICK ESSAY CHECKLIST

### Introduction (p. 118)
1. Does the writer grab the reader's attention from the first sentence?
2. Does this showing-telling introduction provide an appropriate analogy to the thesis statement?
3. Does the writer include a transition sentence that connects the attention-grabber to the thesis statement?
4. Does the thesis statement contain a topic + opinion?

### Body paragraphs (p. 51)
1. Are the topic sentences focused and written with clear diction? Topic sentence = Organizing Element + Aspect of Thesis.
2. Does the writer's topic sentence contain language found in the thesis statement?
3. Does the paragraph organize the evidence according to time, place, or idea?
4. Does the writer explain why the evidence supports the topic sentence, or does the writer merely list the evidence with little explanation and elaboration?
5. When the writer uses direct quotations, does he smoothly blend this text with his own words? (pp. 67–70)
6. Does the writer avoid summarizing plot?

### Conclusion (p. 122)
1. Does the conclusion go beyond summary or restatement of the thesis statement?
2. Does the conclusion attempt to connect the thesis to one larger issue—to the community, to the writer, to other works of literature?
3. Does the writer finish the conclusion by "bookending" the attention-grabber from the introduction or a major detail from the body?

**Additional Suggestion** Read the essay aloud to a friend and ask for honest feedback. This provides an additional strategy for making sure the writer is making the argument clear to the reader.

# EDITING SYMBOLS

**A**   **Add transitional phrase or sentence:** 1) after initial topic sentence, further clarify and identify the path the paragraph intends to take, that is, the organization of material—time, place, idea? (p. 51); 2) add modifier to the end of the topic sentence to further define and specify a general word that appears there; apply this definition to the text. (p. 65)

**B**   **Blending:** 1) blend text more smoothly with the analysis; 2) blend needs to be grammatically correct; 3) explain the text and include it with the writer's words, revealing why this text helps prove the point; 4) don't blend too early, without first setting up the aspect of the topic sentence the quotation is supposed to support—it is not clear how this supports the topic sentence or previous statement; 5) first explain the context of the quotation. (p. 67)

**C**   **Combine some sentences.** This helps eliminate wordiness, extend the elaboration of a single idea, eliminate unnecessary breaks in thought and choppy effect. Use participial, infinitive, gerund, absolute, and appositive phrases, as well as subordinate clauses to combine. (p. 70)

**E**   **Extend the elaboration of an idea:** 1) the writer needs to elaborate and incorporate more textual support; 2) the writer is missing some important textual examples; 3) the writer should extend the elaboration of details, commenting further on this idea before moving to the next; 4) elaboration is vague or merely restates the evidence. (pp. 36, 71)

**EV**   **Textual evidence doesn't provide clear support** for the writer's position or previous statement. Reread the text carefully.

**G**   **Fix any grammatical or punctuation errors!** If the writer doesn't understand the error, see the teacher. RO, CS, //, SV, SF, PA (p. 156)

**L**   The student **merely lists details** without elaborating each image or explaining why these details/quotations provide support for the topic sentence. (p. 75)

**O**   **Off-topic:** 1) evidence doesn't support the topic sentence; 2) not completely off-topic, but either the writer is slipping into plot summary or failing to adequately explain how evidence supports topic. (p. 78)

**P**   **Paragraph needs overall revision:** 1) the organization (time, place, idea) of main points supporting topic sentence needs to be identified or emphasized more clearly (see chapter two); 2) this collection of sentences doesn't provide complete coherence; check logic and word glue, and topic string; 3) paragraphs could use more textual support and analysis—look for additional examples; 4) tie to thesis needs to be stronger. (p. 81)

**S**   **Summarizing** here rather than explaining how these details support the topic sentence. This problem is similar to listing. (p. 75)

**SH**   **Show concrete images** rather than tell these details. The reader can't see any images. Showing text includes direct excerpts from the literary text along with the writer's elaborated analysis. (pp. 35, 84)

| | |
|---|---|
| **T** | **Transitions weak:** 1) check word and logic glue between sentences (p. 58); 2) revise transition so there is closer link between these sentences; 3) transition could be less wordy; 4) maintain topic focus. (pp. 57, 85) |
| **TH** | **Thesis needs revision:** 1) make minor adjustments in style and clarity; 2) thesis contains only a topic, not an opinion; 3) the idea in the thesis is unclear or too general (see chapter three). (p. 91) |
| **TS** | **Revise the topic sentence:** 1) need stronger focus so that all sentences can clearly connect to main sentence; this will help coherence; 2) topic sentence contains an example, a plot detail rather than an organizing idea + aspect of thesis (see p. 113); 3) connect the topic sentence to thesis more clearly, perhaps adding actual words or synonyms from the thesis; 4) this might be too broad or too vague—not sure the reader will understand the meaning; 5) diction is imprecise. (p. 88) |
| **V** | **Vague:** 1) this comment needs to be more specific, precise; avoid plurals; 2) this comment does not really say anything. (p. 92) |
| **W** | **Wordy structures:** 1) this phrase is unnecessary; do not write, "In chapter one it says, 'Hester stands still'"; instead, blend text with the writer's analysis. See **B1**; 2) use fewer words; 3) beware piling adjectives or adjective phrases one after another—either eliminate unnecessary adjectives or reposition some in participial phrases; 4) remove redundant words within the sentence; 5) do not make sentence glue unnecessarily long; use synonyms or pronouns, where possible. (p. 94) |
| **~** | **Redundant:** you've already mentioned this. |
| **WC** | **Word** here is **not the best choice.** Language is jargon or colloquial. |
| **X** | **Revise:** 1) cut the sentence or phrase; 2) revise for clarity and conciseness. |
| **Z** | **Re-examine the structure** of your paper—thesis + topic sentences; do the topic sentences clearly prove the thesis? (See chapter three.) The writer might need to make some adjustments in thesis or topic sentences. (See pp. 113–117.) |
| ⬯ | **Vivid verbs:** 1) revise this "be" verb with a more active verb; 2) avoid the passive verb in this context. (p. 97) |
| **[ ]** | **Vary** some of these **sentence beginnings.** (p. 96) |
| ˆ , | Problem with **comma rule** for 1) **PrPP**; 2) **PaPP**; 3) **ADVSC**; 4) **ADJSC**; 5) **ADV-IP**; 6) **AP**; 7) coordinating conjunction and two verbs, (p. 155); 8) needed when two + prepositional phrases begin sentence; 9) other |

## PEER REVIEW/EDITING ACTIVITIES

Below are four editing activities to use after students have completed a rough draft. All these activities can be easily revised to fit the teacher's classroom context.

### Assignment: Partner Review/Editing

**Directions:**

1. Pick one editing symbol the teacher has either marked on the composition or to which he or she refers during verbal direction-giving in the class.
2. With a partner, write out the revised version of the sentence[s] so that the problem has been corrected.
3. Use chapter two of this writing book.
4. Switch and repeat the process with the partner who hasn't made a correction.
5. If you wish, repeat process with different symbol/same partner or new partner.

### Assignment: Partner-Homework Review/Edit (or In-Class Review/Edit)

**Directions:**

1. The day prior to this assignment, the teacher will require that students bring to class the following day two copies of their composition. This may be a single paragraph, an introduction, a conclusion, or an entire essay.
2. On the day students bring with them two copies of their composition, the teacher will assign each student a partner.
3. For homework tonight, each student will take his or her partner's composition home. (Or this can be entirely for an in-class assignment.)
4. Make an editing sheet. (See p. 204)
5. The student will use the **checklists\*** located throughout this writing book to cover all aspects of the partner's paper. (See below.)
6. Tomorrow each student will have class time to discuss his or her comments with the partner. If a student is absent tomorrow, it is his or her responsibility to make sure the partner's paper with the editing sheet is delivered to school.
7. Each student's editing may be graded based on effort.

> **\* Checklists**
> Showing writing exercises p. 34
> Showing-telling introductions pp.118–121
> Thesis statements p. 112
> Topic sentences p. 50
> Paragraphs p. 51
> Conclusions p. 122
> Transitional glue pp. 58

## Assignment: Partner In-Class Activities for Essays

### Day One: Checking essay structure—thesis statements and topic sentences

**Directions:** Partners should exchange papers, read the thesis statement, and answer the following questions. When both partners are finished answering the questions, jotting their answers on a separate sheet of paper, the partners should discuss the answers.

1. Does the thesis statement include a precise topic + an opinion?
2. Does the thesis merely summarize or only point out an obvious detail or pattern rather than actually argue a position? Explain.
3. Could the reader logically disagree with the thesis statement? (One should be able to disagree if the thesis contains a debatable opinion.)
4. Does the diction include vague or abstract words that contain too many meanings, thus preventing a clear focus? Explain.
5. Has the reader provided some specific suggestions for improved diction?

**Directions:** Partners should read the topic sentences for each paragraph in the body and follow the procedures regarding jotting and discussing listed above.

1. Does each topic sentence clearly help support the argument in the thesis? If not, has the reader offered suggestions?
2. Does the writer include word glue to make the relationship between the thesis statement and topic sentence obvious to the reader? Explain.
3. Is the diction precise and specific? Or does it contain vague and abstract ideas that may be confusing? Has the reader suggested elimination of wordy structures? Explain.
4. Does the topic sentence contain more than one specific idea? Is it too broad? Has the reader suggested that the writer narrow the topic sentence? Explain.
5. Is there a transitional sentence from the topic sentence to the first supporting detail? If not, has the reader suggested one?

### Day Two: The introductory paragraph

**Directions:** Follow each step with a partner.

Step 1: The writer reads the introductory paragraph to the listener.

Step 2: The listener says

> A. Why do you think this introduction would grab the attention of most readers?
>
> *The writer responds....*
>
> B. What do you need to add to the introduction to make it even better, more attention-grabbing?
>
> *The writer responds.... The listener suggests....*

C. What is your transition sentence(s) from the attention-grabber to the thesis statement?

*The writer shows. The listener comments and/or suggests.*

D. What is your thesis statement?

*The writer shows. The listener comments and/or suggests.*

E. What are the sentence structures the teacher is requiring?

*The writer shows the listener the highlighted structures.*

*The listener confirms their existence or points out any problems and suggests solutions.*

Step 3: The listener honestly evaluates the introductory paragraph by marking the following numbers on the spaces next to the individual items mentioned below:

___4 = No improvement needed

___3 = Needs more work in the following areas:
   ___ • The attention-grabber
   ___ • The transition from the attention-grabber to the thesis statement
   ___ • The thesis statement's clarity and impeccable diction
   ___ • At least one example of two different sentence structures
   ___ • The introductory paragraph possesses a somewhat ineffable quality that distinguishes it from most paragraphs because of its audacity, its originality, and/or its creativity

___2 = Needs substantial revision. The writer should review the models on pp. 118–121 and note attention in the areas marked above.

___1 = Little effort shown or the writer may consider meeting with the teacher for additional help.

Step 4: Switch Roles

### Day Three: Checking body paragraphs

**Directions:** Partners should exchange papers, read one body paragraph, and answer the following questions. When both partners are finished answering the questions, jotting answers on a separate sheet of paper, the partners should discuss the answers.

1. Is there a clear transition immediately after the topic sentence? Does the reader understand how the writer is going to organize the information in the paragraph?
2. When the writer includes direct quotations, are these blended as if the words are part of the sentence, or is there an abrupt beginning of quoted material?

3. Is it clear how the textual passages support the topic sentence? Does the writer explain how we should see these details?
4. Is the writer only summarizing details from the story and not explaining why they prove his topic sentence?
5. Is it clear how each sentence helps support the topic sentence?
6. Has the writer provided enough details and commentary to support the topic sentence? Does the reader have suggestions for additional details?
7. Are some sentences too wordy? Are some words too abstract or vague? Has the reader made suggestions for revision?
8. Do some sentences need to be combined, using, for example, a participial phrase, repeat word modifier, analysis modifier, conjunctive adverb, or subordinate clause?
9. Is it clear what the logical and grammatical transitions are? Does the writer use repetition and synonyms for word glue?
10. Are there quotations that need further comment and analysis?

Once each partner has worked with the other on one body paragraph, begin the same process with another body paragraph.

### Day Four: Checking conclusions

**Directions:** Partners should exchange papers, read the conclusion, and answer the following questions. When both partners are finished answering the questions, jotting answers on a separate sheet of paper, the partners should discuss the answers.
1. Does the conclusion avoid summarizing the main points of the paper?
2. Does the writer attempt to discuss what is significant about this thesis? Does the writer attempt to relate the thesis to our contemporary culture in an elaborately extensive fashion?
3. Does the writer attempt to relate the thesis to other works of literature?
4. Are there any wordy structures? Vague or confusing statements that could be more precise?
5. Where and how can the writer extend the elaboration of an idea by providing more concrete detail?
6. Which sentences need combining?

### Day Five: Overall evaluation

**Directions:** After the reader has finished all parts of the writer's composition, the evaluation rubric is used to determine the status of the composition. Once each specific evaluation point that applies to the composition is checked below, the reader will discuss the evaluation with the writer and ways for improving the composition.

**4** ___ The thesis statement is clearly stated; diction is impeccable.
   ___ Introduction includes concrete details and effectively grabs reader's attention.
   ___ Each topic sentence is clearly stated; diction is impeccable.
   ___ The writer has a clear transitional sentence from the topic sentence to the first supporting detail.
   ___ Each topic sentence is supported by extensively elaborated details.
   ___ Each supporting detail clearly relates in an organized fashion to one another and to the topic sentence.
   ___ The writer has employed sophisticated diction.
   ___ Conclusion avoids summary and explains the thesis' relation to other works of literature or a larger community.

**3** ___ The thesis statement is clearly stated; diction needs improvement.
   ___ Introduction's ideas need minor revision, needs to grab attention more vividly.
   ___ The transitional sentence to the thesis statement may need some revision.
   ___ Each topic sentence is clearly stated; diction needs improvement.
   ___ The transitional sentences after the topic sentences need revision.
   ___ Each topic sentence is supported by details, most sufficiently elaborated.
   ___ Some details need to be more extensively elaborated.
   ___ Most details are clearly related to one another and to the topic sentence, though some need additional revision and transitional glue.
   ___ Conclusion is adequate, but the writer may consider a more elaborated literary or contemporary connection.

**2** ___ The thesis statement is not clearly stated; diction needs improvement.
   ___ Introduction doesn't grab reader's attention or needs a closer tie to the thesis.
   ___ Some topic sentences are not clearly stated; diction needs improvement.
   ___ Little extension of elaboration for many details.
   ___ Transitional sentences after topic sentences needed in many places.
   ___ Although a few of the details may support the topic, more work needs to be done on making sure they all relate to one another and to the topic.
   ___ Writer does not employ sophisticated diction.
   ___ Conclusion contains too much summary.

**1** ___ The thesis statement is basically meaningless; diction needs improvement.
   ___ Unacceptable introduction—no showing details!
   ___ No transitional sentences, either between the showing introduction and thesis statement or after topic sentences.
   ___ Most topic sentences are not clearly stated; diction needs improvement.
   ___ Most topic sentences have less than three supporting details; no elaboration.
   ___ Although a few of the details may support the topic, much more work needs to be done on making sure they all relate to one another and to the topic.
   ___ Conclusion incomplete, merely restates thesis statement.

### Assignment: Peer review editing workshop (alternative one)
#### Directions

1. Each student/writer should take a blank sheet of paper and make an editing sheet. (See example, p. 204)
2. Student/writers should place their names, or secret numbers, on the editing sheet.
3. The student/writer turns in to the teacher the editing sheet and paper so that he or she can redistribute papers to students.
4. The teacher redistributes the papers with attached editing sheets.
5. The student/editor should only place the editing symbol on the student/writer's paper when he or she notices a specific problem. For example, the first student/editor might be exploring places in the text **to extend elaboration.** The first editor to use the symbol **E3** would place this symbol next to the sentence on the student's essay, along with a numerical indication that corresponds with the particular editor. For example, if John is the first editor, he will use **E3–1,** indicating that his comment on the editing sheet corresponds with **E3–1.** Since John is instructed to find at least two places on the student paper to make suggestions, he next might use the symbol **E4–1.** Mary might find another example of **E3** and mark **E3–2,** since she is the second editor to use the symbol **E3.** (See the example on the next page.)
6. On the editing sheet, student/editors write their names under editor, fill in the letter code, and explain their comments.
7. Throughout the class period, student/editors will finish editing papers at different times. When one student/editor, for example, finishes editing a paper, he or she should raise his or her hand, and the teacher will provide another paper to edit. During the beginning of the period, one student may have to wait before another paper is available to edit.
8. At certain times, the teacher may assign a grade to the quality of comments a student/editor makes.
9. Students need to write two specific suggestions on the editing sheet, which may include an actual sentence revision.
10. At the end of the period, students will receive their own papers and editing sheets with several suggestions.
11. Student/writers should remember that they are not required to follow all suggestions. The teacher hopes that a few comments will prove helpful or at least help the student rethink aspects of the paper.

### Sample student paper with symbol codes

Dickens shows Scrooge as self-centered and materialistic. Dickens starts by revealing the selfish aspect of Scrooge. For example, Scrooge complains to his nephew that "I live in a world of fools." **E3–1** This pattern continues when Scrooge tells the charity workers that he will donate "nothing."**C** Here Scrooge emphasizes that his practice is not to donate any money for the poor. **E4–1** Instead, Scrooge insists on being "left alone." **E3–2**

### Editing sheet

Writer's Name _____

| Editor | Symbol | Comments |
| --- | --- | --- |
| Mike | E3–1 | Try something like this: "a comment that shows Scrooge is rude even to members of his own family." |
| | E4–1 | You might talk about the irony of the word "nothing" meaning his soul is full of nothing, too, no compassion. |
| Sharon | E3–2 | This isolation prevents Scrooge from not only making financial commitments to his community but also personal ones. Discuss more. |
| Sharon | C | These two sentences could be joined by the conjunctive adverb "in fact." |

### Assignment: Peer review editing workshop (alternative two)

This peer editing approach is adapted from *Acts of Teaching: How to Teach Writing* by Joyce Armstrong Carroll and Edward E. Wilson. The basic difference between "alternative two" and "alternative one" is that the teacher does not touch the writers' compositions or editing sheets during the class period. Instead, the teacher states what specific detail is to be edited. The students face each other in rows of desks or in two circles of desks. The students on one side of the row or circle never move; the others always move.

1. Student/writers create editing sheets with their names on them (see example above), which remain with their compositions during the period.
2. Students sit across from one another in a long row or two; they exchange papers (composition + editing sheet).
3. The teacher states what one detail, punctuation, structure, or "editing symbol" is to be checked. For example, the teacher may say **E3** or **PrPP**.
4. Once the editors have had sufficient time to look for any errors regarding that detail, they make specific constructive comments on the writers' editing sheets. After papers are returned, the designated "movers" move.
5. Teacher directs new partners to exchange papers, states the detail to be checked, and the editors begin perusing the writers' compositions for the detail, make needed comments on the sheet, and then return the papers.
6. The designated "movers" do so when the teacher signals, and the procedure continues. Only the designated "movers" move throughout the period.

# GLOSSARY OF LITERARY TERMS

**Allegory**   a fictional work where characters and/or setting are personifications of abstract qualities. (*Vanity Fair* in *Pilgrim's Progress; Beauty and Death* in the morality play *Everyman; Beatrice* in *The Divine Comedy.*)

**Alliteration**   a rhetorical device that repeats the initial identical consonant sounds in succession. *Sure I had drunken in my dreams, / And still my body drank. The Rime of the Ancient Mariner* (Samuel Taylor Coleridge).

**Allusion**   making a reference to a famous historical, Biblical, mythological, or literary figure or event.

**Analogy**   a comparison of the similar characteristics of two unlike things.

**Anapest**   a metrical foot consisting of two unstressed syllables followed by a stressed syllable. *With a leap / and a bound.* (Coleridge).

**Antagonist**   the character who is opposed to the protagonist.

**Apostrophe**   addressing—speaking to—some abstract quality or non-human entity. (Shelley writes, *"O, West Wind, thou art preserver and destroyer."*)

**Archetype**   derived from Carl Jung, this is a term that refers to a character type, image, setting, or story pattern that can be found in all cultures and from all epochs. *A snake, the temptress, the wise man, the sea, the color red.*

**Assonance**   repetition of vowel sounds. *So twice five miles of fertile ground.* (Coleridge).

**Blank verse**   unrhymed lines of ten syllables each (iambic pentameter).
*It little profits that an idle king,*
*By this still hearth, among these barren crags,*
*Matched with an aged wife, I mete and dole,*
*Unequal laws unto a savage race.* (Tennyson).

**Caesura**   in poetry, a pause in the line marked either by punctuation (a dash, a comma, a semicolon), internal rhyme, or a blank space. *Featur'd like him, like him with friends possess'd.* (Shakespeare).

**Catharsis**   the purging of emotion experienced after a tragedy.

**Closed form**   a poem that follows a specific form and metrical pattern. *sonnet, villanelle, sestina.*

**Colloquial**   language that is informal or familiar to a group of people.

**Connotation**   the meaning of a word other than its strict dictionary definition, the assorted images and ideas associated with a word.

**Conceit**   elaborate comparison—metaphor or simile—between unlikely objects. (John Donne *compares love to a geometric compass in his poem "Valediction Forbidding Mourning."*)

**Consonance**   a rhetorical device used in poetry where the poet repeats the identical consonant sounds typically in the last syllable of words. *That struts and frets.* (Shakespeare).

**Couplet**   the final two lines of a sonnet linked by rime.
*For thy sweet love remember'd such wealth brings*
*That then I scorn to change my state with kings.*

**Dactyl**   a metrical foot consisting of a stressed syllable followed by two un-stressed syllables. *Ever to / come up with / Dactyl tri / syllable.* (Coleridge).

**Declarative sentence**   a sentence that makes a statement. *I have three new books.*

**Denotation**   the dictionary definition of a word.

**Description**   a mode of writing that relies on images to portray a person, place or thing.

**Diction**   the individual words chosen by the author.

**Doppleganger**   a German phrase that asserts that for each person there exists an exact replica of himself, a shadow image. (*Dr. Jekyll and Mr. Hyde*).

**Dynamic/Round character**   a complex character who changes or develops as a result of the actions of the plot.

**End rhyme**   the final rhyme that occurs at the end of lines in a poem. *eyes / cries, state / fate.*

**End-stopped**   final punctuation at the end of a poetic line, a line that is not enjambed. *September rain falls on the house.* (Elizabeth Bishop).

**Enjambment**   occurs when the poet continues the grammatical sentence into the next line.
*Once again I see*
*These hedgerows, hardly hedgerows, little lines.* (William Wordsworth).

**Elegy**   a poem that reflects upon death or another equally solemn theme.

**Ethos**   the personality and emotional quality of a writer.

**Exclamatory sentence**   a sentence that expresses a strong or sudden emotion.
*I love the absolute phrase!*

**Exposition**   a mode of writing that explains a topic or idea.

**Feminine rhyme**   rhyme that results from the sound in two or more consecutive syllables. *despising-arising.*

**Foil**   a character who has traits that contrast with those of another character. *Dr. Watson and Sherlock Holmes, Huckleberry Finn and Tom Sawyer.*

**Foot**   the basic unit used in the measurement of poetry, the foot, contains one stressed syllable and one or more unstressed syllables. *Was this / the face / that launched / a thou / sand ships.* (five feet) (Christopher Marlowe).

**Free verse**   poetry that has no metrical pattern or regular meter.
*All truths wait in all things,*
*They neither hasten their own delivery nor resist it,*
*They do not need the obstetric forceps of the surgeon.* (Walt Whitman).

**Harmartia**   a Greek term that refers to the tragic hero's *error in judgment*.

**Hubris**   a Greek term that means *excessive pride*.

**Hyperbole**   exaggerating a particular point in order to draw attention to it. *No / this my hand will rather / the multitudinous seas incarnadine, / Making the green one red.* (Macbeth). *I have gray hair. I really do. The one side of my head—the right side—is full of millions of gray hair.* (Holden Caulfield).

**Iamb**   a metrical foot consisting of an unstressed syllable followed by one stressed. *dis-grace*.

**Imagery**   the pictures created by words. *I found a dimpled spider, fat and white, / On a white heal-all, holding up a moth.* (Robert Frost).

**Imperative sentence**   a sentence that gives a command. (*Read the first four chapters of the novel* Crime and Punishment.)

**Internal rhyme**   one or more words that rhyme within a line of poetry. *The ship was cheered, the harbor cleared.* (*The Rime of the Ancient Mariner.*)

**Interrogative sentence**   a sentence that asks a question. *What are your favorite novels?*

**Irony**   when the reality is different from the appearance: **Verbal** occurs when what is meant is said in words that carry the opposite denotative meaning; **Situational** occurs when there is a difference between what appears to be true and what is actually true, or between what one expects and what actually happens; **Dramatic** occurs when the audience has information the character does not.

**Juxtaposition**   to place items side by side.

**Language**   refers to the type of language an author uses. *Jargon, colloquial, poetic, scholarly, slang*.

**Logos**   argumentation through an appeal to logical reasoning.

**Loose sentence**   a sentence that begins with its main idea in the introductory independent clause and follows with less important details. *Wesley walked into the bookstore and purchased* Madame Bovery, *a recommendation made by his English teacher.*

**Masculine rhyme**   this rhyme results from the final stressed syllable. *state-gate, brings-kings.*

**Meter**   a regular pattern of rhythm in which the stresses on words occur at apparently equal intervals in time.

**Metaphor**   an implicit comparison between two unlike objects.

**Metonymy**   substitution of a word closely associated with another word, instead of using the actual word itself. *He tried to seize the crown.* (crown= the kingship or head of government.)

**Mimesis**   a Greek term that means the act of imitating reality.

**Modes**   a form of writing that an author may use in composition: *description, exposition, narration, persuasion.*

**Mood**   the emotional quality or atmosphere of a setting. *Anxious, foreboding.*

**Motif**   a reoccurring image, idea, character, or incident.

**Narration**   a mode of writing that retells events in a logical sequence.

**Nemesis**   one's enemy.

**Ode**   an elaborate poem expressed in language dignified, sincere, imaginative, and intellectual in tone.

**Onomatopoeia**   using words whose pronunciation suggests their meaning. *buzz, sizzle.*

**Open form**   a poem that is written in free verse; it does not prescribe to an established form or metrical pattern.

**Oxymoron**   placing together two contradictory words. *Sad joy, wise fool.*

**Paradox**   a statement that appears contradictory or absurd but may be true. *Time, as we know it, is a very recent invention.* (Aldous Huxley) *Art is a form of lying in order to tell the truth.* (Pablo Picasso)

**Parody**   a piece of writing that pokes fun at another serious piece of writing; it is designed to ridicule or criticize the serious work.

**Pathetic fallacy**   a type of personification in which the author attaches human qualities to nature. *The palm fronds would whisper so that spots of blurred sunlight slid over their bodies.* (William Golding *Lord of the Flies.*)

**Pathos**   a Greek term that refers to *emotion, passion, or suffering*; readers of tragedy feel sorrow and pity for the characters; writers may argue by making an appeal to the emotions of their audience.

**Periodic sentence**   a sentence that begins with a series of phrases or subordinate clauses, and builds toward the independent clause. *If by good luck there had been an ash-tray handy, if one had not knocked the ash out of the window in default, if things had been a little different from what they were, one would not have seen, presumably, a cat without a tail.* (Virginia Woolf *A Room of One's Own.*)

**Personification**   a figure of speech that attaches human qualities to that which is not human. *The wind stood up and gave a shout.* (James Stephens)

**Persuasion**   a mode of writing that seeks to alter the reader's point of view on a topic.

**Point of view**   the perspective from which the story is told—first person, third person limited, third person omniscient, objective; point of view also refers to the bias of the speaker or narrator—what has shaped his or her attitudes toward life, characters, and ideas.

**Prosody**   the study of poetic meter and rhyme.

**Protagonist**   the main character in a play or story.

**Quatrain**   a set of four lines in a sonnet.

**Rhyme scheme**   the pattern, or sequence, in which the end-rhyme sounds occur in a stanza or poem

| | |
|---|---|
| *When in disgrace with Fortune and men's eyes* | a |
| *I all alone beweep my outcast state,* | b |
| *And trouble deaf heaven with my bootless cries,* | a |
| *And look upon myself and curse my fate,* | b |
| *Wishing me like to one more rich in hope,* | c |
| *Featur'd like him, like him with friends possess'd,* | d |
| *Desiring this man's art and that man's scope,* | c |
| *With what I most enjoy contented least:* | d |
| *Yet in these thoughts myself almost despising,* | e |
| *Haply I think on thee, and then my state,* | f |
| *Like to the lark at break of day arising,* | e |
| *From sullen earth sings hymns at heaven's gate;* | f |
| *For thy sweet love remember'd such wealth brings* | g |
| *That then I scorn to change my state with kings.* | g |

(William Shakespeare.)

**Synecdoche**   a type of metaphor that mentions a part of something to indicate the whole. *Give me a hand with these boxes.*

**Sarcasm**   a type of verbal irony, in which, under the guise of praise, a caustic and bitter expression of strong and personal disapproval is given; these are comments intended to hurt.

**Satire**   writing that uses humor and wit to criticize a political or social situation and of which there are two types: **Horatian**—a mild form of satire seeking to create change through sympathetic humor, and **Juvenalian**—a caustic and indignant form of satire, expressing anger at examples of corruption and evil.

**Simile**   a direct, or explicit, comparison between two objects using the words like or as. *He is like a snake.*

**Spondee**   a metrical foot that contains two consecutive stresses. *Hum-drum.*

**Static/Flat character**   an uncomplicated character who changes little, if at all, in the progression of the literary work.

**Slant rhyme**   approximate or near rhyme—imperfect rhyme. *Who took the Flag today / Can tell the definition / So clear of Victory.* (Emily Dickinson)

**Sonnet**   a fixed form of fourteen lines; the **Shakespearean** sonnet contains three quatrains and a couplet; the **Petrarchan** sonnet contains an octave of eight lines and a sestet of six lines.

**Syntax**   the order in which words are arranged or grouped within a sentence.

**Tone**   the writer's attitude toward his subject. *curious, joyful, worried, calm, gracious, comic, profound.*

**Tragic flaw**   the flaw in the tragic hero's character that precipitates his downfall.

**Trochee**   a metrical foot consisting of one stressed syllable followed by one unstressed syllable. *Double / double, / toil and / trouble.* (Macbeth)

**Understatement / Litote**   to say something less forcefully than is appropriate. Lady Macbeth, after Duncan's murder, says, *"A little water will wash us of this deed,"* thus suggesting that the crime may be easily disposed of and forgotten. *I have this tiny little tumor on the brain.* (Holden Caulfield)

**Verse**   a line of poetry; poetry that has meter.

**Voice**   the qualities or personality of the speaker or narrator; a speaker's voice may be *angry, wise, ebullient, etc.*

# INDEX

# When It Comes to Reading...Computers Aren't the Answer, Teachers Are!

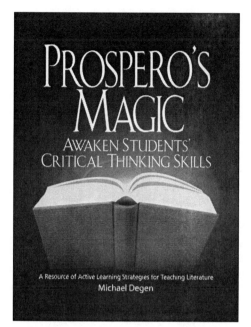

**Learn how to engage students in reading and appreciating any literary work through**
Critical Thinking Games
Lively Discussions
Presentations and Performances

**Table Of Contents**

**Chapter One**
*Critical Thinking Games for Developing Perspicacious Readers*
Includes the tournament of scholars

**Chapter Two**
*Opening Students' Mouths and Minds*
Learning to discuss in group situations
Creating questions for a discussion log
Grading rubrics for discussion

**Chapter Three**
*The Student Presentation*
Short story connections
Discovering the poem

**Chapter Four**
*Jumping Out of the Text:*
*The Student Performance*
60 literary minutes
Great Expectations' meeting in the graveyard
Creating literary courtroom trials
Teaching students how to read Shakespeare
The festival of Dionysus: mythological musicals
Students as contemporary Canterbury pilgrims

**Chapter Five**
*Individualized Project Planning*
The lost adventure of Odysseus:
Create-your-own-book project
Project proposals and evaluations

**Chapter Six**
*The Small Group: A Collection of Ideas*

English teachers, especially, are charged with engaging students with the intellectual creations of the master writers. It is not through anything a computer provides that students will learn to love reading literature; it is the teacher who must provide the environment in the classroom that allows students to work with—indeed, to wrestle with—the author's words and enter the created world of that writer.
— *Michael Degen*

## PROSPERO'S MAGIC
**Awaken Students' Critical Thinking Skills**
**A Resource of Active Learning Strategies**
**for Teaching Literature**
by Michael Degen

Author Michael Degen, recipient of the 2001 Outstanding Teaching of the Humanities Award, shares his "teaching secrets" for getting students excited about literature.

**Prospero's Magic • ISBN 09665125-45**
**$17.95**

# GRAMMAR DOES INDEED MATTER!

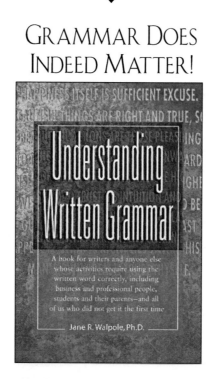

"Some English teachers cheerily assert that grammar doesn't matter," says Jane R. Walpole, Ph.D., "but most professionals know better." Dr. Walpole, who has taught English composition and literature in several community colleges, adds, "If we know how and why sentences work, we are better able to write precisely and effectively."

## Understanding Written Grammar
### by Jane R. Walpole, Ph.D.

A book for writers and anyone else whose activities require using the written word correctly, including business and professional people, students and their parents—and all of us who did not get it the first time, *Understanding Written Grammar* includes explanations of the logic of English grammar plus discussions of such elements as
Sentences, clauses, and phrases
Subjects, predicates, and modification
Punctuation
Sentence combining
Syntax and style

**Understanding Written Grammar**
ISBN 09665125-61
**$14.95**

# Telemachos Workshops

**For teachers of AP, IB, honors, and
regular English students**
Inquire concerning fees

**1.5-hour, 3-hour, and 6-hour workshops
tailored to suit your specific needs**

---

## Workshop 1
**Focus One: Teaching the Essay**
or
**Focus Two: Teaching the Paragraph**
or
**Focus Three: Developing Writing Skills**
The strategies involved in these three workshops
not only address AP and IB objectives, but also those
composition elements required on statewide tests for all
levels of students as they develop fundamental writing
skills: extensively elaborating ideas, using vivid verbs,
focusing on concrete detail, improving coherence, varying
sentence style, and organizing information both
within paragraphs and larger papers.

---

## Workshop 2
**Weaving Grammar Instruction
into the Writing Process**
This is a *how to* workshop that focuses on the instruction
of specific grammatical structures and their immediate and
continual usage by young writers. It is grounded in
the belief that clauses and phrases are tools writers employ
in the work of writing, and that our job as instructors is
to teach students about each tool, about its purpose,
and then require that the tool be used as an integral
part of the writing process.

---

## Workshop 3
**Critical Thinking Games and Other Active
Learning Strategies for Teaching Literature**
During this workshop, the participants will play a number
of critical thinking games based on literature, games
that also reinforce speech and writing skills—skills that are
required for statewide testing—including clear thesis
and topic sentences, coherence, detailed evidence,
and originality.

**NOTES:**

**NOTES:**

## EDITING SYMBOLS

**A**    **Add transitional phrase or sentence:** 1) after initial topic sentence, further clarify and identify the path the paragraph intends to take, that is, the organization of material—time, place, idea? (p. 51); 2) add modifier to the end of the topic sentence to further define and specify a general word that appears there; apply this definition to the text. (p. 65)

**B**    **Blending:** 1) blend text more smoothly with the analysis; 2) blend needs to be grammatically correct; 3) explain the text and include it with the writer's words, revealing why this text helps prove the point; 4) don't blend too early, without first setting up the aspect of the topic sentence the quotation is supposed to support—it is not clear how this supports the topic sentence or previous statement; 5) first explain the context of the quotation. (p. 67)

**C**    **Combine some sentences.** This helps eliminate wordiness, extend the elaboration of a single idea, eliminate unnecessary breaks in thought and choppy effect. Use participial, infinitive, gerund, absolute, and appositive phrases, as well as subordinate clauses to combine. (p. 70)

**E**    **Extend the elaboration of an idea:** 1) the writer needs to elaborate and incorporate more textual support; 2) the writer is missing some important textual examples; 3) the writer should extend the elaboration of details, commenting further on this idea before moving to the next; 4) elaboration is vague or merely restates the evidence. (pp. 36, 71)

**EV**    **Textual evidence doesn't provide clear support** for the writer's position or previous statement. Reread the text carefully.

**G**    **Fix any grammatical or punctuation errors!** If the writer doesn't understand the error, see the teacher. RO, CS, //, SV, SF, PA (p. 156)

**L**    The student **merely lists details** without elaborating each image or explaining why these details/quotations provide support for the topic sentence. (p. 75)

**O**    **Off-topic:** 1) evidence doesn't support the topic sentence; 2) not completely off-topic, but either the writer is slipping into plot summary or failing to adequately explain how evidence supports topic. (p. 78)

**P**    **Paragraph needs overall revision:** 1) the organization (time, place, idea) of main points supporting topic sentence needs to be identified or emphasized more clearly (see chapter two); 2) this collection of sentences doesn't provide complete coherence; check logic and word glue, and topic string; 3) paragraphs could use more textual support and analysis—look for additional examples; 4) tie to thesis needs to be stronger. (p. 81)

**S**    **Summarizing** here rather than explaining how these details support the topic sentence. This problem is similar to listing. (p. 75)

**SH**    **Show concrete images** rather than tell these details. The reader can't see any images. Showing text includes direct excerpts from the literary text along with the writer's elaborated analysis. (pp. 35, 84)

**T**    **Transitions weak:** 1) check word and logic glue between sentences (p. 58); 2) revise transition so there is closer link between these sentences; 3) transition could be less wordy; 4) maintain topic focus. (pp. 57, 85)

**TH**    **Thesis needs revision:** 1) make minor adjustments in style and clarity; 2) thesis contains only a topic, not an opinion; 3) the idea in the thesis is unclear or too general (see chapter three). (p. 91)

**TS**    **Revise the topic sentence:** 1) need stronger focus so that all sentences can clearly connect to main sentence; this will help coherence; 2) topic sentence contains an example, a plot detail rather than an organizing idea + aspect of thesis (see p. 113); 3) connect the topic sentence to thesis more clearly, perhaps adding actual words or synonyms from the thesis; 4) this might be too broad or too vague—not sure the reader will understand the meaning; 5) diction is imprecise. (p. 88)

**V**    **Vague:** 1) this comment needs to be more specific, precise; avoid plurals; 2) this comment does not really say anything. (p. 92)

**W**    **Wordy structures:** 1) this phrase is unnecessary; do not write, "In chapter one it says, 'Hester stands still'"; instead, blend text with the writer's analysis. See **B1**; 2) use fewer words; 3) beware piling adjectives or adjective phrases one after another—either eliminate unnecessary adjectives or reposition some in participial phrases; 4) remove redundant words within the sentence; 5) do not make sentence glue unnecessarily long; use synonyms or pronouns, where possible. (p. 94)

**~**    **Redundant:** you've already mentioned this.

**WC**    **Word** here is **not the best choice.** Language is jargon or colloquial.

**X**    **Revise:** 1) cut the sentence or phrase; 2) revise for clarity and conciseness.

**Z**    **Re-examine the structure** of your paper—thesis + topic sentences; do the topic sentences clearly prove the thesis? (See chapter three.) The writer might need to make some adjustments in thesis or topic sentences. (See pp. 113–117.)

**◯**    **Vivid verbs:** 1) revise this "be" verb with a more active verb; 2) avoid the passive verb in this context. (p. 97)

**[ ]**    **Vary** some of these **sentence beginnings.** (p. 96)

**^,**    Problem with **comma rule** for
1) **PrPP**; 2) **PaPP**; 3) **ADVSC**; 4) **ADJSC**; 5) **ADV-IP**; 6) **AP**; 7) coordinating conjunction and two verbs, (p. 155); 8) needed when two + prepositional phrases begin sentence; 9) other

LaVergne, TN USA
25 September 2010
198451LV00001B/3/P